D0194210

PRAISE FOR *Empowered Judaism:*
What Independent Minyanim Can Tea[ch]
about Building Vibrant Jewish Communities

"This is no ordinary book. This is a call to revolution … a passionate and brilliant manifesto [that] sets out a new course for Jewish life in America…. For an American Jewish community despairing of its future, this book is a prophecy of hope and new vision."
—**Rabbi Edward Feinstein**, editor, *Jews and Judaism in the 21st Century: Human Responsibility, the Presence of God and the Future of the Covenant*

"This moving book reveals a critical new development in the lives of younger American Jews. Not often does one have the opportunity to read such an inside story on dramatically positive Jewish history in the making. Elie Kaunfer's vivid account of participating in the creation of Mechon Hadar, an 'Independent Congregation' community that fosters Jewish liturgical and intellectual rigor, egalitarian ethics and group responsibility, and spirituality at the same time is compelling. His analysis of the strengths and weaknesses of conventional American Jewish congregations is spot-on, and will surely provoke lively and important conversations within and outside those congregations. Equally gripping is Kaunfer's own story of initial resistance to encounters with the Divine, and his eventual immersion into a passionately religious path of Jewishness."
—**Sylvia Barack Fishman**, chair, Department of Near Eastern and Judaic Studies and professor of contemporary Jewish life, Brandeis University; author, *The Way Into the Varieties of Jewishness*

"A roadmap to the future. His incisive understanding of the mindset of early twenty-first-century Jews (especially young ones) informs this accessible and eloquent treatise on building resonant, inspired communities. Kaunfer argues persuasively that transformations in contemporary culture mandate changes in Jewish communal and spiritual structures—and that such innovations have always been integral to the evolution of the Jewish people."
—**Felicia Herman**, executive director, The Natan Fund

"Accessible yet sophisticated…. The practical suggestions about worship are valuable not only to the world of independent minyanim but to synagogue minyanim and sanctuary services as well…. Will challenge both those who want to follow in Kaunfer's footsteps and those who disagree with him."
—**Rabbi David A. Teutsch**, Wiener Professor of Contemporary Jewish Civilization at the Reconstructionist Rabbinical College; editor, *Kol Haneshamah* Prayerbook series; author, *Spiritual Community: The Power to Restore Hope, Commitment and Joy*

"Practical, highly readable…. Read this book to understand the spiritual impulses of a generation of seekers who are not ready to give up tradition and not ready to give up on their own empowerment within Judaism either."
—**Dr. Erica Brown**, author, *Spiritual Boredom: Rediscovering the Wonder of Judaism* and *Inspired Jewish Leadership: Practical Approaches to Building Strong Communities*

"Takes us on an inspiring insiders' guided tour of the new independent minyan phenomenon, which is rejuvenating the Jewish landscape. Egalitarian, joyous, upbeat, participatory, spiritually alive—no wonder young people find a home in the minyanim! Enjoy this testimony to the vitality of Jewish life and the enthusiasm of young people to make it their own."
—**Rabbi Marcia Prager**, ALEPH: Alliance for Jewish Renewal; author, *The Path of Blessing: Experiencing the Energy and Abundance of the Divine*

"Essential reading for anyone interested in twenty-first-century life of Jewish prayer, study, and community…. A great read and a wonderful contribution to the Jewish bookshelf."
—**Riv-Ellen Prell**, professor of American studies, University of Minnesota; author, *Prayer and Community: The Havurah in American Judaism*

"Rabbi Elie Kaunfer has emerged as an insistent and compelling voice for enhanced Jewish life in the twenty-first century. The minyanim of which he speaks are symbolic of a deeper vision: an entire community that is empowered, knowledgeable and committed to the richness of the Jewish tradition. Nothing short of a manifesto for the next generation, a challenge to the Jewish community about what we are likely to fall into by default if we do not take Kaunfer's book seriously."
—**Rabbi Lawrence A. Hoffman**, professor of liturgy, worship and ritual, Hebrew Union College; co-founder, Synagogue 3000; editor, *My People's Prayer Book: Traditional Prayers, Modern Commentaries* series

"Taps into the spiritual yearning of a generation that hungers for a Jewish religious practice that is rich, meaningful and unapologetic. Captures the remarkable phenomenon of a newly emergent movement to reclaim vibrancy and vitality in Jewish life. [An] important and valuable contribution to the Jewish future."
—**Rabbi Sharon Brous**, founder, IKAR

"Remarkable…. A 'must read' for people trying to understand this vital new phenomenon as well as for individuals seeking to connect to Judaism in a new way—be they lay people, scholars, or leaders of the American Jewish community."
—**Rabbi Irving "Yitz" Greenberg**, founding president, Jewish Life Network; founding president, CLAL: The National Jewish Center for Learning and Leadership

Empowered Judaism

What Independent Minyanim
Can Teach Us about Building
Vibrant Jewish Communities

Rabbi Elie Kaunfer
Foreword by Prof. Jonathan D. Sarna

JEWISH LIGHTS Publishing
Woodstock, Vermont

Empowered Judaism:
What Independent Minyanim Can Teach Us about Building Vibrant Jewish Communities

2010 Quality Paperback Edition, First Printing
© 2010 by Elie Kaunfer
Foreword © 2010 by Jonathan Sarna

For information regarding permission to reprint material from this book, please mail or fax your request in writing to Jewish Lights Publishing, Permissions Department, at the address / fax number listed below, or e-mail your request to permissions@jewishlights.com.

Selections from the glossary of *My People's Prayer Book: Traditional Prayers, Modern Commentaries*, Vol. 8, *Kabbalat Shabbat* © 2004 by Rabbi Lawrence A. Hoffman (Woodstock, VT: Jewish Lights Publishing). Permission granted by Jewish Lights Publishing, www.jewishlights.com.

Library of Congress Cataloging-in-Publication Data
Kaunfer, Elie, 1973–
Empowered Judaism : what independent minyanim can teach us about building vibrant Jewish communities / Elie Kaunfer.
        p. cm.
Includes bibliographical references.
ISBN-13: 978-1-58023-412-2 (quality pbk.)
ISBN-10: 1-58023-412-7 (quality pbk.)
1. Fellowship—Religious aspects—Judaism. 2. Minyan. 3. Prayer groups—Judaism. 4. Kehilat Hadar (New York, N.Y.). 5. Kaunfer, Elie, 1973– 6. Prayer—Judaism. 7. Judaism—United States. I. Kehilat Hadar (New York, N.Y.). II. Title.

BM720.F4K38 2010
296.7—dc22

2009044920

10 9 8 7 6 5 4 3 2 1

Manufactured in the United States of America
❀ Printed on recycled paper.

Cover Design: Jenny Buono
Cover Art: Michael Merck, © by iStockphoto.com

Published by Jewish Lights Publishing
A Division of LongHill Partners, Inc.
Sunset Farm Offices, Route 4, P.O. Box 237
Woodstock, VT 05091
Tel: (802) 457-4000   Fax: (802) 457-4004
www.jewishlights.com

For my parents, Rabbi Alvan and Marcia Kaunfer,
who have always empowered me,
and for Lisa:

אַהֲבַת עוֹלָם אֲהַבְתִּיךְ עַל כֵּן מְשַׁכְתִּיךְ חָסֶד.

Contents

Foreword

In 1825, a group of young New York Jews seeking "to promote the more strict keeping of their faith" formed an independent society called Hebra Hinuch Nearim, the society for educating young people. Fired with the spirit of revival, they expressed in their constitution and bylaws "an ardent desire to promote the study of our Holy Law ... to extend a knowledge of its divine precepts, ceremonies, and worship among our brethren generally, and the enquiring youth in particular." To this end, they transformed their worship service, abandoning the age-old Sephardic patterns in which many of them had been raised, and introduced such innovations as "explanations" and "instruction," as well as a different style of leadership and a more democratic congregational ethos. Their goal, they proclaimed, was "to encrease [sic] the respect of the worship of our fathers."[1]

Hebra Hinuch Nearim was the first in a long series of movements in American Jewish life pioneered by young people that aimed, in different ways, to empower Jews and transform Judaism. Each of these movements revitalized and energized Jewish life, responded to a perceived crisis driving Jews away from Judaism, and left a lasting impact. Consider:

- The late 1870s witnessed a "great awakening" led by young Jews who worked for "the perpetuation and elevation of Judaism" in Philadelphia, Baltimore, and New York.[2] They created a wide range of Jewish educational institutions for men and women alike, and many of them eventually became leaders of the nascent Conservative movement.

- The period around World War I saw the growth of the Young Israel movement, designed to "bring about a revival of Judaism among the thousands of young Jews and Jewesses ... whose Judaism is at present dormant."[3] Modern Orthodoxy was shaped by these early

Young Israels. They helped to transform immigrant Orthodoxy into American Orthodoxy.

- The World War II era led to the creation of institutions like Brandeis Camp Institute, created "to inspire [college-age] Jews to be Jews, to link them with Jewish peoplehood, to whet their appetite for more learning, and to encourage them to bring up their children as Jews."[4] Postwar Zionism, transformative Jewish education, the Jewish camping movement, and even Taglit Birthright owe much to what these institutions taught us.

- The 1960s saw the birth of the havurah movement, devoted to fellowship, peace, community, and a new model of Jewish study that sought to meet the needs of "serious young Jews ... deeply involved in honest religious search, who are quite fully alienated from Judaism by all the contacts that they had had to date."[5] The movement, along with the *Jewish Catalogs* that grew out of it, created hundreds of new, close-knit worship communities (havurot), transformed the aesthetics of Jewish life, and focused new attention on Jewish education.

Today's movement of independent minyanim, the subject of this book, continues this grand tradition of youth-inspired religious innovation. Part description and part prescription, *Empowered Judaism* is a manifesto for transforming the way Jews pray and—more broadly—for building vibrant Jewish communities. Rabbi Elie Kaunfer's critique of the twentieth-century synagogue; the lessons he shares from the successful, highly innovative Kehilat Hadar, the New York minyan that he and his friends pioneered; and his description of the recently founded Yeshivat Hadar, the educational institution linked to the world of independent minyanim, all point the way to a new form of Judaism that Rabbi Kaunfer seeks to advance. Its goal, he explains, is "to build a prayer community that speaks to each of its members' spiritual longings, gives participants a sense of community and belonging, and empowers them to find in Judaism a deep sense of meaning and purpose that infuses every corner of their lives."

The founders of the independent minyan movement grew up in a tumultuous era of change in American Jewish life. Their ideology reflects these changes and sheds light on the transformation of Judaism that occurred while they were coming of age. Eight developments, in my view, proved particularly influential:

1. **The Jewish women's movement.** The "second wave" of feminism in the late twentieth century opened up Jewish leadership positions to women, provided women with the tools to study Judaism's central religious texts on their own, and created new norms of gender equality throughout Jewish life. From the beginning, women have played a central role in the world of independent minyanim—indeed, in many minyanim they far outnumber men. Feminist sensitivities have shaped the ethos of the entire movement.

2. **Jewish spirituality.** The late twentieth century also witnessed a renewal of spirituality across the spectrum of American Jewish religious life. Like Americans generally, many Jews during these years shifted the emphasis of their faith from moralism to devotion and the aesthetics of worship. They sought to complement social justice and rational teachings that appealed to the mind with spiritual and emotive religious experiences that appealed to the heart and the soul. Spirituality, as readers of this book will discover, plays a central role in the world of independent minyanim. Communal singing shapes the worship experience.

3. **High-level Jewish education.** The founders and leaders of the independent minyan movement are almost all products of Jewish day schools. The movement as a whole may be seen as the "first fruits" of the new emphasis on Jewish education that took hold at the end of the twentieth century. Rabbi Elie Kaunfer reports here that "the fundamentals" that he gained in day school—familiarity with prayer, understanding of Hebrew, and love of Jewish tradition and learning—became critical building blocks for him and for other founders of the minyan movement. The central values of the minyanim—from the high quality of the service to the excellence demanded of a *dvar Torah*—reflect Jewish education at its best.

4. **Israel.** Traditional Zionist goals play little role in the world of the independent minyanim. You need not live in Israel in order to become an "Empowered Jew." Like young Jews generally, the founders of the minyanim never knew a world without the State of Israel and do not remember the Six Day War. Some are deeply

critical of Israeli policies. Nevertheless, Israel's influence upon the world of the minyanim has been profound. Most minyan leaders have spent substantial periods of time in Israel (more than half of all minyan members have spent four or more months there), and Israeli synagogues and modes of worship have greatly influenced the forms and music of the minyanim. Previous revitalization movements in American Judaism have been totally home-grown or influenced by European Jewish trends. This is the first to reflect a new Jewish world where over 80 percent of all Jews live in two centers of Jewish life, Israel and the United States, and many Jews, as well as many trends in Judaism, travel back and forth between them.

5. **Gay pride.** Jews in independent minyanim grew up amid the gay pride movement and consider discrimination on the basis of sexual orientation to be immoral. Gay Jews have been founders and leaders of independent minyanim, and at least some minyanim actively celebrate gay pride within their communities. Once, gay and lesbian Jews preferred to worship in separate congregations of their own, like New York's Beth Simchat Torah. Today, even independent minyanim that view themselves as observant of Jewish law proudly don the label "gay friendly."

6. **Delayed marriage and childbirth.** In 1960, 77 percent of American women and 65 percent of men had completed three of life's central transitions—financial independence, marriage, and the birth of a first child—by age 30. Today, the corresponding numbers nationwide in the United States are 46 percent and 31 percent, and one assumes that the numbers among Jews are even lower. A great many young Jews now spend ten to twenty years after college in a new stage of life that Kaunfer calls here (after David Brooks) the "odyssey years." Jewish institutions, including most synagogues, were slow to recognize this new reality, leaving many young Jews without a spiritual home. The independent minyanim, created by Jews of this age group, help to fill this void. They represent the first major institutional response to this new demographic reality.

7. **The start-up culture.** Independent minyanim arose amid a cultural celebration of "start-ups," innovative endeavors that take shape in dorm rooms or garages, tap into a cultural vein, and become mass

phenomena. Start-ups are inherently suspicious of big institutions that resist change. Nor do they worry much about competition or failure. If even a small percentage of start-ups make it big, they more than justify parallel efforts that collapse. Independent minyanim reflect many aspects of this "start-up" culture. They too are suspicious of big institutions. They too place a heavy emphasis on sweat equity and technology. And they too are not afraid to fail. The success of the few feeds the aspirations of the many.

8. **Affluence.** Finally, independent minyanim emerged in an era of enormous affluence, one of rising portfolios and outsized fortunes. Jewish venture capitalists considered the minyanim a promising "start-up" investment and rewarded some of their founders with significant funding. To be sure, most minyanim were self-funded. In addition, minyanim require very low maintenance costs—this, as Rabbi Kaunfer explains, is part of what distinguishes them from synagogues. Still, creative innovations of all sorts grow best in soil that is well-nourished by affluent funders. The availability of funding at the right time helped independent minyanim to multiply with wondrous speed.

Today, although funding is much more scarce, independent minyanim remain among the most exciting and successful innovations in American Jewish life. They are nurturing a new generation of Jewish leaders and worshipers and are stimulating new and sometimes controversial ideas—about Jewish prayer, Jewish community, and Jewish learning—that promise to have a long-lasting impact.

From 1825 onwards, young Jews have periodically led the way in promoting innovation in American Jewish life, creating new institutions and setting forth new communal visions. *Empowered Judaism* represents the latest chapter in this uplifting history of religious creativity. This is a book that every Jewish leader will want to read and every serious Jew will want to contemplate.

Jonathan D. Sarna
Joseph H. & Belle R. Braun Professor
of American Jewish History
Brandeis University

Introduction
My Journey to Empowered Judaism

This book is about a lot of different things. On one level, it represents my own story—how I moved from being apathetic and cynical about Jewish life to being passionately engaged in building new Jewish community. It is a first draft of the history of Kehilat Hadar, the independent minyan that profoundly changed me and thousands of others. It is a peek into the inner workings of independent minyanim across the country and a reflection on what factors led to their founding. It is a case for not giving up on traditional Jewish prayer as a mode of connecting to God. It is a "how to" for people who are thinking of creating their own spiritual communities or looking to improve their synagogue.

But at its core, this book is about a vision of Jewish life in the twenty-first century and the opportunity we have of bringing that vision to fruition. In this vision, the future of Jewish life is dependent on Jews—not just rabbis—taking hold of the rich, challenging, surprising, and inspiring heritage that makes up our texts and traditions. It is not about a new "big idea" or innovation for its own sake, but a recognition that the big ideas in Judaism were laid out clearly by our ancestors thousands of years ago. It is about reclaiming those ideas, bringing them to life in this century, and taking them so seriously that they might change your life. The independent minyanim are a great example of this vision in action, but they are just one example. The message of this book is that we have the potential to empower Jews to own—really own—what has been ours for years. We have no time to waste.

PASSIONATE ENGAGEMENT

Have you ever had a job you loved? I've had three. One was a summer job as a reporter for the *Boston Globe*, and one was a two-year job as an investigator of school corruption for New York City. The third was perhaps the best: I was a corporate fraud investigator for the leading securities law firm in the country. Every weekday, for eight hours a day, I would call people from around the country and talk to them about the crimes they or their coworkers committed in corporate America. The challenge was never-ending: understanding the industry (what did Enron do, anyway?), finding the guilt-ridden former employees, and sweet-talking them into spilling the beans. The pay was good and the hours were nine to five. Hard to imagine that such a job existed in New York City, where all my friends were either in school or tremendously overworked.

Then, in early 2001, I discovered something even better than this job. I discovered—not without a fair amount of internal struggle and resistance—that investigating corporate fraud was not my real life's passion. Minyan was.

Not just any minyan, of course. I had attended various minyanim and synagogues throughout my life; I had even run a few of them. But none had ever really caught hold of me in the way that this latest minyan had. We would later call it Kehilat Hadar ("Community of Splendor"), but in April 2001, the minyan had no name. From that first Shabbat morning service, the minyan awoke a sense of passion, mystery, and awe I didn't know I could ever feel. Working with others to grow the minyan, to help other communities like it thrive, and to nurture the vision of Jewish life that it represents became the all-consuming purpose of my life.

> "Empowered Judaism" is a Judaism in which people begin to take responsibility for creating Jewish community, without waiting on the sidelines.

For me, this was a shocking turn of events. For years, I had struggled with my place in the Jewish community. I felt deep down that there must be a real power and mystery to prayer and tradition, but every time I tried to connect to Jewish life, I stumbled. I couldn't find places to engage seriously with Jewish texts. The search became too painful, so I dropped out of Jewish communal life.

I felt alone, but it turns out I wasn't alone at all. In fact, thousands of other young Jews were experiencing the same alienation from mainstream Jewish institutions. But they weren't willing to give up on the possibility of an engaged, vibrant Jewish life. This is the story of how some of those Jews found each other—through social networks and the Internet—and tried to solve this problem by forming their own Jewish communities.

First, this book looks at some of these grassroots Jewish communities—independent minyanim—in detail. What is an independent minyan? How is it different from a synagogue or from minyanim of a generation ago? More than sixty independent minyanim have been started in the past ten years. How do they differ from each other? What are their approaches to community, to prayer, and to Jewish life? What lessons can they offer to the wider Jewish world?

Second, this book looks beyond the independent minyanim to a new vision for Jewish engagement in the twenty-first century. How can we educate and empower a generation of Jews to take hold of their tradition? Can we shift from a mentality of survival to one of meaning? How will we recognize and meet the overwhelming demand for an engaged Jewish life? Can we imagine a new Jewish world?

A VISION OF EMPOWERED JUDAISM

Discovering my own passion for Jewish community took me on a journey that extended well beyond a minyan of young Jews on the Upper West Side. Building Kehilat Hadar allowed me to clarify a vision for a vibrant Jewish future in America—"Empowered Judaism." This is a Judaism in which people begin to take responsibility for creating Jewish community, without waiting on the sidelines. It is a Judaism that recognizes that thousands of Jews—of all ages and backgrounds—are thirsting for a meaningful engagement with critical life questions and want to open up the texts of our past to deepen that engagement. It is a Judaism that has confidence in the wisdom and relevance of our tradition, that doesn't resort to cheap gimmicks to draw people in. It is a Judaism that includes men and women as equal partners in religion and doesn't water down the tradition to be inclusive. It is a Judaism that refuses to cede access to knowledge to a vaunted rabbinical elite but values rabbis as critical teachers who inspire and give people the tools to learn more on their own. It is a Judaism that refuses to close itself off to the larger world and knows it has moral responsibility for the major crises of our modern age. It is a Judaism that trusts in the power of communal prayer and refuses to settle for mediocre attempts at connecting to God. It is, in short, a vision for a substantive Judaism of the future: an "Empowered Judaism."

VISION IN LIVED COMMUNITIES

This vision for an Empowered Judaism is ultimately much larger than any particular independent minyan. But visions are inspired by lived communities. With its dedicated volunteer culture, focus on inspiring traditional davening, high-level Torah study, and egalitarian, universal outlook, Kehilat Hadar attempts to live out a world of Empowered Judaism. Without Hadar, I would never have believed that such a Judaism might ever take root in America. But the seeds of Empowered Judaism are not only alive—they are spreading. Kehilat Hadar grew beyond anyone's dreams—thousands of people have been part of the Hadar community, with hundreds attending any given Shabbat and holiday service. Hadar also inspired other minyanim in cities in America and Israel. More than twenty thousand Jews in their twenties and early thirties have connected to these independent minyanim, and more than sixty independent minyanim have been launched across North America in the past ten years.

As this phenomenon spread, I became more and more invested in making the vision of Empowered Judaism a deeper reality. Together with my colleagues Rabbi Shai Held and Rabbi Ethan Tucker, I co-founded Mechon Hadar, a national institute dedicated to fostering Empowered Judaism across America. Through Mechon Hadar, we run the "Minyan Project," which offers consulting, resources, and education for sixty-plus independent minyanim. Our annual conferences attract minyan leaders from around the globe. Pushing this vision of Empowered Judaism even further, we co-founded Yeshivat Hadar, the first intensive egalitarian yeshiva for laypeople in the Western Hemisphere. Students live out a model of Torah, *avodah*, and *gemilut hasadim*—studying, praying, and volunteering in the community—up to fourteen hours a day. They come from dozens of cities around the world and return to their communities able to energize their peers in a new vision of Jewish life. A whole generation of young Jews is growing up knowing that the vision of Empowered Judaism is no dream—it is a fledgling reality they can connect to and help build.

ONE JEWISH JOURNEY

I am no longer a corporate fraud investigator. I am a rabbi who works with amazing partners and students to bring this vision of Empowered Judaism to fruition. This was never the path I imagined for myself, and in many ways I am an accidental leader—I stumbled into this role of advocate for Empowered Judaism. I tell my personal story here to demonstrate a point that is often overlooked by people hoping to seed change in the Jewish landscape: even for the leaders of this form of Judaism, life is not linear, and serious progress is often the result of messy journeys.

In one telling, my life's path (to date) was obvious, even scripted: the son of a rabbi and Jewish educator goes to Schechter day school and United Synagogue Youth, leads Harvard Hillel, goes to Israel on a Dorot leadership fellowship, uses his network to found an innovative minyan, marries a Jewish educator, becomes a rabbi, and teaches young Jews to build Jewish community through text and substance.

But in another telling, founding a minyan and becoming a rabbi were an unexpected turn: public-high-school prom king explores diversity at Harvard, forms a long-term relationship with religious-skeptic girlfriend, seeks a career as a journalist, moves to New York City but fails to find a Jewish community that resonates with him, works sixteen-hour days as an investment banker for Morgan Stanley, and drops out of communal Jewish life for years. On a trip to Israel, the power of Jewish learning from years past is reawakened in him; he returns to New York

> More than 20,000 Jews in their twenties and early thirties have connected to independent minyanim.

and eventually lands a corporate fraud investigation job. He finally has enough free time and mental space to dream up an ideal Jewish prayer community, and he reconnects with a college friend and a new friend to form an innovative minyan.

To put it another way: surely I drew on the investment of day school (until eighth grade), a warm and loving Jewish home, Jewish leadership opportunities in college, time in Israel, and networks formed over the years. But the "investment" took years to mature and was not a straight-line process. Nor was the outcome assured. At any number of points in my life, I opted for the quickest way out of Jewish community, whether through a romantic partner or through an all-consuming job. But ultimately my life's path—a journey through a host of Jewish communities along with a wide variety of non-Jewish experiences—made my vision clearer when it came to building a robust Jewish community.

Speed Davening: Empowerment as a Kid

My early connection to prayer had very little to do with meaning or an intense connection to God. Because my father was a congregational rabbi, I always had a relationship with shul. I felt very comfortable in the synagogue building and with the synagogue service. Shul was never that meaningful to me as a kid—I am not sure it was meant to be—it was just sort of fun. Sure, there were critically important events taking place on the bimah (platform), but down in our pew, I was content to play with toys and suck on candies. I never felt out of place in synagogue—in many ways it was a second home. Until I showed up at daily minyan.

> I never felt out of place in synagogue—in many ways it was a second home. Until I showed up at daily minyan.

I went to daily minyan with my dad on a regular basis when I was in middle school. Unlike shul on Shabbat, this was a space that felt utterly foreign. At ten years old, I was the youngest person by about fifty years. The minyan was populated by older men (and a few women) who started coming when they said *Kaddish* and then kept on coming. The davening was like nothing I had ever experienced before: people mumbled the prayers audibly. There was no cantor—the men rotated leading services themselves. And it was fast. Extremely fast. The davening was so fast that I was convinced they weren't saying all the words—how could someone really pronounce *all* those Hebrew words in that amount of time? I remember listening during *Aleinu,* trying to catch them skipping words. But they were saying them all, just much faster than I ever thought possible.

I resolved to learn how to daven the way they did—as fast as humanly possible. This wasn't a spiritual decision, but a social one—I felt out of place not keeping up with the people sitting around me. I was unfamiliar with most of the prayers, but I knew *Ashrei* from Shabbat, and I decided that I would practice saying that prayer quickly. I remember gearing up mentally as they approached *Ashrei* (to save time, I had already turned to the right page, waiting for them to arrive). When they started, I kept pace, probably for the first two lines. Then the old men sped past me in a blur. I made it to perhaps the sixth line when they were already moving on to the next psalm. As the weeks passed, I inched forward, until finally, months later, I could daven *Ashrei* as fast as they could. Now I just had to do that with the rest of the service.

Even though I was motivated to speed daven for social survival, I was surprised by the spirituality embedded in that service—not that the chapel regulars would have ever called it "spiritual." There were no melodies, no page announcements—just straight, fast davening. And yet there was an amazing rhythm to it. It wasn't boring; it was other-worldly. The sounds that filled the chapel, the mumbling of those words that I could barely keep up with, were a contrast to the American cultural life I was taking part in ("must-see TV," sports, and baseball cards). I felt transported by the strangeness of the sounds and also attracted to their performance. I was able to connect to God in those fast, mumbly prayer-filled mornings. I thought that "real" davening, as it was meant to be, was taking place right in that chapel, and I was the only kid who had discovered it.

Harvard Hillel: Peer-Led Community

Years later when I started going to Harvard Hillel as a college freshman, I saw yet another form of davening—a peer-led community of young people. This was similar to the chapel service at home in that no clergy member was running the show. But it was radically different in feel and style. This service had no mystery or longtime history, and it lacked otherworldly spirituality. It was chiefly a social environment—people were welcoming at *Kiddush*—but the service itself was overly predictable and plodding. The Torah readers were so-so. Same melodies, same rhythm, every week. I became a leader of that minyan with one goal in mind—to move things along faster to get to *Kiddush* quicker. I had no passion to try to remake the service, and I didn't really believe a better way was possible. For me, even as a leader of the minyan, college was a cynical davening time—prayer can't really engage people, I figured, so let's just get it done as quickly and efficiently as possible.

The Holy Land: Davening with Clear Intention

When I went to Israel on a Dorot Fellowship following graduation, my spiritual life opened up and my understanding of the possibilities of prayer was radically altered. In college, there were three flavors of minyan. In Jerusalem, there were hundreds. What's more, people seemed to daven as if they *meant* it. They exuded this sense that something could happen in prayer. Take the Leader Minyan in Jerusalem, for example. It was the polar opposite of the "let's get it over with" ethos I had come to develop in college. The people at the Leader Minyan were perfectly happy to spend seven hours davening what should be a two-hour service. I was both repelled and drawn in. And the melodies they used—I had never heard any of them. Yet they were resonant in a deep way. Here they didn't repeat a melody once or twice; they repeated it for fifteen or twenty minutes. It was like a mantra experience, but with the familiar words of the siddur. This prayer style was not just different, it bordered on scary. What if prayer could be really, deeply meaningful? How would that change the way I related to Judaism and God? These were questions I was running away from in college, and the experience at the Leader Minyan forced me to confront them.

Cognitive Dissonance: Spiritual Davening sans Women

Still, I was unable to fully let myself go into a deep relationship with prayer. I spent most of that year in Israel confounded by an empirical fact—of all the moving davening experiences available in Israel, none of them allowed women to participate equally. I was confused and somewhat angry about this. Why was it that the values I had grown up with were seemingly incompatible with a meaningful, powerful davening experience? Despite their spiritual draw, I didn't let myself fully experience the davening offerings in Jerusalem because I was upset at the lack of egalitarianism in this form of compelling religious expression. By writing it off as fundamentally immoral and unethical because of its approach to gender, I sidestepped the challenge of what it would mean practically to have a prayer life that had the power to move me. I simply couldn't handle a world in which God played a real role in my life and I could connect to divinity in prayer. I much preferred to stay on the sidelines, sulking in righteous indignation at their lack of egalitarianism.

> People seemed to daven as if they *meant* it. It was like a mantra experience, but with the familiar words of the siddur.

A Wandering Jew

When I moved to New York after a year in Jerusalem, I started a journey away from Jewish community that lasted six years. I first lived on the Upper West Side and bounced around various synagogues and minyanim. But my friends and I never quite felt integrated into the communities there, and the davening itself didn't draw me in. I followed my serious girlfriend to Greenwich Village. She taught me about poetry—a different spiritual endeavor—and I cloistered my prayer life into a solitary—and extremely fast—performance in the morning. Shabbat became a time of reading and relaxing, but not a time of prayer. I threw myself into my jobs—first investigating fraud in the New York City public schools, and then working at Morgan Stanley as a junior banker in municipal finance. The pace of that job was punishing: in before 9 a.m., out after 11 p.m. It left me no time for serious Jewish reflection (or for much of anything else), and my spiritual life hit a nadir.

Drawn Back to Jewish Communal Life in Israel

In August 2000, I left Morgan Stanley and went to Israel to decompress. After a few weeks, I wandered back to the Pardes Institute of Jewish Studies, a yeshiva I had attended five years earlier. There I experienced three weeks of intense community and study that lurched me out of my worldview. Unlike five years earlier, I was so burned out from my job that I didn't have the energy to defend myself against the power of Jewish community—and the presence of God. I went to a Shabbat dinner, and instead of cynically dismissing the singing at the Shabbat table, I simply participated—and enjoyed it. I learned Talmud with a *havruta* (a study partner) and became engrossed in a text that finally was speaking to me. I could feel myself losing a battle to ignore the possibility of God in my life. It was exhilarating—and scary.

I moved back to New York after a few months and had a painful breakup with my girlfriend. I took my time finding a new job, living off my bonus from Morgan Stanley. I continued to learn Talmud with an old college friend. And I was finally ready to search out a meaningful relationship to God through prayer.

A New Vision

Despite this desire to connect to God through prayer, I felt frustrated. None of the options—even in Jewishly robust New York City—seemed to take seriously the possibility that traditional prayer and practice could offer a real and profound encounter with the Divine while still supporting a worldview that promoted gender egalitarianism and openness to the wider world. Drawing on my memories of experiences in Jerusalem, I awoke to the possibility of a prayer life that was more than just a performance, but that actively worked to connect to God. I had a hard time settling. I started to dream up an altogether new possibility: what about just starting something fresh? I floated the idea to a few friends, who—for other reasons—had been thinking along similar lines, and I gave myself six months to start a new minyan.

At the same time, I started a job at a law firm as a corporate fraud investigator. The job was wonderful—it challenged and engaged me, and I felt I was doing good for the world. But its real blessing was a nine-to-five schedule. I could spend my free time after work dreaming up a Jewish community that would legitimately forge a deep connection to God through traditional prayer, without giving up modern values. One friendship and one chance encounter made this pipe dream a reality. Mara Benjamin, whom I had met just a few months earlier, would join me at various synagogues on the Upper West Side, and during *Kiddush* we shared our frustrations together. Then one Friday night, leaving an Orthodox synagogue, I ran into Ethan Tucker, a friend I had not seen in years. He and I had led the Harvard Hillel egalitarian minyan together years earlier, and I felt the irony of us both "settling" at this synagogue we didn't really connect to. We resolved to start something new, and because he was also a friend of Mara's, the three of us came up with a plan. We met at a bar in April 2001, hammered out a vision in a couple of hours, and launched the minyan a few weeks later.

Encountering God in Community

Kehilat Hadar (as we named the minyan in October 2001) became the focal point of my contention that I could encounter God in a community that shared my values and still believed in the search for the Divine. I spent every waking moment thinking through the logistics and contours of the minyan, and while I still worked at my job in corporate fraud investigation, the minyan became my real passion. I remember that very first service, when Mara led *Shacharit* in Ethan's apartment, and she used melodies I had never heard before. I was drawn in. My long battle to pretend that prayer wasn't powerful and God couldn't play a real role in my life was lost. I remember crying during *Shacharit*, because it felt like the end of a long journey. It was a journey that had taken me far away from the spiritual side of Judaism, yet one that led me back with fresh goals and energy. In truth, that morning was not the end of the journey, but a first step in a much longer path to build a world of Empowered Judaism.

Why Become a Rabbi?

In 2002, a year after I started Hadar, I decided to become a rabbi. Five years later I was ordained at The Jewish Theological Seminary. This was certainly not my life's plan, and in some ways it ran counter to the lay-led ethos of Hadar. After all, I founded Hadar as a corporate fraud investigator, living out my strong belief that a person doesn't need to be a rabbi to run an inspiring minyan. But the Jewish world still needs rabbis— rabbis who are committed to opening up the power of the Jewish tradition and who believe in empowering others to take responsibility for their Jewish lives and communities. In other words, rabbis as teachers are in critical demand. And after a year running Hadar, I knew that my life's focus was not only to build one specific community but also to spread the model of Empowered Judaism. I couldn't predict exactly how this would play out at the time, but I knew it would require me to be first and foremost a teacher of Jewish texts and tradition. I started rabbinical school with the faith that this career would lead to a fulfillment of my innate knowledge that I wanted to do something significant to build Jewish community in America.

Taking Hadar's Vision to the Next Stage

While I was in my final year in rabbinical school, I co-founded Mechon Hadar (the Hadar Institute), an organization devoted to building a world of Empowered Judaism. My partners in this project—Rabbi Shai Held and Rabbi Ethan Tucker—shared my passion for a new vision of an engaged American Jewish life. Since the minyan started in 2001, dozens of other communities—independent minyanim—had sprouted up across the United States and Israel. Through its Minyan Project program, Mechon Hadar responded to some of the needs faced by these communities, networking the leaders in conferences and through the Internet to share skills and best practices.

Perhaps the most audacious move we did at Mechon Hadar was to found Yeshivat Hadar, the flagship educational institution of Empowered Judaism. Yeshivat Hadar is North America's first-ever egalitarian place of intensive Jewish study and practice that is not a professional school. Yeshivat Hadar serves as a Torah nerve center for young Jews interested in living out Empowered Judaism. In three years, more than a hundred men and women, mostly in their twenties, have spent sixty hours a week learning Jewish texts in the original, davening three times a day, working for social justice, and building community with a diverse group of Jews. I teach Talmud to the beginners in the program, the most challenging and inspiring experience of my professional career. Yeshivat Hadar represents my gamble that the American Jewish community is finally ready for a place of community building, text skills, and meaning that is open to the world. It is a 7 a.m. to 9 p.m. instantiation of my belief that Judaism is relevant to the modern world and that we must train young Jews to be able to take hold of Jewish tradition and put it to work in communities across America.

MOVING ON

Although I have devoted my life to building a world of Empowered Judaism, I have since moved away from the Upper West Side and the minyan where it all started for me. Kehilat Hadar is rooted on the Upper West Side, and life in that neighborhood became too expensive for my family. I met my wife at Hadar's first Shavuot Retreat in 2002, and we now have a daughter. We moved to Washington Heights and are working with a rabbi (who davened at Hadar as a student) to transform a hundred-year-old synagogue. Although there is much optimism at the shul, we are just at the beginning of that project.

> When you stop running away from the possibility of encountering God, when that scary possibility of meaning becomes real, wonderful things can happen.

Once in a while my family and I return to the Upper West Side for Shabbat and to daven at Hadar. It is filled with people in their twenties, people I don't know, who are looking for the same kind of community we were looking for eight years ago. Many of them were in middle school when we started Hadar. It is painful to leave the community I poured so much of my soul into, but so very inspiring to see others taking up the mantle and pushing it forward—growing, innovating, and changing in new and inspired directions. And it is a reminder to me that when you stop running away from the possibility of encountering God, when that scary possibility of meaning becomes real, wonderful things can happen.

I continue to embrace a vision of empowering Jews of all ages to find spiritual meaning in prayer and in community. The inspiration behind Kehilat Hadar—to create a minyan that resonated with our sense of spiritual yearning and that reflected our most deeply held values—propelled me and like-minded friends to make our vision a reality. As you will see in this book, others had somewhat different visions, which led to the formation of independent minyanim with a slightly different focus or emphasis. Overall, however, the drive behind the independent minyanim has been remarkably uniform across the country and in Israel—to build a prayer community that speaks to each of its members' spiritual longings, gives participants a sense of community and belonging, and empowers them to find in Judaism a deep sense of meaning and purpose that infuses every corner of their lives. By looking at what independent minyanim can teach the wider Jewish world about how to build vibrant Jewish communities, I hope to illustrate the ways in which these grassroots communities are the first step to a world of Empowered Judaism.

1
Kehilat Hadar
A Model of Empowered Judaism

This is the story of Kehilat Hadar—one community that exemplifies Empowered Judaism in the twenty-first century. It is not a perfect community, and it is not going to "fix" American Judaism. It has a tremendous amount to learn from past and contemporary Jewish communities. But it also can serve as a model of what Jewish life can look like when a small group of laypeople feel empowered to act on their vision of Judaism. Fundamentally, Kehilat Hadar succeeded because it had a resonant vision, was willing to define clear boundaries while remaining open to anyone hoping to share that vision, and energized hundreds of people to take hold of their own Jewish life and express it in community.

CRAFTING A COMMUNITY

If you could design your own prayer community from scratch, what would it look like? This is the project that Mara Benjamin, Ethan Tucker, and I embarked on in April 2001. We were all in our twenties, had each been living on the Upper West Side of Manhattan for a few years, and shared a very clear vision of a prayer community. One evening, sitting at a back table at the Abbey Pub at 105th Street and Broadway, we wrote down our plan, and Kehilat Hadar was born. What led us to that moment?

A Millennial Moment: The Turning Point
In New York City in the early 2000s people from all walks of Jewish life were exploring new spiritual paths: Orthodox folks were experimenting

with egalitarianism; people returning from intensive time in Israel were looking to reengage with a vibrant prayer community in the States; people with nontraditional backgrounds, who would never dream of separating sexes in their communities, sought out a vibrant, traditional service. Better yet, these people were starting to notice each other through Shabbat meals and social networks, and they even started to pray together at some of the new options on the landscape.

By 2001, the Upper West Side was already home to a few start-up minyanim. There were the long-standing start-up minyanim of the 1960s and 1970s—Minyan M'at and the West Side Minyan—that met at Ansche Chesed, which was, at the time, an unaffiliated synagogue. In the 1990s, Kehilat Orach Eliezer (KOE), Rimonim, and the Friday night minyan at Shaare Zedek were founded. The Drisha Institute started a popular Rosh Hashanah and Yom Kippur minyan. But there were also a few others that had sprouted since 2000 to offer Friday night davening. Two that were influential for Kehilat Hadar both met in apartments about once a month: the "113th Street Minyan," organized by rabbinical students Laurie Hahn and Lauren Thomas, and the "Steinmetz-Silber Minyan," which met at the home of Dr. Devora Steinmetz and Rabbi David Silber. They were both traditional and egalitarian, and the leaders used vibrant melodies in the service. The living rooms were packed with people and, perhaps most significant for me, I didn't know most of them. I felt for the first time that I was not alone in my search for a particular kind of prayer community.

Two other critical factors were at play in New York City at this time: the start-up culture of the Internet world and the power of e-mail. Even though by 2001 the Internet bubble had just burst, the possibility that recent college grads could start a successful venture was still so fresh in the collective consciousness that no one batted an eyelash at young people who said they were going to start something new.

Meanwhile, the most powerful community-organizing tool to date—e-mail—was still fresh enough that people were reading e-mails and responding to them. The last time I had tried to do any community organizing—in college in 1994—the only way to mobilize people was via the phone tree. E-mail was the critical venue for getting the word out to people, and it was free and easy. (Technology is still a critical part of Kehilat Hadar—see "Maximizing Technology," p. 57.)

In the midst of this energized cultural and social environment, Mara, Ethan, and I connected over the fact that no one in our wide social network had yet organized a start-up minyan for Shabbat morning (of course, a much bigger challenge than Friday night because of the need for a *sefer Torah* [a Torah scroll] and for enough skilled people to lead the multifaceted service). We each attended a range of synagogues and minyanim in the area, but we didn't belong to any of them and didn't attend any particular one with regularity. We were not founding a breakaway from a specific shul; we were completely under the radar, starting something new that expressed our own vision of a vibrant prayer service.

What was this vision? On paper it was simple: a fully traditional liturgy and Torah reading; a commitment to full gender egalitarianism; a short (five-minute) *dvar Torah*; a lay-led ethos with high standards of excellence; a service that doesn't drag and engages the daveners through music. The trick was pulling it off.

By the end of our second meeting at the neighborhood bar, we had a plan: we picked a date (April 28, 2001) and a place (Ethan and his wife Ariela's apartment on 110th Street and Broadway). We brainstormed a list of a hundred people to invite through e-mail and found a *sefer Torah* to borrow. We carefully chose the leaders for that first service, and at 9 a.m. on Shabbat morning, we showed up and wondered: would anyone else come?

The answer was a resounding yes. Sixty people crammed into the tiny living room in Ethan and Ariela's one-bedroom apartment, and by *Musaf* people were spilling out into the hallway. The entire service, which included one of the longest Torah reading portions of the year, was over in two hours and fifteen minutes. But it was not a rushed service—it was joyous and filled with melodies most of us had never heard before. The small room worked to our advantage, because the sixty people felt energized and part of something larger than a one-time minyan, even on that first Shabbat. Because the minyan was entirely new, there was no "insider" or "outsider" feel. Aside from Ethan, Mara, and me, everyone was new to the endeavor, and people felt excited to meet others who were attracted to the minyan.

GROWTH AND EXPANSION

In the next eight years, the minyan—later named Kehilat Hadar—developed in ways that we couldn't have imagined on that first Shabbat. Hadar continued to meet every other week until 2005, when it increased to three of four weeks, and then, in 2008, it expanded to meet every week. The Shabbat morning crowd grew from 60 to an average of 180 on Shabbat mornings, and the e-mail list exploded from 100 to 2,800. Services grew to include Rosh Hashanah and Yom Kippur, Purim, Shavuot, and Simchat Torah, drawing in total over 1,000 people in a given year. Hundreds of people led services, read Torah, and gave *divrei Torah*. In 2002, Hadar launched a weekly *beit midrash* (study group), held at the Jewish Community Center (JCC) in Manhattan. The minyan started a social-action team that focused its efforts on Darfur and homelessness. Originally founded as a biweekly Shabbat morning prayer service, Hadar grew into a community of Torah, *avodah*, and *gemilut hasadim*—study, worship, and acts of lovingkindness.

Much has been made of the innovations at Kehilat Hadar. But, in reality, I believe the core reason Hadar succeeded is because it did *not* attempt a big-picture reinvention of Jewish tradition or practice. Rather, Hadar tackled a number of discrete issues with a larger vision toward excellence, inspirational davening, and rethinking some basic assumptions about how American egalitarian worship communities can be constituted.

Youthful Energy, Youthful Appeal

One of the most striking features of the minyan was its youth. Because most people in 2001 who were comfortable on e-mail were in their twenties and thirties, and because most of our social networks were made up of people in that age range, the vast majority of people who came to the first minyan were in their twenties. Although this was not a stated goal of the minyan, it soon became a defining characteristic. We actually tried in the very early days to actively combat this "twenties only" feel. The next few services at Hadar were hosted by Len Sharzer, a surgeon turned rabbinical student who had grown kids of his own. He invited people from his shul community to join the minyan, and a few of them came to the first few meetings. We also contacted people in our social networks in their forties and fifties, but word spread so quickly among people in their twenties and thirties that we never quite attained the generational diversity we would have liked. Also, Hadar was appealing to a group of people who had not found a home in a synagogue community. Although some older adults might have been attracted to the style of Hadar, many would have had to actively leave a community they felt a part of in some way.

Although our ideal vision was a multi-generational community, there was something energizing about a minyan of people mainly in their twenties that was critical to Hadar's founding spirit. The youthful vibe and willingness to experiment with new ways of doing things certainly defined Hadar's culture. Jewish events and organizations that target young people are often styled to capitalize on the dating or networking scene. But at Hadar, youthful energy was channeled in another way: in a yearning desire to connect to God, while not taking oneself too seriously. There was also a sense of optimism—these were not burned-out veterans of Jewish communal life, but hopeful activists looking to strike a new path. That attitude filtered throughout the prayer and other programming at Hadar.

> We all bring to the community our ripened fruit, the experiences and ideas we have developed in our lives, the patterns and rhythms that define us. The challenge is to be open to new ideas and experiences (budding fruit) without rejecting the ripened fruit of our past.

Choosing a Name, Reflecting a Vision

We waited five months before choosing a name for the minyan. In some ways this demonstrated our resistance to being defined at all. Once there was a name, people would necessarily start to attach labels to it and make associations with it. But we also knew that we couldn't go on forever simply as "the minyan." When we set out to choose a name, we had two major criteria: a Hebrew word with two syllables that was easy to pronounce, and one with no previous association with any other labels. I carefully read through Psalms in order to come up with a number of options.

In the end, although we almost went with *sulam*, meaning "ladder," we chose *hadar*. We intentionally did not name the community Minyan Hadar, because we aspired to be something more than just a minyan. We chose Kehilat Hadar (Hadar Community), because of its reflection of our values: a belief that prayer can be meaningful and that community thrives when old and new coexist, and a desire to provide a spirit of welcoming to people of all ages and backgrounds. *Hadar* also expressed some of the hopes and aspirations we had for the minyan and the community (*kehilah*) we were forming. The following is a deeper explanation of the name that I shared with the community at the time:

> *Hadar* is a noun meaning "splendor" or "glory," and it is also a verb meaning "to glorify, respect, or honor." It appears numerous times in *tefillot*, including in the *Kaddish* (*Yithadar*) and *Ashrei* (*Hadar k'vod hodecha.... Uch'vod hadar malchuto*).
>
> Yet the name embodies even more. The word *hadar* is found in relationship to the three classic Jewish lenses: *bein adam l'atzmo* (our relationship with ourselves), *bein adam l'havero* (our relationships with others), and *bein adam laMakom* (our relationship with God).
>
> **Bein adam l'atzmo (our relationship with ourselves).** In the Torah, the *etrog* is referred to as *pri etz hadar* (fruit of the beautiful tree, or beautiful fruit of the tree). In the Talmud, there is a discussion about what exactly this means. Rabbi Abahu offers the following comment: Don't read *hadar* as "splendor"; rather, read it as something that dwells (*dar*) on its tree from year to year (Babylonian Talmud, *Sukkah* 35a). Rashi takes this to mean that the *etrog* is the only fruit that remains on the tree from one season to the next. Therefore, an *etrog* tree has well-ripened fruit from years past coexisting with newly budding fruit from the current year.
>
> We see this as a metaphor for an ideal internal relationship: we all bring to the community our ripened fruit, the experiences and ideas we have developed in our lives, the patterns and rhythms that define us. The challenge is to be open to new ideas and experiences (budding fruit) with-

out rejecting the ripened fruit of our past. We hope to make our prayer community a space where people strive for that internal integration.

Bein adam l'havero (our relationships with others). Hadar is used in the Torah as a verb in the following verse from Leviticus 19:32: V'hadarta p'nei zaken ("Pay respect to the elder"). Our minyan aspires to be a place where everyone respects each other, from simply introducing yourself to someone new to creating a culture of hachnasat orchim (welcoming guests).

Bein adam laMakom (our relationship with God). There is a rich tradition in Rabbinic and kabbalistic literature that God is in need of salvation—people are not the only ones in need of saving. This is one understanding of the somewhat cryptic phrase we say repeatedly during the Hoshanot on Sukkot: Ani v'ho hoshia na—Save me and God.

Psalm 104:1 states: Hod v'hadar lavashta ("You dressed in splendor and glory"). We traditionally say this line when we put on the tallit, and the Rabbis imagined God dressing in a metaphoric prayer shawl of light. The hope we have for this minyan is that through our prayers and actions, we will provide that comforting covering to God, doing our part in contributing to God's salvation. The challenge to strive toward that goal will remain a motivating force behind our activities as a kahal (community).

A New Model of Leadership

From the beginning, one of the salient features of Hadar has been its volunteer leadership. Oftentimes, volunteer-led enterprises are known for their inclusion and democracy, but not necessarily for their efficiency and productivity. Perhaps the most unusual aspect of Hadar, and what made it different from other minyanim before it, is this ability to combine a volunteer ethos with a focus on "getting things done."

Minyanim thrive or falter on their core leadership in the early years. Only two months after its founding, both Ethan and Mara moved away to other cities (reflecting the increased mobility of this age group), leaving me to continue what we had started. In preparation for their move, we looked for two replacement leaders and chose Adam Wall and Debbie Kaufman. When they started as *gabbaim* (organizers) with me in summer 2001, I hardly knew either one of them. Our selection criteria were based more on instinct than knowledge. Adam—a manager at a construction firm—was old friends with Ethan, and he had a hunch Adam would make a good *gabbai*. We asked Debbie Kaufman—who worked in public television—to join the team because she had done *hagbahah* (lifting a *sefer Torah*) with particular gusto a few weeks earlier and seemed to have the excitement to push the minyan forward.

Luckily, our instincts were correct. Adam and Debbie turned out to be exactly what the minyan needed: energetic, stable, extremely competent leaders with the time and desire to move the minyan out of the start-up phase. The three of us would remain *gabbaim* together for the next three years and become incredibly close friends. Over the next year, we grew the *gabbai* team to six, adding Debbi Bohnen, Josh Greenfield, and Jessica Lissy. Together, we enshrined in Hadar a culture of "getting the job done" by imposing certain expectations on ourselves.

A Small Core of Strong Voices

What were the structures that led to our culture of getting things done? Part of the success was simply the size of the leadership. Eschewing the model of a thirty-person, or even an eight- to ten-person board or leadership council, we kept the leadership very simple in the beginning: three to six people who had ultimate responsibility for the day-to-day operations. In such a small group, there was nowhere to hide from responsibility, and everyone's voice was critical to the operation. Hadar was a top priority in our lives, and we were driven by a sense of shared mission and vision of what the community could be. The six of us were working in the secular world. But in those first couple of years, our jobs were secondary to the work we put into the minyan. We would e-mail each other every day—day and night—to make decisions and address logistics, and we committed to attending pretty much all the Hadar programming.

On top of the daily e-mail traffic, we had a weekly meeting. By this point in my life, I had been to hundreds of meetings in various contexts—Jewish and secular—and most of them were basically a game of counting down the painful minutes until they were over. But Hadar meetings were different. First, we broke some taboos—while most meetings are judged by how long they run (the shorter the better), with most averaging two hours, we decided to set the normal meeting time for three hours (7 p.m. to 10 p.m.). This extra hour paradoxically made the meeting run much more smoothly. Oftentimes, in a two-hour meeting, the entire goal is to run through the agenda items as quickly as possible, and when discussion is getting serious, the timekeeper is nervous because the packed agenda won't stand a chance unless "we move on." But this tends to cut off debate artificially. With a three-hour limit, we were able to really delve into critical issues during the one time each week that we sat face-to-face.

Evaluation and evolution. The *gabbai* meetings were also an opportunity to evaluate ourselves and build on what we had created, sharpening our ideas of what Hadar was about and how the community should develop. Every week, we started with a brief review of the previous Shabbat's service. This didn't take long—maybe five or ten minutes—but it gave us a forum to articulate what "good davening" looked like and the ways in which any particular week stacked up. We spent the most time evaluating our own actions as *gabbaim*. (Do we need to make announcements at the end of services? How can we make calling people up to the Torah move smoothly?) When one of us made a public goof, we'd joke, "You're fired." In truth, these conversations were done in a shared spirit of loving feedback for each other.

Keeping it light. Humor was a critical part of the *gabbai* culture. We took our commitment to Hadar very seriously, but at the same time, we never hesitated to make fun of ourselves (and the people in the *gabbai* group had a talent for self-deprecating humor). Being a volunteer organization afforded us the freedom to fail—the knowledge that if our venture didn't work out, we could shut Hadar down without having to lay off any staff. This recognition of our minyan's fragility allowed us some decent perspective on all the many discussions whose results we took so seriously, and we didn't hesitate to mock ourselves for all our neuroses. Ultimately, humor allowed us to keep our meetings light, even when we were dealing with critical needs of the growing community.

Policy making and accountability. The longest discussions in our meetings were reserved for policy decisions, which also helped us clarify the guiding principles of Hadar. How do we respond to someone who made numerous errors while leading davening, but who wants to lead davening again? Should we cosponsor an event that will take time away from our activities within Hadar? How should we set a kashrut policy that respects the diversity of the community? These were thorny issues, and we spoke about them for the bulk of the meetings. But two features characterized those discussions. First of all, everyone spoke and offered an opinion; and second, we were not politicking or grandstanding. We legitimately cared for the health of the community and its standards, and we looked at each problem from one key standpoint: how will this affect Hadar's ability to maintain its formula of success?

The meetings were designed around a culture of action and accountability. We agreed that if we made a decision in a meeting, we would carry it out, and we held each other accountable over e-mail in the following days. During the meetings, we often asked each other, "Are you writing this down?" (meaning, "Are you going to follow up on this decision in the week ahead?"). This gave people the hope and encouragement that the time they spent in meetings would actually lead to a result "on the ground."

Getting It Right

Of course, much of the ethos of Hadar was not to reinvent Judaism, but to execute it a bit better than we had seen it done elsewhere. This manifested in hundreds of little pre-planned decisions and details that added up to a well-run minyan. We never wanted the fact that we weren't run by professionals to mean that we were less than "professional." We also felt that getting the details right would gain buy-in from the community and foster goodwill. Here are a few key examples.

Keeping up the energy. On Simchat Torah, the key to exuberant dancing with the Torah is continued upbeat energy. Those who have been to *hakafot* (dancing with the *sifrei Torah*) know that energy tends to lag as someone desperately tries to come up with a new song to sing. Or people belt out a tune for the first and second rounds, but flag by the end of the sixth or seventh round. To prevent this, we went into Simchat Torah with a list of songs and a rough order of when to do each one. (Which song will kick off the round? Which song will end it?) We did some simple math, and figured that each of the seven *hakafot* shouldn't last more than seven minutes if we were going to finish all the dancing in less than an hour.

Coming prepared didn't mean there was no room for adjustments in the moment, but it meant we didn't get caught flat-footed without knowing which song would come next, losing the energy we had built up.

Bringing people into the circle. Another energy lag on Simchat Torah is that there is always a group of people who linger on the edge of the dancing but, for whatever reason, don't join the circle. There is an easy solution for this: invite them in. I had been to so many Simchat Torah celebrations in which the energy was depleted by people talking around the perimeter—so much so that the dancing itself was often a sideshow to the schmoozing. But at Hadar, people wanted to dance, even if they didn't always start out dancing. So I would dance on the outer ring of the circle, looking for people who were clapping along, but not yet in the circle. Almost everyone I invited would join in, and as a result, the bystanders were the sideshow, and the dancing remained the focus.

Streamlining rituals for large crowds. Hand washing at meals is often a logistical black hole at Jewish gatherings, as the crowd lines up single file at one communal sink. On the minyan's first Shavuot retreat, we set up twelve washing stations side by side to accommodate our crowd of 250 people. We also decided to make *Kiddush* communally but to ask each table to make *Hamotzi* (the blessing of the bread) on its own. We saved twenty minutes on dinner, and people felt as if the meal moved along, even with the large crowd.

Saving announcements for e-mail. Announcements take up a tremendous amount of time in most synagogues and minyanim. We greatly feared that as Hadar expanded, announcements would become more and more onerous, and, I submit, people don't remember the details of shul announcements anyway. To avoid spending live airtime on community announcements, we used e-mail to spread the word about upcoming programs.

Spreading the word: creating a forum for community engagement. From our inception, we recognized that Hadar was part of a larger ecosystem of Jewish communities on the Upper West Side. Because so many Jewish organizations were interested in reaching Jews in their twenties and thirties, and because we were one of the few organizations that had managed to attract a critical mass of those Jews, we were often asked to announce other programs, and we wanted to encourage the development of a rich, diverse community beyond Hadar. We created a community postings announcement list (and later webpage), to which anyone could post any Jewish communal activity. We also spread the word about programs and services that Hadar couldn't offer but were available elsewhere in the community, like a spreadsheet of synagogues and restaurants that had a sukkah on Sukkot. In the world of denominational synagogues, it is almost unheard of to announce a program from another synagogue (unless it is specifically meant for cross-community programming), but our announcements helped create an outlet for other organizations to compete in the marketplace of programming for young Jews and also positioned Hadar as the go-to place for information about local Jewish life.

Changing a liability into an asset: innovative meeting locations. Not having a building to call home presents a massive number of challenges to Hadar. In the first year of Kehilat Hadar's existence, we met in fourteen different spaces. We tried to meet at a number of synagogues, but no synagogue on the Upper West Side had room for 200 additional people in a separate room on Shabbat morning. Our meeting sites ranged from a Latino cultural center, to a rooftop apartment space, to a Franciscan community center. We moved on from each place either because we outgrew the space or because they couldn't accommodate our schedule.

> One of the advantages of not having a permanent building to call our own was that we were free to program in more creative ways.

But one of the advantages of not having a permanent building to call our own was that we were free to program in more creative ways. For instance, in advance of Tisha B'Av, one of the members of the Hadar community suggested that we meet outdoors. He recalled all the moving Tisha B'Av services he had participated in as a kid in summer camp and figured we could re-create that on the Upper West Side simply by meeting outdoors. So in August 2001, we held Tisha B'Av services on a grassy hill in Central Park; 180 people came (at that time, it was by far our largest service).

Knowing when to call it quits. Sometimes the trick to doing things right is to know when you're in over your head. The first Purim we had at Hadar was a sight to behold—250 people crammed into the Franciscan Community Center on 97th Street. There was no room to sit, even on the floor. But following the *Megillah* reading (no *spiel*, no costume parade—just straight, great *Megillah* reading) we had a party at a Hispanic cultural center. It was a phenomenal party, with DJ Aaron Bisman (later the founder of JDub records). The cover charge was low, alcohol was plentiful, and the music was uplifting.

The next year, word spread about the Hadar party, and the JCC asked to cosponsor with us. We did, and 600 people came. Bisman was the DJ again, but the party was not the same: too many people there for the sound system to handle, too much schmoozing, too many people getting too drunk. The intimate feel of the year before gave way to a big, institutional party vibe.

The third year, we decided to go on our own—no cosponsor. But we rented a site that was outside our core neighborhood. Even though 150 people made the trek, the room (a high school gym) was too big, and the place felt empty. Also, our cover charge was fifteen dollars, and people left with a feeling that the money they paid was just not worth it.

The year after that, we had no party. In fact, Hadar hasn't held a Purim party since. The lesson we learned was this: we aren't the experts in every Jewish program, and we didn't have the best take on how to run a party. So for years afterward, we have publicized a number of other Purim parties and happily encouraged people to go to them. But we had no compulsion to try to be what we're not. The freedom to say about a program, "That worked one year, it doesn't work now," is incredibly liberating.

VOLUNTEER ENGAGEMENT

The lifeblood of Hadar is its volunteers, and the community only functions with an engaged and energized volunteer crew. So the key question is this: how do you attract volunteers to a new enterprise and keep them motivated?

Success Is Contagious

How many times have you been to a minyan where the following announcement is made: "Raise your hand if you can make the minyan next week. If we don't get enough volunteers, we won't be able to have

minyan." This is essentially the guilt-trip form of volunteer recruit-
ment—the "world will fall down without you" mode of motivating volunteers. Although this makes each volunteer feel very important, it also
sends the message that the entire volunteer enterprise hangs by a thread.

At Hadar, we did not broadcast a sense of desperation, even when
we might have been most tempted to in the early days. People were
inspired by the constancy of the minyan and the ability of a small, committed group of people to get things done. This then led them to ask
how they could get more involved. Success inspired more volunteers.

But even success is not enough to motivate everyone. Ultimately,
most people need to be asked directly to contribute. This is why the leadership at Hadar actively sought out volunteers one person at a time. When
you receive a group e-mail asking for help, you are often tempted to let
someone else answer. But when someone comes up to you and asks you to
do something personally, you feel important and valuable, and it is much
harder to say no. At Hadar, we worked on figuring out who would be able
to complete a task and then asked that person, one-on-one, to do that task.

Making Volunteers Feel Appreciated

The flip side of volunteering is thanking those who come forward to volunteer. Yet in most congregations, the thanking of volunteers is done in
a long roll-call list at the end of services or a program, when all people
want to do is leave. With the ease of communication through e-mail,
Hadar made sure to add another forum: a personal thank-you via e-mail
to each volunteer. This became a signature feature of volunteering at
Hadar (especially for service leaders)—within two days, people received
an e-mail thanking them specifically for the work they had done. Because
this was via e-mail, the thank-yous often led to a return thank-you from
the volunteer (after all, *gabbaim* were volunteering as well) and often
some important feedback about the program we would not have otherwise received. Fundamentally, volunteers need reinforcement and gratitude, and a recitation of names at the end of a long program isn't enough.

Developing Volunteer Leaders

If scouting for volunteers is critical to success, then how do you know
whether any particular volunteer is ready for a crucial role in the community? I found that volunteers often show their abilities in the small,

low-risk tasks and, if successful there, can be tapped for more important jobs. In the early days of Hadar, we had to set up our own chairs every week before davening (people came early to services and spent a sweaty, frantic half hour dragging out chairs and setting them up in rows). I noticed the people who came on time, who took initiative setting up the chairs, who remembered the detailed way in which we decided the chairs should be aligned, and who did it with a smile. They were ready for the next stage of leadership.

Another example: when Kehilat Hadar produced its CD of melodies, we needed a volunteer who could process the orders and mail them out. It was not a glamorous task, but it was something that needed to be done accurately (and not ignored). Our volunteer—then a college student—handled that job and then took on more and more responsibility, until she became one of the six *gabbaim* of the community four years later. Even mundane tasks require skills, and they offer an opportunity to discover future leadership talent.

The Leadership Team

As an expanding organization, Hadar soon needed a broader group of committed volunteers to carry out the many tasks of organizing our community. To expand the leadership and create a pipeline for future *gabbaim* and other key leaders, we added a layer to the structure of Hadar called the Leadership Team. (We named everything at Hadar a *team* rather than a *committee*, something I learned from the educational organization Limmud in England. After all, no one likes committee meetings, but everyone wants to be part of the team!)

To join the Leadership Team, people didn't simply opt in. We asked them to apply. This was in some ways heresy ("How can you ask people who aren't going to be paid to apply for a volunteer job in their own community?"), but we wanted people to take their volunteer role seriously, and if they couldn't commit to writing something about their goals, then they might not be right for the job. We asked them two questions on the "application": (1) What is your vision for Hadar? and (2) In what ways could Hadar improve? Though we almost never rejected an application, the process served to elevate the status of the volunteer job and make it something people had to seek out and exert some effort to acquire.

PRAYER: BALANCING TRADITION AND CREATIVITY

One of the clear dividing lines between egalitarian and non-egalitarian synagogues is the limits of liturgical flexibility. At Hadar, however, we broke the mold, deciding from our very first meetings to use a full traditional liturgy. Although most egalitarian syngagogues in New York's Upper West Side prayed in Hebrew and used a traditional siddur, they often skipped certain prayers or did not repeat others that are traditionally repeated. The rationale in most of these minyanim was often based on time constraints: "We don't want services to drag on." Although this kind of creative approach certainly reinvigorates the service, it often unsettles people seeking a sense of familiarity in their prayer life. At Hadar, we decided not to compromise on any of the traditional liturgical choices. Why? Because we believed in the power of the traditional liturgy as a means of connecting to God. We felt we could save time in other areas (shorter *divrei Torah*, less wasted time in the transitional moments of the service). We wanted to decouple the de facto union in American Judaism between full women's participation and a scaled-down service.

Adding Imahot—A Culture of Cooperation

There was one early exception to our insistence on traditional liturgy: the option for the prayer leader to add the *imahot* (matriarchs) to the first blessing of the *Amidah*. We developed a unique solution to this problem: instead of forbidding the addition, we decided to allow the prayer leader to choose whether or not to add their names in the middle of the blessing—as long as he didn't alter the final line of the blessing. More important to me than the end result was the process of reaching this decision. This might sound unremarkable, but it demonstrated one of the most important contrasts between Hadar and other communities I had participated in.

For the past twenty years, adding *imahot* has been a particularly hot-button issue in egalitarian prayer communities. People noticed that only men were cited in the first blessing of the *Amidah:* Abraham, Isaac, and Jacob. To fix this problem, some liberal liturgists wrote an additional line that mentioned the corresponding four matriarchs and altered the final blessing to read: "shields Abraham and remembers

Sarah" (see the appendix). When I was in college, this was an issue that tore apart our tiny, thirty-person Shabbat morning minyan. Traditionalists (at the time, myself included) felt that we should not alter any of the words of the *Amidah*, no matter how much our egalitarian leanings told us that mentioning men only was a thing of the past. But reformers felt they could not say a prayer that excluded the matriarchs. After half a dozen meetings and study sessions—many of them quite emotionally charged—we took a vote. *Imahot* were voted out (years after I graduated they were voted in), and people who were angry with the decision left the minyan.

Discussing this issue at the founding of the minyan, we had no angry fights, no vote, no walking out. Ethan and our friend (now colleague) Rabbi Shai Held had done much thinking about the issue and concluded it would be halakhically acceptable to add *imahot* in the body of the first paragraph, but not change the final line of the blessing. Ethan, Mara, and I decided to leave it up to the person leading the prayers to make the alteration in the body of the prayer (but not allow a change at the end). With only three people dreaming up this minyan from scratch, we had the luxury of making policy decisions without politicking a wide range of constituents. We were not going to become derailed on (legitimate) ideological debates instead of cranking out the core of what was needed—a well-run, vibrant, and egalitarian minyan. We made a decision and moved on.

Testing the Boundaries of Tradition

One of the earliest tests of Hadar's policy to adhere to traditional liturgy came in our fourth meeting of the minyan. A person we asked to lead davening told us that she had written a special *Al Hanisim* prayer for Gay Pride Day, and that day coincided with the day she was to lead services. She asked the *gabbaim* whether she could include it in the *Musaf Amidah*.

The very fact that she thought to ask the leadership whether this was appropriate was an important step in setting the culture of the organization. Hadar was never a liturgical free-for-all, and I believe that there is a very large silent majority who appreciate that people check in with the leadership when any liturgical change is proposed. In those early days of the minyan, these critical policy decisions were made within the very small group of leadership—at that point still the three founders (one of whom was openly gay). We certainly sympathized with the position of this volunteer service leader but also recognized that springing a new, sui generis prayer on a community that was very much still in formation might have a significant negative impact. This was not a political statement—we certainly agreed with the message of the prayer—but more a traditional statement: people expect the text of the *Amidah* to remain constant. We offered her the opportunity to teach her prayer in a class following the minyan but did not allow its inclusion in the service. This was a difficult test of our values in the early weeks of the minyan, but one that helped define certain expectations of what our service was: a traditional liturgy.

Breaking the Mold to Respond to Disaster

Although Hadar remains quite conservative with the words of the liturgy, we have had a few instructive countervailing examples. In 2004, when the tsunami hit South Asia, Hadar's scholar-in-residence, Rabbi Held, wrote a prayer for the people affected by the disaster:

> Ruler of Creation, Master of the world:
> Have mercy on all those who are suffering from the
> raging waters and the storming waves.
> Have compassion on Your creatures—Look, O Lord, and
> see their distress;
> Listen, God, and hear their cries.
> Strengthen the hands of those who would bring relief,
> comfort the mourners,
> Heal, please, the wounded.
> Grant us wisdom and discernment to know our obliga-
> tions,
> and open our hearts so that we may extend our hands
> to the devastated.
> Bless us so that we may walk in Your ways,
> "compassionate ones, children of compassionate
> ones."
> Grant us the will and the wisdom to prevent further disas-
> ter and death;

Prevent plague from descending upon Your earth, and fulfill Your words,
"Never again shall there be another flood to destroy
the earth."
Amen. So may it be your will.

Because of the power of e-mail and listservs, the prayer was circulated
worldwide—largely because it expressed the feelings of prayerful people
who looked in vain to the liturgy to deal directly with such a catastrophe. Significantly for our decision to include it, the prayer was an addition to the service following the Torah reading, as opposed to an
insertion in one of the critical prayers of the liturgy, such as the *Amidah*.
This space in the service is traditionally considered more flexible
regarding new prayers (for example, the relatively recent prayer for the
government and State of Israel are inserted at this point). Weighing this
factor, as well as the urgency of the need to respond prayerfully to this
catastrophe less than a week old, led us to include it in the service at
Hadar.

Expressing Emotion through Prayer
Of course, ritual creativity is not only expressed by penning a new
prayer. One of the most powerful creative prayer moments at Hadar
took place on Simchat Torah in 2004. That morning, after services had
already started, someone told me about a terrorist bombing in the Sinai
in which a number of Israelis were killed. No one else in the community knew about the attack, so we were faced with the twin challenges
of letting people know bad news and continuing to celebrate Simchat
Torah—a holiday marked by extreme joy and dancing. Rabbi Shai
Held, Julia Andelman, and I huddled in the back of the service and
came up with a plan: Shai would speak briefly during *Shacharit* (something never done at Hadar), and Julia would lead the first *hakafah* with
a special melody.

Shai spoke movingly about the message of the *Kedushah* as one of
yearning for a world we do not yet live in, and he broke the news about
the attack. Then Julia led the first *hakafah* to a slow melody. The community followed her into a circle and marched around slowly, singing
the plaintive *niggun* (wordless melody). The circle spiraled upon itself,

and the people drew tighter and tighter until it felt like we were all supporting each other by the closeness of our steps and the intensity of the *niggun*. The contrast to what we all had experienced on Simchat Torah in the past—wild, joyous dancing—was palpable, and people cried freely. Then we transitioned for the next *hakafah* into the joyous dancing we have always known at Hadar's Simchat Torah celebration. Although we often think of youth culture as looking for ways to express joy in religious settings, that morning demonstrated the ways in which Hadar also allowed people space for grief and mourning in an authentic religious space.

The Minyan's First Sefer Torah

The same spirit of openness to innovation played out in perhaps one of the most powerful community moments in Kehilat Hadar's history. In 2005, Professor Shuly Rubin Schwartz received a Torah scroll written in memory of her husband, Rabbi Gershon Schwartz *z"l*. Rabbi Schwartz used to daven at Hadar on occasion, and his children who lived in New York would also attend. After he passed away suddenly one Pesach, a colleague of his commissioned a new *sefer Torah* to be written in his memory. Shuly decided to donate the *sefer Torah* to Kehilat Hadar, as the first-ever *sefer Torah* owned by the minyan.

This was a significant moment for Hadar, not least because of the logistical problems solved by owning a *sefer Torah*. For years, we had borrowed a *sefer Torah* from the Drisha Institute. A *gabbai* would go to Drisha on a Friday and move the *sefer Torah* to a community member's apartment (sometimes taking it on the local bus to get there). Then on Shabbat morning, another *gabbai* would arrive early at this apartment, take the *sefer Torah* from the bleary-eyed host, and carry it to the location for davening. After services, we reversed the process. No wonder owning a *sefer Torah* was such a cause for celebration!

The *gabbaim* brainstormed the proper way to welcome this gift and to mark the significant milestone. We wanted to design a ceremony that engaged the entire community directly with the *sefer Torah*. We also thought it best to perform this ceremony on Shavuot, the holiday that officially celebrates the receiving of the Torah. This also allowed us to welcome the gift of Torah at one of Hadar's program highlights of the year: the well-attended Shavuot retreat in the Berkshires.

On the eve of Shavuot, before the all-night learning began, everyone on the retreat (250 people) gathered in the rustic shul of Camp Ramah in the Berkshires, and Rabbi Held spoke about the importance of each individual taking hold of Torah in a personal way. Then, in a ritual meant to reinforce that message, we sang a *niggun* and a community member brought the *sefer Torah* into the back of the room. The people standing in the rows passed the scroll to one another, and everyone in the room actually held it for a few seconds. (The *gabbaim*, fearing a ceremony that could last more than an hour if not timed well, practiced passing objects from one to another to estimate how long the whole experience would last. The answer: fifteen minutes.) The last person to hold the *sefer Torah* after it had been passed around the room—the very same person who had stored the borrowed Torah in her apartment all those years—put it into the *aron kodesh* (ark). People cried as the power of the music and the scene of the Torah literally being received by each person in the room sank in.

Many people told me afterward that they had never held a *sefer Torah* before. This was the most direct and clear way we could think of to send the message that this *sefer Torah* belongs to everyone in the community, and it is the responsibility of each one of us to take hold of it.

BALANCING INCLUSIVENESS AND INSPIRED SPIRITUALITY

One of the defining challenges of any lay-led minyan is the following dilemma: how to balance inclusive service leadership with a quality spiritual experience. In theory, a lay-led minyan should have no problem with this. Because it is founded on the premise of including a large number of active volunteers, instead of a small number of professionals, in leading the services, the minyan should easily be able to include all the participants in whatever way they hope to contribute. However, not all lay daveners and Torah readers are blessed with the same skills. Well-meaning but less-competent volunteers can actually detract from the larger mission of creating an inspiring prayer experience. A minyan must walk a fine line between balancing opportunities for ritual and communal leadership with a focus on inspired and meaningful prayer.

Kehilat Hadar's Hybrid Approach to Selecting Prayer Leaders

We recognized that volunteers have a wide range of skills in prayer leadership and Torah reading. So we developed a few key values and strategies to try to strike the proper balance.

Establishing standards for Torah reading. Torah readers at Hadar are asked to read a minimum of two *aliyot*. This was designed with one goal in mind: to give people who wanted to read Torah enough of a challenge so that they could not try to learn the entire reading in one night. The biggest risk to Torah reading performance is not really from the true beginner who works hard to learn how to *leyn* (read publicly from the *sefer Torah*). In my experience, it comes from the more experienced person who thinks she can learn the Torah reading on short notice, but in fact needs more time. I clearly remember kids in youth group staying up late at night to learn the Torah reading, only realizing too late that they could not learn it well enough to read it properly in time for the service. By asking people to read a minimum of two *aliyot*, we set a standard that precluded people who might try too late in the game to learn the entire section.

Ensuring that Torah readers show up. A related problem we tried to address by encouraging people to read two or more *aliyot* was the constant switching of Torah readers, which is prevalent in lay-led minyanim. Although, of course, this has the advantage of including the widest number of people in the Torah reading, it has the distinct disadvantage of creating a revolving-door effect for the Torah reading. The constant switching of readers often leads to a slower service. People lose their place in the Torah, they never get a chance to find a rhythm, and, worst of all, having seven readers increases the chances that someone will forget to show up at shul or that the *gabbai* will forget to assign all the *aliyot*. At other minyanim I had attended, AWOL readers inevitably led to someone trying to read the portion on the fly, a painful experience for everyone in the room. At Hadar, we worked hard to create a culture where this would not happen.

Avoiding the "insider-outsider" dynamic. The problem with giving too much responsibility for leading prayers and reading Torah to a small, competent core is that you create an insider-outsider dynamic in the minyan, and you burn out the people who have the skills to lead well. Part of what we did to combat that at Hadar was to actively seek out new, competent people to lead and read Torah—what I called "scouting." At Hadar, we didn't have rules about allowing only regulars to lead services. On the contrary: we were excited to have visitors who brought new and different melodies and styles to the davening. When I heard about people visiting the minyan who lived elsewhere and were known as "good daveners," I would work hard to schedule them in advance to lead at Hadar. Similarly, the *gabbaim* at Hadar kept on the lookout for new talent that might wander into the minyan. We gave *aliyot* to newcomers and listened to their performance. Often, just by hearing someone bless the Torah, you can tell whether he has the skills and comfort to be a good prayer leader.

At the same time, we also decided to take a number of risks—we didn't rely on the same five "go-to people" all the time, but sought out untested people. To hedge our bets, we would balance the service with other solid daveners who had a positive track record. Taking these gambles sometimes stumbled, but it often paid off. I have found that the most competent people are often reluctant to make themselves known and need to be sought out and asked to lead. One measure of the health of the minyan lay in its ability to actively seek out new people to become prayer leaders.

Cultivating future leaders. Even though we set certain standards for minyan leaders, we very much wanted to encourage people who wished to develop their skills to become leaders in the future. We did not assume that whatever you learned by age eighteen was the limit of your potential as a ritual leader. So we offered classes in a range of practical skills: how to lead services, how to read Torah, how to read Haftarah, how to lift the Torah, and so on. The goal of these classes was to offer intimate and supportive environments for people who were looking to push themselves to become competent leaders of prayer and contribute to the community. When a particular student in one of these classes was ready to lead services, she would invite her peers from the class to be a supportive presence in the davening that day—standing nearby, singing loudly. So much of leading well is feeling supported by the congregation, and these classes provided an opportunity for a mini peer group to support the leader.

Scheduling prayer leaders far in advance. A critical part of ensuring a quality spiritual experience in services is competent scheduling of daveners and Torah readers. In many lay-led communities, the harried volunteers are barely able to keep up with the scheduling for the following week, forcing leaders to have only a few days to prepare. As a result of needing fewer people to lead on a given week (if one person reads the entire Torah portion, there are six fewer people to schedule), we were able to free up the scheduler's time to work on planning the calendar well ahead of time. The davening calendar is usually scheduled three months in advance. This pace of scheduling allows for some wonderful opportunities.

First, someone who needs more time to prepare well can reserve a spot on the calendar three to four months in advance with ease. Second, it allows the *gabbai* to thoughtfully plan out the service on a particular day. If someone new were leading davening, the *gabbai* would often "anchor" that person with a more practiced veteran. Each service allowed for some experimentation and risk taking with the leaders, but it never had an entirely untested lineup. That was critical to maintaining the balance between a solid performance of the liturgy and an openness to new potential leaders.

Providing feedback for continued growth. One of the challenges of a lay-led community is that there are very few opportunities for real growth by the prayer leaders. Often this is because there is no framework for constructive feedback. People think: "Since this is a volunteer-driven community, the very fact that you stepped up to lead is all we could ask. Thank you very much." But at Hadar I found that people, in the right context, were looking for ways to grow and develop their skills as leaders. They wanted to prepare with someone, and afterward they wanted to hear ways in which they could improve. Now, we did not always get this right. There is a temptation to focus only on the areas of improvement or to offer feedback in a framework that is unhelpful (such as at *Kiddush* immediately following the services). But shying away from any opportunities for preparation or feedback ultimately erodes opportunities for spiritual experiences at a lay-led minyan.

Putting preparation into action. How did we enact this culture of preparation and feedback at Hadar? We started with a goal of having someone with the requisite skills listen to a first-time Torah reader or prayer leader. This was a huge shift in culture, because most people are unaccustomed to peer tutorial or review. In some cases, it backfired: the person felt overly critiqued and offended. But most of the time we found that the prayer leader appreciated the opportunity to work collaboratively with someone who cared about his abilities and skills and wanted the best experience for the congregation.

Eventually, recognizing that leaders at all skill levels want to improve, we created a peer feedback group. This was composed of the best and most experienced daveners at Hadar, who wanted to learn and grow from each other, to share melodies, and to ask questions they hadn't worked up the nerve to ask. The peer feedback group was our most successful strategy for improving skills (outside of a formal class). The group bonded beyond the content of the discussions, and they served as informal cheerleaders for each other when any of them led davening.

Addressing Alienation

When this all started in 2001, a lay-led minyan that erred on the side of inspired spirituality versus radical inclusion was unusual. Regardless of their original intent or ethos, the havurot that had been in existence for more than thirty years when Hadar started had come down squarely on one side of this approach: anyone can lead or *leyn*, and the more people who do it the better. There were rarely any mechanisms for ensuring quality or even offering feedback for people who performed a less-than-competent davening or Torah reading.

In many ways, the stance Kehilat Hadar took on this question was the core of what made it both successful and innovative, but also what led to its greatest challenge when it came to inclusion. To be clear— someone is *always* going to be alienated from any community. In communities that practice complete openness to leadership, there is often an unintended outcome: by allowing anyone to lead davening, the quality invariably suffers, which, in turn, alienates people who desperately want to experience a worship environment that is powerful, not just inclusive. Thus, although any community can claim full openness to ritual leadership, they may be alienating the people who simply want to participate as members of the congregation and who want a competent prayer leader.

EMPOWERING THE COMMUNITY IN PRAYER

One of the core questions of the minyan has always been this: how can we increase the participation of the daveners in the service, both as a group and as individuals playing specific roles? Even in very active congregations, I found there are always certain areas of worship in which people feel unable to participate.

Teaching Hagbahah

A classic example is the act of lifting a *sefer Torah*, or *hagbahah*. Many people feel intimidated by the physicality of this act, and even in egalitarian congregations, women tend to avoid it entirely. I remember as a college student for the first time seeing a woman lift the *sefer Torah* and being wowed by her confidence. But rarely did I see a woman do that again, either in synagogues or at Hadar. The problem is not one of opportunity—as a *gabbai*, I asked dozens of women to lift the Torah. But they all turned me down. The problem was one of training and confidence.

On our second Shavuot retreat, one of the Hadar community members offered a *hagbahah* training class. Although it was open to anyone, all the people who attended were women. He taught them how to lift the scroll with ease (it's not about strength—it's all about technique). And at the next service following the class, one of his "graduates" lifted the Torah for the first time. Without this path to empowerment, no amount of cajoling or opportunities would have inspired someone to try to perform an unfamiliar ritual act. But once people had the opportunity to learn in a safe setting how to perform the ritual, they were eager to try during services.

Creating a Comfortable Space for Prostration

Perhaps one of the most unfamiliar acts in Jewish prayer is prostration—lying face down with hands and feet stretched out, in an act of complete submission. Most of the year it is absent from Jewish prayer, but on Yom Kippur, it is a critical feature of the *Avodah* section of *Musaf*. As a kid in shul on Yom Kippur, I remember that the rabbis would invite the congregation to prostrate together with the clergy. But no one ever took them up on the offer. I would sneak to the back of the sanctuary and prostrate there at the appropriate times, but I always felt self-conscious—why would no one else join me? Part of it was logistics (it's hard to shove your way past other people in the pew to get to the aisle), and part of it was a modern squeamishness regarding overt displays of piety. Part of it was also a collective lack of initiative—no one wanted to be the only person doing this unusual act. But most significant was that no one was quite sure how to prostrate, and no one had ever taught them.

When Hadar held its first Yom Kippur service in 2002, we faced the same challenge. How would we empower a group of worshipers—none of whom had ever davened Yom Kippur services together—to experiment with prostration during the *Avodah* service? As part of our general preparation for the High Holidays, Hadar offered a series of classes that addressed various aspects of the *machzor* (High Holiday prayer book). I taught one on the history of prostration. During the class, I physically demonstrated some of the positions for prostration (in the Babylonian Talmud, *Shevuot* 16b, kneeling, bowing, and prostrating fully are all treated as separate acts). Then at the end of the class, I asked everyone to get up and experiment with full prostration. I mentioned that this was probably most people's first time trying this, but we were going to try it together, just to experience the power of prostration. A roomful of thirty people pushed their chairs to the side and, following my verbal cues about which words corresponded to which body movement, learned how to prostrate.

At Hadar on Yom Kippur, we stopped the service and asked people to fold up chairs before the prostration-filled *Avodah* section of *Musaf*. We gave people the opportunity to spread out in the room and find enough space to fully prostrate. When the time came, the people in that class, plus a few dozen others who had done this before in other settings, formed a core of prostrating daveners. Those fifty to sixty people provided enough of a critical mass to create a ritual space that made prostration culturally acceptable for the moment, and dozens of others joined them. It was the first egalitarian service I had ever attended in which the majority of people in the room prostrated during *Avodah*.

Empowering Worshipers through Music

For many, the easiest way to connect to prayer—and become an empowered, active member of the congregation—is through music. Yet, so often, the music used in prayer is tired and staid. Why? Sometimes people have an emotional attachment to the same melody no matter what ("I came here to sing *Avinu Malkeinu* the way I always have!"). And sometimes the person leading the service (in a lay-led service) is unsure about introducing a new melody. (What if people don't pick it up? What if it falls flat?) As a result, everyone may desire a new melody, but the leaders rely on the "tried and true" ones as safe choices when leading prayer.

At Hadar, we recognized that introducing new melodies into the davening is very difficult, because by the time people pick up on the melody, the prayer is over.

We decided to create community sessions specifically for learning new melodies. Julia Andelman was one of the pioneers of this initiative. In the lead-up to the High Holidays, Julia led classes on melodies for Rosh Hashanah and Yom Kippur and then introduced these melodies in the davening. She would also teach classes on new melodies for Shabbat and then coordinate with the daveners for that Shabbat to use them in davening. The most popular model was a dinner on Friday night during which Julia taught melodies. The next morning, while the melodies were still fresh in our heads, Julia led davening, using the tunes we had learned. This model overcame the usual objection to new melodies, where people bristle at something new mainly because it is unfamiliar, not because they don't like it.

> For many, the easiest way to connect to prayer—and become an empowered, active member of the congregation—is through music.

JEWISH STANDARD TIME NO MORE

I do not believe in Jewish Standard Time. This is the odd but widely accepted notion that Jewish events are simply expected to run at least fifteen minutes late. But despite evidence to the contrary, Jewish events actually can run on time. Do Jewish people miss airplanes at a higher rate than non-Jewish people? Not at all. In other words, when things run on time and have an expectation of running on time, people adjust. But if people are accustomed to things running late, people show up late, expecting not to miss anything. When everyone has an incentive to be the last person to show up, the people who show up on time are punished for their punctuality by having to wait around.

We fought the notion of Jewish Standard Time in several ways at Kehilat Hadar. We had a very strict rule from day one that we would start the minyan on time, no matter how many people were there. People often complain about the late ending time of synagogue services, but in my experience, the best place to "save time" is at the beginning. The tendency to start late at the beginning of a service is borne of a desire either to wait until there is a critical mass so people don't feel like they are praying by themselves or, more significantly, to have a minyan for the early *Kaddish*. But at Hadar we treated those problems as distinct: find ways to attract ten people at the beginning and you don't have to worry about starting late. We accomplished this by asking all the leaders in a given service to show up early to help with setup. Together with the *gabbaim*, this guaranteed us a minyan at the start.

Culture of Enforcement

The real trick in running things on time is enforcement. Everyone can aspire to start on time, but what happens when things go wrong? This happened at Hadar on the fourth time we ever held services. The person who was asked to lead *Shacharit* did not show up by our start time of 9:30 a.m. This was a true dilemma because, of course, the person had prepared and was excited about leading services, and she also had never led at Hadar before (given that it was only the fourth service ever). On the other hand, we were consciously trying to build a culture of on-time davening. We waited for three minutes past the start time, and then I ended up leading the first part of services. Our would-be leader showed up at 9:40 a.m., and she took over leading before *Barchu* (the formal call to prayer). We sent a clear message that the "silent majority" of people who valued and expected on-time services were going to trump the individual. From the individual's perspective, of course, this was a harsh position. But part of the culture of the minyan is that the individual leader does not hold captive the rest of the congregation, and certain standards are worth enforcing even when there are costs associated with them.

Shavuot Retreat: Tough Love

Perhaps the clearest example of Hadar's attitude toward time is on our Shavuot retreat, a highlight of the Hadar calendar. More than 250 people trek up to the Berkshires each year for a holiday filled with all-night learning (six or seven different sessions each hour), dawn davening, a massive *tisch* (a gathering for *divrei Torah* and singing), and plenty of downtime in nature. Most significantly, it runs on time.

Hadar's approach to retreat scheduling began with transportation. I had been to countless Jewish conferences in which the chartered bus left thirty to sixty minutes past the stated departure time. This was a constant annoyance. "Why did I leave work so early?" I would think, as I sat on a hot bus going nowhere. For Hadar's retreat, we decided to leave a fifteen-minute grace period for the buses. They were called for a 3:45 p.m. departure, and we planned to leave at 4 p.m. sharp, no matter what. Of course, we were tested. Amazingly, all but three people had boarded the buses by 4 p.m. (by that time, Hadar already had a clear culture of starting on time). What to do—wait for the other three (who knows when they would arrive?) or leave without them? We made a tough call: leave on time. By cell phone, we helped the stragglers find their way to the retreat by train, and by sticking to our schedule, we showed Hadar's respect for people's time.

The Shavuot retreat itself was a novelty for Jewish conferences. The schedule actually reported the real times for events, not a rough estimate of when activities might happen. This meant dinner started when we said it would, and davening and classes did, too. People were floored at the end of the holiday that the retreat actually ran on schedule—they had never expected a Jewish conference to run on time. And they were so grateful for it! People had simply given up on the possibility that a conference schedule could actually report the real times of events.

Building in Downtime

The main reason that sessions always run late in Jewish conferences is the burning desire to overprogram. How many times have you been to a conference where no breaks are scheduled, people zone out, and a spontaneous "ten-minute break" is called? "It's 2:17 p.m. Let's all be back here at 2:27 p.m. ready to start." Everyone nods their head. Then no one returns at 2:27 p.m. Although it is human nature to remain on break as long as possible, it is also poor conference planning to assume no need for a break. People always complain at the end of a conference:

why didn't we have more time to connect to each other "in the hall-way"—that is, when no formal programming was taking place?

The best part of the Shavuot retreat was the ample free time. For both days of the holiday, we had free time from lunch until *Mincha* and dinner. Four hours of free time. Both days. People had simply never experienced a conference that offered them that much time "off." We did have programming options (some learning, meditation, hikes), but nothing communitywide. The mental space of afternoon free time allowed people to relax, meet each other, and connect without constantly being herded to the next program.

This is not to say that Hadar's ultimate purpose is to run a precision operation exactly according to plan. In that very retreat, the most powerful moment occurred on the second night, before dinner. Most people had entered the dining hall, and all of a sudden in the back, a few people spontaneously started to sing and dance in a circle. For whatever magical reason, people started to join them, until every person in the room was dancing in concentric circles. It was not part of our plan, but it was the highlight for so many people—an unprogrammed expression of joy and celebration.

Feels Like Five Minutes

My larger point about time is this: honor a schedule, and the rare moments that run over will be for good reason. This is best expressed through Hadar's *dvar Torah* policy. Hadar famously has a five-minute limit on its *divrei Torah* during services. Most *divrei Torah* in synagogue have a nominal time limit, but none are as short as five minutes (who could imagine a rabbi speaking for less than ten minutes?). More important, very few limits are enforced. How do you enforce a time limit on speaking?

The only hope is to enforce the time limit culturally. The second time Hadar ever met, the speaker went on for eighteen minutes. We honestly felt as if the entire venture was at risk in that one moment. But the next week we made sure to find a good speaker who we knew would adhere to the time limit (she spoke for four minutes). We also made it known publicly that the time limit was five minutes, and, for better or worse, the time limit became an integral part of the culture: people even referred to the time limit in their talks ("Since

I can't really solve the problem of evil in a five-minute *dvar Torah*….").

This is not to say that the be-all and end-all of Torah teaching can be encapsulated in five minutes. In truth, there is something better than a five-minute *dvar Torah*—a *dvar Torah* that *feels* like five minutes even if it's longer. Rabbi Shai Held is the master of this. He always spoke for more than five minutes. But his content was so deep and rich that no one ever complained that he spoke too long—it felt like five minutes, in that people were unaware of the passage of time, but instead were wrapped up in the content. In many ways, any time limit is meant as a fail-safe for something gone wrong. If someone delivered a "bad" *dvar Torah*, at least it only lasted for five minutes (as opposed to the many *divrei Torah* I have heard that were bad but lasted closer to twenty minutes). But the possibility of transcending the time limit, which can only be done with real content and skill, is the higher purpose and possibility. Five minutes is for most of us, and "feels like five minutes" is for the best of us.

Prayer That Transcends Time

This principle applies to prayer as well. Hadar was originally founded on the radical notion that a service that is egalitarian could run as fast as a nonegalitarian service. In college I was always confounded by the fact that the Orthodox Shabbat morning service started eating *Kiddush* while the egalitarian traditional service—using exactly the same prayers—took thirty to forty-five minutes longer. The sixth time Hadar met, in June 2001, we actually finished the entire service in two hours. This was a breakthrough that was critical for the community—we had demonstrated that we didn't need to cut parts of the service or race through the liturgy at breakneck speed in order to finish davening in a reasonable amount of time. It is a matter of eliminating the "dead time," finding quality Torah readers who make minimal errors (mistakes always slow down a service), starting on time, and insisting on a brief *dvar Torah*.

But there is something even better than a two-hour service—a service that *feels* like two hours. By that I mean a service in which your experience is so positive that you don't even feel tempted to look at your watch. This is ultimately an "empowered" service, where partici-

pants are so engaged that time becomes irrelevant. This is the fundamental difference between length and pace. Pace is the critical element;
length often correlates with it, but not always.

Boundaries Lead to Openness

This speaks to the larger framework in which Hadar operates—one in
which clear boundaries—like time—are set, not for the sake of boundaries themselves, but for the sake of opening new possibilities. When
basic expectations are clear, people feel freer to open up and experiment
in prayer. In lay-led minyanim of a previous generation, often the service was "dealer's choice"—the leader could choose to cut various prayers
or interject explanations or dedications in the middle of the service.
Although this can be meaningful for the leader, it creates an environment in which many worshipers never feel fully comfortable losing
themselves in the prayer.

When the expectations are clear, however, there is some amount
of letting go. That is why on our Shavuot retreat, in the context of a
strict schedule, there was openness to spontaneous dancing. And in the
context of davening where there is a fixed liturgy and a general emphasis on timeliness, there is openness to spend more time on the *Kedushah*.
This for me was a major mental shift: I moved from having the goal of
"beating the time" of the Orthodox service to creating a framework of
efficiency that would allow for more openness in certain areas of the
service.

THE CHALLENGE OF BEING "WELCOMING"

In recent years, the synagogue world has become obsessed with welcoming people into the worship space—and not just *Kiddush*, but the service itself. People report that various worship services are "unfriendly"
when they are turned off by the social space in the synagogue or minyan. The solution has been to develop a culture of "welcoming" during
services to combat the perceived stiffness and "unfriendly" atmosphere.

Social Space versus Prayer Space

Developing a sense of friendliness and being welcomed is complicated,
and the solution is not simply to have a greeter at the door handing you

a prayer book. First, we have to distinguish between the social space of *Kiddush* and the prayer space of a service. Let's start with the prayer service. It seems to me that the focus on a welcoming environment in synagogue comes in the wake of a lack of spiritual expectations. In other words, if people were fundamentally wowed by the spiritual experience of prayer, the focus on how much their neighbor smiled at them (or whatever metric of friendliness is used) would be much diminished.

Think about an inspiring experience that was also empowering—say, your first rock concert with fifty thousand people. Even though there are no greeters, and no one really talked to you, you would never claim, "Wow, that U2 concert was really unfriendly." And even if you didn't know the words to the songs, there is something about the spirit of an amazing rock concert that transcends the social demands of friendliness. There is no focus on mundane social interaction in an inspirational space. But when there is no spirit to grab hold of, then people focus on the social interactions, and rightly so. For me, the solution is not to add more smiling people in services, but to make the services more inspirational.

Rows versus a Circle

This also relates to the decision to sit in rows as opposed to a circle. I have heard beautiful explanations about why minyangoers should sit in a circle in prayer: the Shekhinah (the feminine aspect of God) is to be found in the face of the other; we are all equal, so no levels of hierarchy should be imposed during a worship service; community is best found in this formation; and the like. But the human dynamic created by sitting in a circle (or in rows that face each other) is one in which everyone is looking at everyone else. This, in the best of circumstances, can feel "friendly." ("How nice that you are smiling at me from across the room!") But that form of supposed intimacy may actually undercut the possibility of intimacy with God. Fundamentally, the construction of prayer space involves openness to a certain amount of vulnerability in front of others. But openness to vulnerability is a very difficult atmosphere to engender, and sensing that people are watching you can cause you to become self-conscious and retreat from the possibility of true openness in prayer. Although sitting in straight rows may seem "unfriendly," it actually opens the possibility of transcending the human social dynamics that are always present in a room of worshipers. In that formation the sounds of prayer, not the faces of the worshipers, are elevated in importance.

I once stumbled on a *tisch* on Saturday evening at the Satmar rebbe's winter home in Florida. The Hasidim were gathered around the table, singing extended melodies that the rebbe began in a weak voice. Suddenly, at the peak of one of those melodies, the lights went out (they were on a timer, I later found out). The singing increased in intensity. Why did the lights go out at a critical moment in the singing? A Hasid later explained to me that the previous Satmar rebbe decreed the lights to go out during a *tisch* because the Hasidim are so vulnerable at that moment that they don't want to see each other cry. It is hard to let go in front of someone else.

So when we walk into a prayer space where no one says hello, it may be because the community is trying to cultivate the *kavannah* to be open to God. Fundamentally, the spiritual aspect of the Rabbinic rule not to interrupt davening with speech between the *Shema* and the *Amidah* reveals a deep truth about human behavior—a focus on the mundane social interactions can mitigate the possibility of real connection to God.

This is not to say that there is no room for saying hello to a stranger who sits down next to you in services. There are moments for those interactions during the service. And arguably, a greeter can be helpful in guiding people who are walking into a service for the first time, offering him a siddur and pointing him to the right page. But the concept of a greeter is also problematic. The greeter is ultimately disempowering for the rest of the congregation. Why? Because if it's Harold's turn to be the greeter, then everyone else is officially relieved of that responsibility. If there is a culture of welcoming, then there should be no need for an individual greeter. Although a

> Although sitting in straight rows may seem "unfriendly," it actually opens the possibility of transcending the human social dynamics that are always present in a room of worshipers. In that formation the sounds of prayer, not the faces of the worshipers, are elevated in importance.

greeter may be better than nothing, the complete reliance on an official role of a rotating group to be welcoming discharges in an unhealthy way the collective responsibility to welcome others to the worship space.

Aliyot *as a Measure of "Friendliness"*

Aliyot represent another common metric of friendliness. "Welcoming" shuls give *aliyot* to new faces, and "unfriendly" ones don't. One shul I used to attend has a policy of giving *aliyot* only to members (and, the somewhat appalling exception seemed to be, famous Jews), but most minyanim have no official policy on giving *aliyot*. I sometimes heard complaints from people at Hadar who felt slighted that they did not get an *aliyah*.

But here also, it is important to analyze the deeper issue. First of all, there is the simple math: 25 meetings a year (when the minyan met only twice a month) x 7 aliyot per time = 175 aliyot for the year. But 200 people show up each week, so even with perfect distribution, people would only get an *aliyah* once a year.

Aliyot *as a Culture of Appreciation*

In the early days of Hadar, we decided to try to build a culture of appreciation through the *aliyot*. Specifically, we wanted to reward people who arrived early to set up and make minyan, so the third *aliyah* was always given to the first non-*gabbai* who arrived at shul. Often this was a first-timer, who was surprised but pleased to learn of this policy.

In the first few years at Hadar, we took this policy to its greatest extreme on Simchat Torah. In many synagogues, the *aliyot* on Simchat Torah morning are reserved for people who are big supporters of the shul. It is perhaps the most insider-ish *aliyah* one can imagine. But at Hadar, with no *machers* ("big shots") that we needed to honor, we kept our Shabbat *aliyah* policy in place: whoever arrived first that morning would receive *Hattan/Kallat Torah*—the final *aliyah* of the Torah.

We made a big deal of this opportunity in the announcements in the weeks leading up to Simchat Torah. It was, to my knowledge, the first democratic offering of that *aliyah*: anyone who had the energy to come early to services could experience the magic of standing at the Torah as it is finished.

The stratagem was also a neat incentive for people to arrive early in the morning after one of the latest nights of the Jewish calendar (on

Simchat Torah on the Upper West Side, especially pre–9/11, thousands of young Jews milled about until late in the night). And it worked. That first year, we had one of our largest crowds ever on Simchat Torah, and people arrived early to vie for the *aliyah* spot. The second year, after all the hype surrounding this opportunity, someone actually showed up at services at 6:30 a.m., just to guarantee his spot (another person came at 7 a.m.). Although this took it to a bit of an extreme, the message was clear: this community values and celebrates people who come to shul on time, and everyone has the chance to be a "*macher*."

One last welcoming metric regarding *aliyot:* How does the *gabbai* offer *aliyot?* At Hadar, *gabbaim* say more than, "Are you a Kohen or a Levi?" The offer is preceded by an introduction. "Good Shabbos. My name is Elie. Welcome! Would you like an *aliyah* this morning?"

The Problem of Kiddush

When it comes to a welcoming spirit, *Kiddush* is an entirely different story. I think *Kiddush* was invented to torture all but the most socially outgoing among us. All of a sudden a space that was filled with people trying to connect with the Divine morphs into a cocktail hour, where anyone *not* speaking to his neighbor feels left out. Here I have much more sympathy for the concerns of a welcoming atmosphere. This is where charges of cliquishness and "unfriendliness" abound. But let's analyze this a bit more closely.

When people say that a minyan is "unfriendly," they often mean this: I stood around at *Kiddush* and no one came up to say hello to me. I used to feel that way myself at a minyan I attended from time to time on the West Side. I would play a little game with myself: see how long I could stand just outside a group of people who were talking to each other without anyone acknowledging my presence. The game often ended with me becoming frustrated and walking away, thinking, "I can't believe no one talked to me, and I was standing next to them for ten minutes!" But this is fundamentally another symptom of feeling disempowered. I never took on the responsibility to initiate the conversation with anyone. If I had gone up to someone at that *Kiddush*, introduced myself, and asked his name, and he had turned his back to me or ignored my "hello"—*that* would have been unfriendly! But someone engaged in conversation who does not notice someone standing alone outside the group is not necessarily being unfriendly.

One of the challenges at Hadar was the sheer size of *Kiddush*. In a small minyan with twenty-five people, there is really no excuse not to reach out to the person standing in the corner. But with two hundred people in the room each week, and with the transient population we attracted, there were always a dozen first-timers at Hadar every Shabbat we met. Worse, people who had been coming for six months felt awkward about assuming that those they didn't recognize were "new." Given the size of the community, it was a reasonable worry that they might "welcome" someone who had been coming for two years! This left a tremendous burden on the *gabbaim*, the only public face of the minyan, to scout the *Kiddush* room for people who looked like they were not talking to anyone, and bring them into the fold.

We tried a few strategies to transform *Kiddush*. One of the most interesting was a "*Kiddush* class." Ten minutes into *Kiddush*, we held a class in the back room to study some aspect of prayer. This was meant to address a few problems: expand people's knowledge of prayer, offer more Torah than can be contained in five minutes, and provide a safe haven for people who did not feel comfortable schmoozing at *Kiddush* but wanted to find a way into the community. We ran the class for a year, and only attracted about five to ten people each time (turns out more people wanted to schmooze than we thought). But for those five to ten people, it was a healthy way to deal with *Kiddush* anxiety.

Sharing Shabbat Meals

The best metric I have for a "welcoming" community is one in which people invite each other over for Shabbat meals. By this I don't mean the planned meal invitation (which is also crucial for building social fabric in community), but the spontaneous *Kiddush* invitation: "Oh, this is your first time here? Would you like to come to our house for lunch?"

I had experienced this previously in Orthodox shuls but found it to be relatively rare elsewhere. For an entire year, I davened at a shul on the East Side that was very warm (in that people talked to me at *Kiddush*), but I never once received an invitation to a Shabbat meal. (This could be, in part, because people did not actually regularly have

Shabbat meals in their homes.) Some lay-led minyanim I encountered came up with a partial solution to this problem. The *gabbai* would make an announcement at the end of shul: "If you need a place for lunch, come see Rachel during *Kiddush*." This always seemed somewhat self-defeating to me. First of all, many times it was not clear who the coordinator—Rachel—was. But more important was the language—"If you *need* a place for lunch...." It put the onus entirely on the meal seekers and made them feel as if they were needy. Many times I ate alone on Shabbat, rather than go through the somewhat humiliating experience of approaching a coordinator and labeling myself as someone who "needed" a place.

We thought that spontaneous invitations should become more universal and so set out to make it happen at Hadar. We believed that the issue had to do with empowerment: how could we foster a culture in which people felt empowered to invite newcomers to join their Shabbat meals?

We wanted to make sure that the solution really changed the community's culture and didn't just rely on a greeter or announcement. Hadar experimented with ways of creating that culture, starting with "underground hosts"—people who were assigned to be on the lookout for people who didn't have lunch plans, but were not announced as such. The idea was to subtly create an environment in which no one official took care of someone, but invitations seemed to just bubble up as part of the *Kiddush* culture. Although that worked well sometimes and started to spread to the greater community, it was not the most efficient way of identifying people looking for a meal. (Person X—aware of the underground hosting—would meet someone, realize she had no plans for lunch, and then have to seek out Person Y—the designated host—to host her.) Hadar ultimately returned to the public announcement from the front, which, although imperfect, certainly sends a message that the community is interested in helping people feel like part of the community through shared meals.

Inviting people to meals is not only important for welcoming first-timers but also for strengthening the connections among regular minyangoers. One sign of a healthy and integrated community is one in which longtime attendees continue to meet each other and break out of their subgroup safety zones in a minyan.

I once went to a meeting of a longtime minyan on the Upper West Side. I was shocked to hear that one of the biggest complaints among minyangoers was that the people there, who had been coming to the minyan for years, did not know each other's names, and they were too embarrassed to ask at this point in the minyan's history. I saw this at Hadar as well. As a co-founder, I knew a lot of the people who came to the minyan over the years, but I was always stunned to realize that longtime attendee X had never spoken to longtime attendee Y.

Shabbat meals are a great way to make these connections, but we found that most minyangoers usually attended meals with the same group of friends again and again, rarely meeting people outside their own social networks. Hadar set out to mix things up and began organizing hosted meals every month or so. Today we do this through a simple Internet sign-up: ten days before a given Shabbat, people sign up online to host a meal or be hosted at one. We close registration on Monday before Shabbat, and a volunteer mixes and matches the hosts and guests based on age, location, food preferences, and gender balance. By Thursday morning, the hosts contact the guests with all the details of what to bring. In this way, we are able to provide a communal Shabbat meal experience that creates a forum for meeting new people.

The culture of meal hosting has turned out to be one of the defining features of the independent minyanim nationwide, with more than 90 percent of people who responded to a national survey reporting that they had been hosted by their peers through the minyan. In my vision of the future of American Jewish life, the real test of whether a minyan is welcoming is not whether you get offered an *aliyah* or whether someone hands you a siddur on your way in. It will be defined by the ease in which you are drawn into each other's homes to share a meal together on Shabbat.

E-mail Welcomes

A final note on welcoming: because people who come to Hadar are often moving to New York, many for the first time, we often rely on e-mail introductions to welcome someone to the community. The loose social networks of other minyanim play an important role here. When someone wrote to us to say he was moving to Los Angeles, we were able to connect him via e-mail to the leaders of a minyan there. Similarly, when someone left Washington, D.C., to come to New York, the minyan leaders there could e-mail Hadar and tell us to be on the lookout for their former community member. The power of receiving a personal e-mail from a minyan leader even before you set foot in the minyan cannot be overestimated. In that way, we are able to welcome new people to town through the social network that spans the minyan world.

LOW OVERHEAD, HIGH COMMITMENT

One of the simplest aspects of Kehilat Hadar is its finances. In the very early days of the minyan, the costs were extremely low and consisted solely of food for *Kiddush*. After six months, when we started renting space for Shabbat morning, having outgrown apartment living rooms, the costs grew somewhat to include rent. But in 2001, the cost of rent for a Saturday morning hovered around fifty dollars per hour.

As a result of its relatively small operating budget, Hadar had the luxury of developing the program side of its operations without having to do extensive fundraising. Imagine a Jewish community in which costs and budget are simply not on the daily radar screen of the leadership. It meant that we could focus on the core program areas of the community, without worrying about how to raise money and how to spend it effectively. In that first year at Hadar, I was advised by a few not-for-profit entrepreneurs to start asking people who attended for money, because only when people pay something will they gain "buy-in." But I resisted that approach—in large part because we just couldn't justify taking in money that we didn't need to spend. Instead, the buy-in mechanism came around shared community and volunteering.

Fundraising

As the minyan grew and the frequency and popularity of meetings increased, as well as the size of the room we needed to rent, we had to rent a larger space and running Hadar became more expensive. The budget for the minyan currently stands at around $165,000 (about one-third of which is a pass-through for the Shavuot retreat, where fees cover expenses). Hadar pays some people for critical jobs: a scholar-in-residence to bring the highest-level teaching at critical moments, a community member to keep the finances, and a custodian to set up the chairs. But by far the largest category in the budget is rent.

How does the minyan raise money? When people sign up on the Internet to reserve a spot for High Holiday services (no assigned seats or tickets, just a way for Hadar to know how many people are coming and when to cut off sign-ups because of limited space), they are prompted to make a suggested donation, which is $250 per person ($180 for students). Although people can give any amount of money (as low as eighteen dollars), the vast majority contribute within the range of the suggested donation. (Now, as rent prices continue to climb, Hadar also sends an e-mail at the end of the calendar year asking for a donation.)

> Because our finances are very clear (we post our budget online for all to see), there is a sense that no donated money is wasted.

Because our finances are very clear (we post our budget online for all to see), there is a sense that no donated money is wasted. Also, because very few people give more than the suggested amount, there is no sense of "catering to the *machers*." In a very real way, the community lives within its means and does not rely on a few vaunted members to bankroll the budget. People know that their $250 donations make a relatively significant impact. The time that could be spent strategizing about fundraising, stewardship of donors, gala events, and the like is focused instead on community programming and services. This has helped us build a culture based on the quality of the experience without wringing our hands all day about how to fund it.

Engagement without Membership

Hadar has no official category of membership. After all, membership is often a means of raising money, so we wondered whether membership would still be useful if we raised enough money through voluntary donations. For us, the answer was ultimately no. As explored in chapter 3, membership certainly has its upsides and downsides. Although it can offer people a sense of ownership and belonging, it excludes those who are not members. Especially in a transient community like Hadar, we could not afford to alienate new people who come to the minyan, because within a year or two, those people could often be at the core of the leadership. Membership, when stripped of its financial obligations, seemed an inefficient way for us to create buy-in and belonging. And for a generation of people who do not see their identity expressed in membership, the category of *member* is simply less appealing. This means the minyan has to work at offering people other ways to become connected.

MAXIMIZING TECHNOLOGY

By Aaron Kasman, current gabbai at Kehilat Hadar

Information technology (IT) touches almost every part of Kehilat Hadar's operations in some way: collecting donations, event registration, outbound e-mail blasts, and advertising events, to name just a few. Several factors influence the way we think about IT and why it matters so much. Consider how our approach differs from that of conventional synagogues:

- **We have no central office.** Hadar doesn't have a central office, and we have very few paper files. Most of the work we do in organizing the community is delegated to volunteers working at different times in different locations, necessitating technological solutions to make communication easier.

- **There is high turnover.** Hadar's leadership turns over quickly, so storing reference documents is critical. There's also turnover among those who are working on the technology solutions themselves, so solutions need to be transferable as people move on.

- **We are committed to keeping costs low.** Hadar is very budget-focused, making free and open-source software highly desirable. (Check out www.techsoup.org for deals for not-for-profits.)

- **Our population is Web-savvy.** Hadar doesn't send snail mail— at all. Aside from a few fliers that we distribute at services, all of our communications are Web-based.

CONTENT MANAGEMENT SYSTEMS FOR YOUR WEBSITE

Kehilat Hadar was early on the Web scene with a "Web 1.0" site that served the community well. However, among the major challenges was that any changes that went beyond basic edits of content, such as setting up a calendar for the following year, required more advanced IT skills. In early 2009, we launched a new site that leverages a content management system (CMS). This allows a wider range of nontechnical people to edit the site. It's fairly intuitive to use and requires just a little orientation to get it up and running.

There are numerous popular CMS systems out there. We picked Drupal (see www.drupal.org for more details). Why Drupal? Because it has let us build tremendous functionality into our site without a single line of code written. (A bit of custom work was done to *theme* our site, but not to address functionality.) We have been able to add a calendar, manage community postings, and integrate simple forms, all by reusing a few of the hundreds of optional modules available at drupal.org. We also use our Drupal-based website to create several areas of resources for our leadership, essentially the minyan equivalent of a corporate Intranet. Furthermore, we've been able to make good progress on our goal of making as much of the setup as possible available to non-techies. For example, one of the *gabbaim* who does not have a technical background set up the form for our communitywide learning project. By bypassing the IT person, lay leadership is further empowered, the IT operations are demystified, and very practically, there's a reduced bottleneck on waiting for IT people to complete needed tasks.

GOOGLE FOR DAY-TO-DAY TASKS

A few highlights from Google, all currently free:

- Google Analytics allows you to easily view statistics about the number of visitors to specific parts of the website.
- Google Documents allows you to jointly edit documents (in real time, if necessary) and then refer to them later.
- Google Spreadsheets has a terrific feature that lets you set up a form that members of your community can use to sign up for events, sell their *hametz* (leaven products) before Passover, etc.

- Google Alerts are a convenient way to be notified when your minyan's name (or any other topic of your interest) appears online in the blogosphere or news media.

- Google Calendars can be directly embedded into webpages to publicize your minyan's events. We use an internal Google calendar to schedule meetings for *gabbaim*, keep track of who is on vacation, etc.

- Gmail lets you converge your mailboxes. E-mail sent to my Kehilat Hadar account lands in my Gmail box, but I can also *send* e-mail from that address from my personal Gmail account.

STAY CURRENT

The information that Hadar offers is being consumed through more and more media and devices (such as the iPhone), and we need to stay current with how we get our message out. We try to engage with the latest social media: we tweet on Twitter and have pages on Facebook and LinkedIn. We're experimenting with the best ways to use RSS feeds. These feeds let members of the community easily follow new updates from Kehilat Hadar (and other sites) in their favorite newsreader, such as Google Reader, rather than having to come to our site to get the updates. It also lets other websites automatically aggregate our content into their site. And our main events calendar can also be viewed in your Google calendar (a feature that Drupal provides).

FLOURISHING BEYOND THE FOUNDERS

Kehilat Hadar is now in its ninth year of existence, and for more than four years, I have not been part of the day-to-day leadership. This points to the stability of the structures that are in place at Hadar and, more important, attests that there is an active and growing community of Empowered Jews who remain committed to living out this vision of Judaism. Even more than the continued existence of Kehilat Hadar, I am proudest of the ethos behind the founding of the minyan: we can build vibrant Jewish communities that empower people to take ownership of a vision and bring it to reality.

2
Independent Minyanim Nationwide
Significance and Impact

Jews across the country are looking for new ways to connect to the substance of their religion and tradition. In New York City, thousands of young Jews found that connection through Kehilat Hadar. But Hadar turned out to be more than just a local minyan; it became a model of grassroots religious community that spread dramatically across the United States and Israel. These communities became known as "independent minyanim."

What is an independent minyan? They are defined by the following characteristics:

- Organized and led by volunteers, with no paid clergy
- No denomination/movement affiliation
- Founded in the past ten years (distinguishing them from the havurah movement—see below)
- Meet at least once a month

The term "independent," like any term, is imperfect. These minyanim do not see themselves as independent from the wider Jewish world. On the contrary, they see themselves as filling a need not being met by existing institutions, but as operating within the larger Jewish community, not outside or against it. The founders, myself included, are grateful to a host of mainstream Jewish institutions that offered us the confidence to dream of something new and the skills to build it. They are also aware of the ways in which they do not provide all the services necessary for Jewish life (burial, daily minyan, and so on).

So what is "independent" about these minyanim? They are independent of the existing labels that mark Jewish institutional life. They do not see themselves as aligned with one denomination or as breaking away from one. They are marked by a wide variety of Jews with diverse backgrounds coming together to form communities. This particular form of religious expression had no place on the Jewish map, so these minyanim started to refer to themselves as "independent." The best analogy to this is the political affiliation of "independent." People who claim to be Independents say that the platforms of the Democrats or Republicans don't represent their views (although there is some overlap). But Independents haven't opted out of the political system—they use the same voting booths, vote on the same days, and pay taxes to the same government. They simply avoid a label that doesn't reflect who they are.

The growth of independent minyanim is nothing short of astounding. By the end of 2001, there were five independent minyanim nationwide. By 2003, another twelve had started, and by 2005 an additional eighteen minyanim had been launched. As of 2009, there were more than sixty independent minyanim across the country. They were originally founded in the largest Jewish urban areas, including New York, Los Angeles, Boston, and Washington, D.C., but have since cropped up in cities such as San Francisco, Denver, Atlanta, and Philadelphia, as well as in smaller communities, including Charlottesville, Providence, New Haven, Palo Alto, Minneapolis, Kansas City, and Princeton. Using numbers of attendees and e-mail list subscribers, researchers have estimated that twenty thousand people attend independent minyanim in a given year.[1] Because of the frequent fluctuations in minyan congregations—partially the result of a young, mobile, primarily urban population—the overall number of people who have been involved in minyanim may be much larger. The vast majority (more than 80 percent) of minyangoers are under age forty.

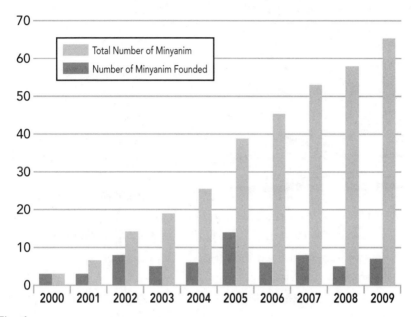

Fig. 1.

Growth of independent minyanim in the United States, 2000–2009. Includes six minyanim in Israel. Data courtesy of Mechon Hadar.

WHAT CHARACTERIZES THESE MINYANIM?

As I watched these minyanim grow—and was in touch with the founders of new communities—I was eager to know more about these grassroots communities and what made them tick. In 2007, I helped conduct a national survey of independent minyanim with leading social science researchers Prof. Steven M. Cohen, J. Shawn Landres, and Michelle Shain. In 2008, Mechon Hadar held a national conference for independent minyanim and used the event as an opportunity to gather more data.[2] These two studies begin to present a picture of the independent minyanim and the ways in which they differ from a typical synagogue:

- The majority of minyanim hold Shabbat morning services, and about 75 percent hold Friday night services.

- About half of the minyanim attract crowds larger than fifty for each service.

- About 40 percent meet in a Jewish institution (synagogue, JCC, other), while 27 percent meet in people's homes; 7 percent meet in a church.
- More women than men attend the services, but more men than women lead the services.
- Some 75 percent reported some joint programming with other Jewish institutions.
- Space rental and food-related costs are the biggest expenses for most minyanim.
- The most popular meeting-space setup combination is prayer leader in the middle of the room and chairs in rows; 25 percent have a *mechitza* (the barrier separating men and women in prayer).
- 80 percent of minyanim offer classes or other opportunities to learn to daven/*leyn*.
- One-third of minyan founders remain leaders in their minyanim.
- Only 32 percent of minyanim have an official category of membership, and only one-third of those with membership offer special benefits to members (High Holiday seats, for example). Only two minyanim charge more than $300 for membership.
- 70 percent count both men and women in a minyan. The remaining 30 percent count either ten men and ten women, or only count men.
- About 50 percent of minyangoers are married.
- Of the attendees, 46 percent grew up in a Conservative synagogue, 20 percent in an Orthodox synagogue, and 18 percent in a Reform synagogue. Currently, the largest percentage of minyangoers (about half) does not claim any denominational affiliation; these "nondenominational" minyangoers hail from a variety of denominational backgrounds.
- Minyan attendees' Jewish identity is quite strong: 90 percent say "being Jewish is very important to me"; 77 percent attend services more than once a month; and 84 percent say they have a "strong sense of belonging to the Jewish people."
- Minyangoers' top two reasons for being involved are to be part of a community (86 percent) and to participate in meaningful prayer (85 percent).

- Minyangoers reflect a diverse spectrum of Jewish educational experiences: 40 percent went to elementary Jewish day school, 67 percent were part of a Jewish youth group, 65 percent went to Jewish summer camp, and 80 percent were involved in Hillel. Some 87 percent understand a simple Hebrew sentence.

These independent minyanim, while deeply rooted in tradition, offer a new approach to Jewish community. Why have they experienced such explosive growth in the past decade?

ODYSSEY YEARS: THE SEARCH FOR MEANING MESHES WITH MINYANIM

Much of the independent minyanim phenomenon is grounded in a new demographic category that has emerged in America. Thirty is the new twenty. People are delaying marriage, children, and long-term careers for at least a decade after college graduation. David Brooks, writing in the *New York Times*, has termed this time of life the "odyssey years." Young Jews are no exception, and given their socioeconomic background, they often lead the charge to explore during the decade following college. In addition, there is tremendous mobility in this age group, and significantly, it's focused in urban areas. By and large, young Jews have stopped settling down in the suburbs at the age of twenty-four. They flock to large urban areas and tend to move from one big city to another as they seek jobs or schooling. Although these twenty- and thirtysomethings uproot themselves frequently, they still yearn for community and a sense of feeling at home, a yearning perhaps made stronger by their increased mobility and instability.

> Although twenty- and thirtysomethings uproot themselves frequently, they still yearn for community and a sense of feeling at home, a yearning perhaps made stronger by their increased mobility and instability.

Lack of Institutional Affiliation

Like most of America, the Jewish world has not caught up with the "odyssey generation." There are plenty of institutions for Jewish children and teens—Hebrew schools, day schools, camps, synagogues. College students are often served by the Hillel movement, whose expansion in the past twenty years redefined what it means to be a Jew on a college campus. But following college graduation, there is no institutional net attracting Jews in the odyssey years. The synagogues—ideally built as a one-stop center for Jewish community across all ages and stages of life—typically appeal to parents with children in school or to older adults.

So in the 2000s, Jews in their twenties and early thirties found themselves in an institutional universe that served every age but their own. Most dropped out of Jewish engagement altogether. The dropouts included not just those with very little Jewish background but huge numbers of young people with high levels of Jewish education. Luckily, a few decided to see whether they could create their own institutions to fill this gap.

Informal Networks Reflecting Mobility and Transience

Given this cultural context, how did this minyan phenomenon spread, and spread so quickly? In a twentieth-century model, a central agency looking to get its message across might carefully study the institutional landscape and choose pilot cities in which to launch spinoffs. But the growth of independent minyanim was not the result of a coordinated effort to franchise; rather, the boom was unplanned and haphazard, relying on the power of individual initiatives and informal networks. The rise of sixty independent minyanim in the past decade was fueled by the mobility and transience of young Jews and relied on the power of each motivated individual who saw something in one city and said, "I can do that in my town." In its most basic form, the spread of independent minyanim can be traced to networks of founders formed years earlier, a core of successful minyanim that served as a model, and a critical mass of Jews with diverse backgrounds looking for an alternative form of religious expression.

Growth through Viral Networking

Here's a concrete example of the social networks that facilitate the proliferation of these minyanim: when we started Kehilat Hadar in 2001, a college friend of mine came to visit for Shabbat. Having grown up in a

Modern Orthodox family, he was living in Washington, D.C. and davening at an Orthodox synagogue. But because we were friends, and because he felt comfortable enough with the traditional service we were holding (despite the full participation of women in the service), he came to Hadar. What he experienced was something he hadn't known to be possible: a vibrant, traditional service that "felt Orthodox" when he closed his eyes, but included women in all roles of worship. Later that fall, he felt frustrated by his Orthodox synagogue: all the men were offered the opportunity to lead the biblical verses traditionally recited on the evening of Simchat Torah. The rabbi pointed out that this was an attempt to include "everyone" in the davening. But, my friend noted painfully, this definition of "everyone" excluded half of the participants—the women. He resolved to start his own minyan and, having seen Hadar in action, he called me up. I gave him all the materials we had, and together with other people in his DC network, he created DC Minyan in March 2002.

Another friend of mine spent a year in Washington, D.C., in 2004 on a fellowship, temporarily leaving his community in Brookline, Massachusetts. He became active at the DC Minyan and was very sad to leave the community at the end of his fellowship year, knowing that nothing like that existed at home. When he and his wife returned to Brookline, they decided to introduce their own version of DC Minyan to the community and founded the Washington Square Minyan in 2005.

Two Israelis who were living in Brookline that year experienced egalitarian traditional davening at Washington Square Minyan for the first time in their lives. When they finished their academic appointments in Boston, they returned to Jerusalem and, inspired by the model they had seen, founded Baka Shivyoni in 2006—a traditional minyan with increased participation of women. Over the course of five years, these three minyanim were founded, each inspired by a previous new minyan.

Here are a few significant features of this viral expansion:

- **Rapid growth.** These minyanim sprang up relatively quickly due to the mobility of the founders.
- **Urban Jewish settings.** The places each of these minyan founders moved to or visited were urban areas with critical masses of Jews.
- **Distinctive character.** The minyanim were not carbon copies of each other, even when it came to core issues of women's roles and

seating. Each minyan reflected the particulars of the founders and their local Jewish constellation.

- **New, unique institutions.** With the exception of Baka Shivyoni, these minyanim are not breakaway minyanim from an established shul, and their founding did not cause a rift within an existing synagogue. Rather, the local synagogues continued to serve their core population, and the minyan founders, who were at most on the periphery of a synagogue, stepped into a new role as leader.

KEY ELEMENTS IN FOUNDING INDEPENDENT MINYANIM

A few key factors in combination made the founding of new minyanim possible, including:

- **An inspirational experience.** Almost every new minyan founder had a transformative experience with an existing minyan that showed her that a new paradigm was possible.
- **A personal tie with someone else who started a minyan.** The would-be founder received encouragement, technical advice, and resources from someone who had already founded an independent minyan.
- **Dynamic networks.** Most minyan founders have strong ties with minyan leaders in other communities and broad networks in their own communities that help their minyan expand.
- **Freedom from institutional ties.** Founders are typically "under the radar" in the Jewish community in which they start their minyan, affording them a freedom to innovate and create without directly challenging an existing synagogue.

COMMON INFLUENCES ON MINYAN LEADERSHIP

It turns out that minyan founders—distinct from minyangoers—have quite a lot in common.

Israel. Israel is *the* model of variety and diversity when it comes to prayer and Jewish community. My own experience of spending a year in Israel after college, wandering into the various vibrant minyanim in

Jerusalem, offered me new models of what could happen in prayer. The 2007 study of independent minyanim nationally found that the general independent minyan population has significant experience with Israel: 96 percent have been there once and 82 percent have been there twice or more.[3] Perhaps more significant, 52 percent of independent minyan-goers have spent more than four months at a time in Israel, giving them the opportunity to experience the power of the religious expression of Israel firsthand. On average, the founders of independent minyanim have spent even more time—at least a year—living in Israel. While there, they often formed tight bonds at study programs or fellowships: Pardes, Hebrew University, the Conservative

> The fundamentals gained in day school are critical building blocks for the founders of the minyanim.

Yeshiva, Yakar, Wexner, or Dorot. These and other institutions offered people the educational background, experience with vibrant prayer, and leadership opportunities that they drew upon later when founding minyanim. They also served as a critical social network.

Hillel. The 2007 national study found that 80 percent of the attendees of the independent minyanim attended Hillel in college. Minyan founders often had a leadership role within the Hillels, running student programming and minyanim. Hillel essentially offered a fertile training ground for how to be a grassroots organizer without the day-to-day help of clergy. But Hillel also served as a laboratory in which values such as pluralism and a welcoming atmosphere were a critical part of the espoused Jewish culture. When Hillel leadership alumni started minyanim, they had a clear sense of how to engage Jews of diverse backgrounds.

Day school. The 2007 national study of minyanim found that only 40 percent of the minyan attendees have gone to Jewish day school—though the minyanim are often mischaracterized as attracting only day school graduates. However, the *founders* of the minyanim have, by and large, attended day school at least through eighth grade. The fundamentals gained in day school (familiarity with prayer, understanding of Hebrew, love of Jewish tradition and learning) are critical building blocks for the founders of the minyanim.

Loyalty to institutions is not a given. The minyanim were founded by a group of people living a generation after Watergate. They have no loyalty to an institution simply because it is an institution. This is part of the misunderstanding in the denominational challenge to independent minyanim. Denominational loyalists are confounded when graduates of denominational institutions "spurn" a denominational synagogue in favor of a minyan (assuming for a moment that the choice is zero-sum, which I doubt it is in reality). According to the minyan study, most founders were never loyal to the denomination—they liked (or disliked) each discrete experience without signing on to a larger movement loyalty statement.

Perhaps even more interesting: minyan founders are suspicious of all institutions—including the very institutions they have founded! In my experience, people are not loyal to a minyan per se; they are loyal to the particular mode of community the minyan represents. This gives people some perspective on the minyan and a bit of humor relating to all the hype surrounding the minyan. The outside Jewish world may love (or hate) the minyanim as institutions, but the attendees are loyal only as long as the minyan keeps providing a community that responds to their needs. If that fundamentally changes, I predict people will leave minyanim and start founding other institutions.

New understanding of "affiliation." The traditional Jewish community views collective communal success through the lens of affiliation: Jews either join an institution (that is, they pay dues) or they are "unaffiliated." *Affiliation* in this dichotomy has very little to do with attendance (according to the 2007 study, only 39 percent of synagogue members attend services more than once a month, while 77 percent of minyangoers do). Yet a third relationship to affiliation exists: we can feel connected to a particular religious community without attending, paying money, or even living in the city where the community is located. For example, minyangoers report that they are affiliated with an *average* of five different Jewish communities. This does not necessarily mean that they are physically present at five different communities during any given month. But it means someone claims affinity to a minyan that their friends go to in another city, and they attend when visiting them. Or they attend a community's yearly retreat; even though they only attend once a year, they count themselves within that community. A mobile and urban population has an entirely different understanding of what it means to "affiliate."

Integration with the non-Jewish world. Even though three-quarters of minyangoers report that their closest friends are Jewish and 90 percent say being Jewish is "very important" to them, they are not shut off from the secular world at all. In fact, according to the national minyan survey, 58 percent of them have had a romance with a non-Jew, 24 percent in the past year. This integration with the larger secular world—for better or worse—leads to particular outcomes in the minyanim. Most minyangoers are comfortable meeting in non-Jewish spaces, such as the Women's Building in San Francisco, a Latino cultural center in New York, or a church in Denver. The social action projects of these minyanim often focus on the secular world, such as lobbying for justice in Darfur and building houses through Habitat for Humanity. In many cases, minyangoers are looking to engage with the outside world but are interested in doing so with other Jews.

WHAT IS THE DIFFERENCE BETWEEN INDEPENDENT MINYANIM AND THE HAVURAH MOVEMENT?

Despite the clear sense that independent minyanim are a product of the larger contemporary cultural moment, one of the most common questions I have been asked over the years is this: "How are independent minyanim different from the havurah movement?" After all, the havurah movement is that famous collection of grassroots Jewish communities that placed a strong emphasis on spirited prayer, the inclusion of women, and organizing outside the synagogue, without the leadership of traditional clergy.

Before I delve into some of the similarities and differences between the independent minyanim and the havurah movement, let's consider the question itself. One of the valences of the question comes down to this: you are not so new, and therefore you aren't so valuable. A funding and media culture that values innovation, often for its own sake, is not interested in the "same old, same old." So if we are just repeating the patterns of the previous generation, what is all the hype about? Even more troubling is the tenor of the question from the adherents of the havurah movement, who sometimes patronize members of the independent minyanim: "Oh, how nice—the next generation is doing the same things we did. Wait until you face the roadblocks we faced and then we'll see how successful you are." The other valence of the question is this: the havurah movement "failed," and (implicitly) you, who have strong parallels to the havurah movement, will also fail.

Keep in mind that the supposed failure of the havurah movement depends on what the metrics of success were meant to be. Did it bring down the synagogue structure and the organized institutional Jewish world—a world it was in active rebellion against? No. Did most American Jews gravitate toward the havurot's engaged and intense way of Jewish practice? Not even close. But did it normalize female participation in traditional Jewish prayer? In many ways it did, serving as the outside catalyst of a feminist movement in Reform and Conservative communities that ultimately ordained women. The members of the havurah movement made Jewish education a centerpiece of the larger communal agenda, successfully demanding that federations allocate more funds for Jewish education.

So I engage this question of "What is different?" in a spirit of fellowship with the founders of the havurah movement, noting that the American Jewish community has changed a great deal as a result of the havurot. In many ways, the havurah movement normalized some of the core givens that the independent minyanim have in their communities (egalitarianism in some form, participatory and engaged prayer, placing a strong value on Jewish education).

The real surprise is not that havurot and minyanim share similarities, but that modern synagogues and other institutions of nineteenth- and twentieth-century Jewish life persist. Judaism has always been a religion of grassroots community organizing, and the rabbinic model of the twentieth-century synagogue is perhaps the most foreign to the traditional Jewish heritage. (Riv-Ellen Prell, in her article "Independent Minyanim and Prayer Groups of the 1970s: Historical and Sociological Perspectives," points out how even in pre–World War II America, Jews were organizing prayer groups in their homes.) Groups of Jews who know how to pray and want to eat, daven, learn, and perform *gemilut hasadim* together have traditionally created their own communities throughout Jewish history. The real question is not how are independent minyanim new, but how are suburban synagogues—a product of the early to mid-twentieth century—a departure from a Jewish organizing heritage shared by minyanim, havurot, and dozens of Jewish communal structures of years past?

Nevertheless, there are some critical differences between the independent minyanim and the havurot; perhaps most striking is the difference in motivation and influence. Only a handful of independent minyan founders and leaders grew up in a havurah or were members of a havurah. Interestingly, the havurah movement itself did not produce the next generation of minyan founders, even if some of the goals of these minyanim and the havurot are the same. Instead, other environments—Israel, Hillel, day schools, camps—were more significant in forming the networks that fostered these minyanim.

Shifts in Culture, Shifts in Demographics

The Jewish world looks extremely different from the one that gave rise to the havurah movement. Although most of the havurah movement leaders did not have a significant day school background, the Jewish day school explosion of the past thirty years produced thousands of Jews who could potentially be the knowledgeable leaders and participants in the independent minyanim. In addition, the mixing among those with Orthodox backgrounds and those without is very prevalent in the minyanim in a way unthinkable in a previous generation. The leaders of the minyanim drew from an Orthodox world that was increasingly frustrated by the lack of inclusion of women and a non-Orthodox world that was increasingly frustrated by the lack of traditional prayer.

Differences in Scale

The havurot always struggled with how to maintain a clear commitment to intimacy—many of them were founded for people not only to pray together but also to really live in Jewish fellowship (as *haverim*, friends). By contrast, the first independent minyanim were responding to a larger American culture that was more transient and mobile, and also attracted large numbers from their inception. At Kehilat Hadar, for instance, the number of daveners ballooned to more than 150 within the first few months. In the independent minyanim, there was never a chance for intensive, fellowship-based intimacy. Although this poses other challenges for the minyanim, leaders don't struggle with how to deal with growth and the ways in which it undermines an intimate group, as the havurot did.

Well-Educated Laity

Havurot are proud of the fact that many of their participants went on to become major Jewish professionals and professors. Many of the top leaders of today's institutions, including a major federation and three rabbinical seminaries, are run by self-identified alumni of the havurah movement. In contrast, the independent minyanim, by and large, are not run by (future) Jewish professionals or rabbinical students. At Mechon Hadar's National Independent Minyan Conference in 2008, in which thirty-two minyanim sent ninety-one leaders, only three were rabbinical students. The independent minyanim offer a place for an educated laity—educated in ways unimaginable in the 1960s—to run a prayer community.

> Independent minyanim offer a place for an educated laity to run a prayer community.

Divergent Worship Styles

Another difference between havurot and minyanim is the style of the worship itself. Although some might point to these differences as marginal in the larger scope of Jewish life, the cultural space created by each is quite different when these factors are considered one by one:

- **Truncated services versus full services.** While havurot davened the traditional Hebrew liturgy for the most part, almost all of them cut various "objectionable" parts of the siddur and emended some traditional practices, such as repeating the *Musaf Amidah.* In contrast, almost all the independent minyanim perform a traditional liturgy with little deviation. This reflects a focus less on the creative retooling of the siddur, and more on the vibrant performance of traditional liturgy.

- **Circular arrangement versus rows.** The layout of the havurot is often circular, and the layout of most independent minyanim is straight and in rows, leading to a very different aesthetic of davening (see chapter 4).

- **Brevity versus discussion.** Many havurot services center around a long Torah discussion; the minyanim, in contrast, prefer a short *dvar Torah* without discussion.
- **Countercultural leadership structure versus hierarchical structure.** The leadership structure of havurot was reflective of the radical democratic tendencies of the 1960s counterculture and often involved large groups of decision-makers. The leadership structure of the minyanim reflects a ceding of control to a small group of capable volunteers.

Different Goals

The havurah movement also grew out of a clear rejection of the institutions of Jewish life and a desire to remake them. Much like the counterculture of the 1960s, the goal of the havurot was to do battle with the institutions of Jewish life that were, in the view of the havurot leaders, holding back progress. By contrast, the independent minyanim have a different relationship to the organized Jewish world. They see themselves as filling in a critical gap in Jewish life, not as working to replace existing institutions.

WHAT SYNAGOGUES CAN LEARN FROM INDEPENDENT MINYANIM

My father was a pulpit rabbi for twenty-five years, and I have tremendous respect for the community built in healthy synagogues. At their best, they model (often much better than independent minyanim) what it means to care for people who are vulnerable, to educate and engage children, and to provide important services for the elderly. But by and large, they have not unlocked the power of prayer. Perhaps one of the lasting impacts of independent minyanim will be to spur the synagogues to treat the issue of prayer as critical to their future.

I was once at a national conference, speaking on a panel, when a man in the audience stood up to ask a question. He complained that his synagogue was not attracting young people, and he asked, in a desperate tone, "What can we do to attract Jews in their twenties? Tell us what we can do!" The problem is this: most synagogues see independent minyanim only as a way station for a population that they hope to bring into the synagogue. In their ideal scenario, the synagogue will continue to do what it does, just with more people in their twenties. But the members of independent minyanim are not a demographic treasure trove to be raided, co-opted, or lured. They are the expression of a particular type of Jewish practice and engagement, one that is very different from the typical American synagogue.

Diversification of Worship

There are fundamental differences in the overall approach to worship between synagogues and independent minyanim. The independent minyanim do not represent every Jew in the twenty- to thirty-year-old age range—far from it. But most people of that generation have a particular connection to worship that is markedly different from those who grew up in the 1940s and 1950s and now heavily populate the aging American synagogue. Here I don't make a value judgment about what is "good davening" and what isn't, but I

> You can't satisfy everyone's davening needs in one service.

want to clearly state that you can't satisfy everyone's davening needs in one service. Synagogues have made a particular choice when it comes to the style of the synagogue service, and that is the right of the congregation. But don't expect everyone to sign on to that style without trying to consider alternatives that speak to a different form of spiritual expression.

I once had a phone consultation with the clergy of a large suburban synagogue. The young assistant rabbi had a particular vision of prayer—inclusive, participatory, engaging—in short, an Empowered Judaism approach—that was at odds with that of an old-line cantor—performative, soloist. I mentioned that the young rabbi's preferences were shared by many in the independent minyanim, and the cantor seemed to recognize that there was value in that style of prayer. But at one point he asked, "Is there any place for a thirty-second aria in the middle of the Kedushah in the form of prayer you are talking about?" In other words: Could we meet in the middle? I responded in a way I hope was sensitive, but the basic answer was no. All it takes is one excessively performative moment in the middle of a service to make the congregation into the "other" and alienate worshipers who wish to engage as full participants. This is not to deny that some people love the operatic cantorial service, but it cannot be blended with a participatory service with real integrity. Synagogues and independent minyanim offer different approaches to worship and community life. A false merger of these populations (especially in the name of institutional perpetuation) would only lead to a dilution of religious expression, by both the synagogue and the minyan.

Possibilities for Synagogues

What can an Empowered Judaism ethos offer to synagogues, even without a fundamental shift in their approach to prayer or community?

Treat the davening problem with some urgency. In my experience, many pulpit rabbis have given up on improving the davening at their synagogue, instead turning their attention to creating top-notch Hebrew schools or exceptional programming. But fundamentally, a synagogue's main program is still worship services, and when the leadership has despaired of making any improvement to the service, then no progress will be made.

Allow for discussion and feedback about the style of worship. Most people in synagogues have no opportunity to offer any form of feedback on the worship service. The structure and style of the service are often viewed as givens, either because the professional leadership won't change or because denominational affiliation assumes a certain style of worship that won't change (Orthodox shuls mumble; Reform temples use English, and so on). But synagogues could open up a critical dialogue in their communities by giving people an opportunity for meaningful feedback on the style of worship and having a conversation about what people appreciate and what could be changed.

Imagine new possibilities by experiencing other models of worship. It is hard to consider new modes of synagogue worship without seeing a variety of other models. Too often, synagogue leaders and members only know their own form of worship. A collective trip to vibrant prayer spaces in Jerusalem or to independent minyanim in America could open up possibilities for changes in the synagogue.

Create a culture of gratitude. Independent minyanim run based on the volunteer power of the community, and one of the critical currencies in engaging volunteers is positive feedback. Synagogues, by contrast, engage paid professionals. Laypeople may assume that the clergy don't need to be thanked (after all, it's their job). Also, because the paid staff does the lion's share of the work, volunteer engagement may be undervalued. Most synagogues thank people only during announcements at the end of services, when most people aren't paying attention. What would it look like for synagogue clergy and volunteers to thank each other with meaningful, thoughtful feedback over e-mail or through handwritten notes?

Consider the power of new music. One of the hallmarks of the independent minyanim is their "new melodies" classes. Synagogues could introduce new melodies into the worship service through a variety of mechanisms. Instead of a scholar-in-residence program, consider bringing in a musical scholar-in-residence who would teach congregants a new set of melodies. With a willing cantor/prayer leader, these classes could create buy-in throughout the congregation and allow for the introduction of new melodies in a nonthreatening environment.

Create an alternative prayer space. Although synagogues have historically welcomed minyanim that start at different times (the early service versus the main service), few have minyanim for alternative prayer styles. This often frustrates those with divergent ideas of what it could mean to engage in meaningful prayer. Synagogues could broaden their appeal if they were open to multiple forms of davening—and didn't just tolerate them, but supported them—without feeling threatened.

Use real estate to attract new audiences. One of a synagogue's major assets is its real estate. By limiting the use of that real estate to only one form of religious expression, the synagogue misses an opportunity to advance new forms of Jewish expression. If a synagogue is willing to lend an extra meeting room to an independent minyan, this asset can be doubly valuable. To the extent the synagogue exists to further the Jewish people, and not just further a particular form of Judaism promulgated by the clergy, the synagogue will advance its mission by opening itself up to other forms of expression.

THE FUTURE OF INDEPENDENT MINYANIM

So what is the future of the independent minyanim? Or, to put it in a way I often hear, what will happen when these minyangoers start to have children? In the past ten years, this model of Jewish community has exploded within the twenties and thirties demographic across the United States. What will the next ten years bring?

First, I believe the independent minyanim located in urban areas will continue to be populated mostly by Jews in their twenties and early thirties and will not, by and large, evolve into child-centered communities with the related needs of bnei mitzvot, Hebrew school, and so on. More than any other factor, this is dictated by the real estate market. Most people who would love to stay in the urban areas that are homes to the largest independent minyanim are forced to leave once they have children because the price of housing is simply too high. So when people ask what will happen to the minyan as it ages, my experience suggests that it simply won't. Most people past their mid-thirties leave the urban area, and a new crop of college graduates moves in.

Understanding this phenomenon is critical to understanding the future of any particular minyan. The institution itself is actually quite stable, because it caters to a demographic that is constantly replenishing itself. A more significant question is this: what will the former attendees of these minyanim do when they move out of the urban areas? Below are a few possibilities.

The proliferation of independent minyanim. Empowered Jews will form minyanim outside the super-urban Jewish areas of the United States (for example, New York City, Los Angeles, Boston). Already we have seen the spread of minyanim in different areas of the country—places like Columbus, Ohio; Princeton, New Jersey; Denver, Colorado; and Charlottesville, Virginia now have independent minyanim. The founders of these minyanim are either alumni of larger, urban independent minyanim or are in the same social network as those urban minyangoers.

The minyanim in these areas are, by definition, different from their urban predecessors. These new minyanim do not have a critically large base of attendees to draw on and are relying on the active attendance of a few families. But significantly, they have not taken the path of least resistance by melding into the existing synagogue structure. The founders of these new independent minyanim have sent a message by their actions: we have seen the possibilities offered by the independent minyanim, and we don't want to give up on that model, even in a different geographical area.

Minyan-synagogue hybrids. Alumni of independent minyanim will join synagogues but will launch their own minyan within the synagogue. The best example of this is in Teaneck, New Jersey. Two married former Kehilat Hadar *gabbaim* moved to Teaneck when they outgrew their one-bedroom apartment on the Upper West Side. They joined a synagogue that was well attended and warm but whose main sanctuary services didn't offer the vibrancy they had experienced at Hadar. The synagogue offered a twice-a-month "parallel minyan" that had started in the 1980s, but it offered a Torah-discussion-oriented approach rather than the kind of vibrant, participatory (and child-friendly) service that this couple sought.

So they started a new minyan within the synagogue. It is not, strictly speaking, an independent minyan—all of the participants are members of the larger synagogue. But the service they put together is largely based on the model of an independent minyan: it is participant led, includes the full liturgy, and incorporates new melodies on a regular basis. Although the rabbi initially resisted the minyan (concerned that, if it met every other week, and the "parallel minyan" met on the alternate weeks, there was always an alternative to the main sanctuary), he eventually supported it as a healthy sign of growth in his community. Significantly, the minyan has drawn in new people in addition to a number of longtime synagogue members. When clergy are open to this model, it represents a real possibility for change within a synagogue structure.

Minyanim as training grounds for synagogue members. Many alumni of independent minyanim will attend synagogues, but as more active members than they would have been without their minyan experience. One former *gabbai* at Kehilat Hadar moved to Salt Lake City. There was no critical mass to start a minyan in her new community, but she and her husband joined the synagogue (with their two children) and immediately became active members of the synagogue leadership. She drew on her models of success and the practical skills she developed in the minyan to offer real contributions to her new community. One rabbi on the outskirts of Washington, D.C., has stated that he loves the existence of DC Minyan, an independent minyan founded in 2002—it serves as a feeder for his synagogue of engaged, knowledgeable laypeople.

Rabbis will bring the independent minyan ethos to their communities. The vast majority of people who attend independent minyanim are not rabbinical students. But many rabbinical students attend independent minyanim. When these students become rabbis and fan out across the synagogue landscape, they may introduce various features of the minyanim into their synagogues. They will know that "standard" suburban synagogue services are not the only model in twenty-first-century Judaism, and they may incorporate the values of the independent minyanim into the mainstream synagogue. Some of them will even found their own start-up rabbi-led communities—such as Kavana in Seattle or IKAR in Los Angeles—taking the independent minyan ethos and applying it to a new environment.

Minyan participation as a deviation from an otherwise unengaged Jewish life. Some minyan alumni will simply drop out of organized Jewish life. This is a sad potential outcome, but my sense is that part of what animates the attendance at the minyanim is a connection to the vibrancy of Jewish prayer and community. If that vibrancy is missing, and if it is simply too difficult to transform a synagogue, people may become frustrated and go back to their pre-minyan Shabbat routine: sleep through services and find other ways to engage with their spiritual side. Because this generation does not join out of guilt or institutional obligation, but out of a search for meaning, then if the meaning is absent, some will not join at all. This is the outcome I fear the most, because it means that people who would otherwise be engaged will stop contributing to Jewish life.

REAL CHALLENGES FOR INDEPENDENT MINYANIM

Many of the supposed challenges to independent minyanim are not real issues. The most common one I hear—"Wait 'til the minyan has to deal with people who grow up and have kids"—simply ignores the real-estate pressure that is moving young families out of range of the urban minyanim. But make no mistake: independent minyanim have critical challenges before them.

Compromising core values. Fundamentally, minyanim thrive because they have come up with a formula that favors excellence, even in a participatory service. The pressures at any given time to compromise standards in favor of inclusion are immense and may sometimes be correct and necessary. But, fundamentally, to forget that excellence is a critical part of a minyan is to undermine the reason the minyan was started in the first place. A minyan does not exist simply to satisfy the most recent volunteer's request—rather, it is part of a new order for how religious community can be organized. To lower standards by adopting short-term fixes will threaten any minyan over the long term.

Preserving the institution instead of the idea. Minyanim were launched because founders had a particular vision of community and engagement. The minyan itself is not the end goal—the vision of community is. The challenge is not to confuse the preservation of the goal for the preservation of the institution. Minyanim face the challenge of remaining focused on achieving the vision of a vibrant, traditional, engaged community rather than preserving the way things "have always been done."

Triumphalism. Independent minyanim represent a breath of fresh air in an often tired spiritual landscape. However, they don't have all the answers and should never pretend to have solved all the problems of Jewish communal life. The leadership of minyanim I have interacted with is unusually self-critical, but that self-criticism must be consciously reinforced to prevent a certain complacency from settling in.

Settling for Shabbat-only Judaism. Minyanim do a very good job of meeting their constituents' needs for a prayerful Shabbat community. But what about daily minyan, regular Torah study, engagement with Israel, and questions of peoplehood? Right now, all but the largest minyanim have not answered these needs. How do they plan on growing or partnering with other institutions to connect people to a wider sense of Jewish life?

Meaning as the only driving force in community. The minyanim are responding to a new phase of American Jewish life: people join out of inspiration, not obligation. But obligation and responsibility are age-old Jewish values. How can the minyan culture foster a sense of obligation without guilt?

Sidelining rabbinic leadership. Minyanim have demonstrated that rabbis are not needed to help form engaged prayer communities. But well-educated rabbis are still critical for halakhic consultation, pastoral care, and high-level teaching. How might minyanim engage rabbinic leadership without ceding the value of a participant-led community?

Inability to learn from other models. Although the minyanim constitute an implicit critique of existing models, it is a mistake to dismiss as irrelevant the major institutions of the Jewish world. I have learned a tremendous amount from well-functioning synagogues about what it means to care for and serve a diverse population. I have also learned about the deep and abiding love older Jews have for other Jews—no matter what their background or where they are located along the spectrum of Jewish life—and this is inspiring to see. Minyangoers would lose something real by not connecting to the greater Jewish world.

THE LASTING SIGNIFICANCE OF THE INDEPENDENT MINYANIM

Regardless of what the alumni of the independent minyanim go on to do, it is clear that the minyanim themselves will have made a significant impact on American Jewish life. There are two broad categories of impact. First, independent minyanim have stepped into a demographic vacuum in the Jewish institutional constellation and provided a meaningful and engaging option for Jews in their twenties and early thirties. This is a new demographic that does not fit neatly into the existing world of Jewish institutions (too old for Hillel, too young for a family-oriented synagogue). This population has grown significantly in recent years, and the minyanim are the first major response that has been replicated across the country. If the minyanim serve only to meet the needs of this fifteen-year period in a Jew's life, they will have made a significant contribution to American Jewish life, in the way that camps and Hillel did for younger Jews.

Second—and perhaps more significant—independent minyanim have refocused the energies and resources of the larger Jewish world. This shift in focus, which could outlive any institutional presence of the minyanim, is perhaps their greatest opportunity for impact. Here are a few shifts in perspective brought about by the minyanim:

- **Vibrant, egalitarian, spirited prayer communities are now possible in the twenty-first century.** Those who had given up on the ability of American Jews to connect deeply with religion and modernity while forming community saw a workable alternative that inspired and engaged them.

- **In order to create spirited, vibrant religious communities, we do not need to reinvent Judaism.** The minyanim are not innovative in a groundbreaking, "new big idea" way. They took the power of traditional Judaism and made it compelling and energizing.

- **Empowered young Jews can make real change on the landscape, so we need to focus on how best to empower young Jews.** The minyanim were the outcome of a long educational and experiential process for their leaders. How can American Judaism invest its resources to make those opportunities for education and real, deep empowerment possible on a wide scale?

The independent minyanim are one answer to the crisis of meaning in American Judaism. I see these minyanim as the most recent response to the perennial question: how can we connect to the age-old truths in Jewish tradition even as our world evolves rapidly? As an optimist, I look forward to the next contributions of Empowered Jews who struggle to answer that question.

3

The Diverse Landscape of Independent Minyanim

Voices from the Field

This chapter contains a selection of essays from seven minyanim in the United States and Israel that convey a range of lessons for building vibrant Jewish communities. In unique and innovative ways, they deal with a wide range of challenges, including:

- Creating vibrant children's services
- The question of membership
- How to engage volunteers meaningfully
- Appealing to a pluralistic community
- Supporting life-cycle events without clergy
- Sharing space with a synagogue

Their experiences reflect the diversity of the independent minyan landscape and the particular advantage of a decentralized network, each solving its local challenges in its own way.

CREATING ENGAGING CHILDREN'S SERVICES AT DC MINYAN IN WASHINGTON, D.C.

By Sarah Gershman, www.dcminyan.org

Children's services can be engaging and content rich, reaching children at each particular age and stage of life.

I started the Tot Shabbat program at DC Minyan when my son turned one. I was finding it more and more difficult to be in the main service with him, and I wanted to create an alternative prayer space for us.

As I thought about what I wanted the Tot Shabbat to look like, I realized that my guiding influence was not other children's services (I had not been to any), but rather a music class I took when my son was six months old. I was impressed by the teacher's sophisticated and creative approach to music and excited to bring some of her ideas to our Tot Shabbat.

The music teacher focused on family music—not children's music. She stressed that music transcends age and can be enjoyed by all. Just as there is no reason to teach kids nursery rhymes without bothering to teach them to appreciate jazz, so too a Tot Shabbat program should not be limited to kids' Shabbat songs. There is no reason why even the youngest children cannot learn basic *tefillot*, as well as have an opportunity to communicate with God.

We based our Tot Shabbat on the Shabbat morning davening, while still making it accessible to even our youngest participants. We included some of the best elements of Jewish celebration—*niggunim*, dance, and singing filled with *ruach* (spiritual energy).

We began with about five families. Within a year, the number grew to twelve to fifteen, though not everyone would attend each week. Most of the families were regular DC Minyan attendees and about a third were families who just came for the Tot Shabbat. A few families became more involved in DC Minyan through participating in Tot Shabbat. When we started, most of the kids in the minyan were under two years of age and several were infants.

We met in a carpeted classroom during the Torah reading at the main minyan, at around 10:30 a.m. The kids' service lasted about thirty minutes, followed by *Kiddush* (grape juice and snack) in the main lobby of the Washington, D.C., JCC.

Lessons Learned

Build the structure around davening. We began with *Modeh Ani* and ended with *Ein Keloheinu* and *Adon Olam*. The middle included *Shema*, *V'ahavta*, *Ki Mi'tzion*, *Etz Chaim Hi*, and even the beginning of the *Amidah* (which has great choreography for walkers). We also included lots of other songs, but always after the *tefillot*—and before *Adon Olam*.

Make talking to God the focus. Before *Shema*, for example, we took a few moments of quiet for both the kids and the adults to say whatever they wished to God. We also made a point of going around the room and giving everyone a chance to say thank you to God for something.

Include the *parsha* (Torah portion) of the week. Even the most seemingly inaccessible *parshiot* have lessons for kids. Taking the time to mine the text and find those lessons can be one of the most rewarding elements of the experience for the adults. Take *Parshat Tazria-Metzora*, for example. The Torah goes into a lengthy discussion about a condition called *tsaraat*, a physical manifestation of a spiritual impurity. In addition to afflicting the body, *tsaraat* can also afflict someone's house. This can lead to a great discussion about the home—what makes the home feel safe, happy, and loving, and what does not, such as when people are mean to each other. We tried to get to the essence of the *parsha* in a way that was most accessible to children.

> Like the davening itself, develop an energy and rhythm that includes warming up, building the intensity, and winding down.

Involve the parents. Make it clear to the parents at the outset that their participation is vital. Kids learn more from watching their parents participate than they do from the leader. Make sure the parents have an opportunity to contribute. In *Parshat Vayeitzei*, when Leah gives birth to and names seven of her children, we went around the room and each parent told us the meaning of his or her child's name and why this name was chosen. This exercise was not only fun for the kids, but it also served as a wonderful experience of sharing for the parents.

Vary the energy. Don't sit the whole time. Allow moments of dancing, moving, freezing, and so on. At the same time, don't keep getting up and down. Like the davening itself, develop an energy and rhythm that includes warming up, building the intensity, and winding down. This keeps kids engaged in a manner that is predictable and also indirectly teaches them about the flow of the Shabbat morning service.

Use props. Puppets, stuffed Torahs, scarves (great for dancing), dolls, stuffed Shabbat objects, and hats all make great Tot Shabbat props. The little ones were more interested in watching Ali the alligator sing *Hinei Mah Tov* than they were in watching me. For *Adon Olam*, we gave each child an animal puppet and incorporated the various noises into our singing. For *Mah Tovu*, our current leader invites the children to stand under a tallit, our *ohel* (tent).

Find concrete metaphors to teach Jewish principles and values. Judaism is filled with these. To teach the concept that *mitzvah goreret mitzvah* (one mitzvah leads to another), we made a mitzvah train. Each child or parent named a favorite mitzvah and we went around the room singing, "Chug-uh, chug-uh … mitzvah!"

Don't forget the babies. Often in a multiage group, it is easy to focus all the attention on the older kids who can do more. Try to have something for everyone and encourage the older kids to be helpers. For example, ask older children to hold the puppets for the entertainment of the babies. The younger children learn a great deal from watching the older ones participate.

Assign responsibilities. Kids will learn to take ownership over the davening when they have a way to help out. *Hagbahah* (lifting the toy Torah), *petichah* (opening our "ark"), passing out Torahs, dressing a Torah, and cleaning up are all great jobs for kids.

Focus on joy. Sing *niggunim*. What better thing to do with preverbal children than to sing songs with no words! And get up and dance.

As I learned at our music class and then at DC Minyan, Tot Shabbat can be a meaningful and wonderful family experience, no matter how young the children are. Further, such a service can be just as spiritually meaningful and enjoyable for the parents as it is for their children. Designing a prayer experience for our youngest daveners encourages the

> Designing a prayer experience for our youngest daveners encourages the parents to go back to the beginning and rediscover the essence, in its simplest form, of what it means for a person to communicate with God.

parents to go back to the beginning and rediscover the essence, in its simplest form, of what it means for a person to communicate with God.

The Question of Membership at Washington Square Minyan in Brookline, Massachusetts
By Yehuda Kurtzer, www.wsminyan.org

What does membership mean in an independent minyan? Do members of minyanim have different expectations from members of synagogues, federations, or Jewish community organizations?

The question of how to structure membership or other models of financial and volunteer participation is especially thorny for an independent minyan. First, participants in independent minyanim tend to see themselves as free agents in how they identify with their minyan and other communities. Membership connotes belonging, and belonging connotes an ownership that runs in two directions: members collectively own the institution, and the institution owns its members.

A second challenge comes in the financial expectations that tend to accompany membership: in colloquial terms, membership has its privileges; in practical terms, there are expectations of discounts on activities and certain rights of belonging. And together with these rights and expectations also inevitably comes a barrier between insiders and outsiders. If participants expect to be able to fluidly enter and exit the community, establishing an arbitrary barrier of membership risks closing in a circle of insiders.

The third challenge is more systemic in the world of start-up programming targeted at a younger demographic. The tendency of Hillels on campus not to charge for programs can generate a sense for college graduates that Jewish life should be free; Birthright Israel—with its prepaid trip model—reinforces this idea. A real question for independent minyanim is: how will the people who benefit from it be motivated to pay money, for many the first-ever act of supporting a Jewish institution?

When we launched the Washington Square Minyan in January 2005, we were sensitive to these concerns. We also found ourselves in a community with several synagogues whose leadership appeared to be mismanaging their fiduciary responsibilities—synagogues that were pro-grammatically or infrastructurally overextended, running over budget, and otherwise in perpetual need of funds. In starting our minyan, we wanted to ensure that the locus of the community's attention would be the project at hand; that we would focus on spiritual and communal via-bility, and not merely on whether we could pay for what we wanted to do. We also believed that a good product would ultimately sell itself, and more effectively than a concerted effort at the outset to raise money in the interest of creating the product. So the few of us who were creat-ing the minyan pooled some resources to cover the cost of operations for the first few months.

We were surprised by the success of the minyan. Right from the outset we attracted a vibrant and excited crowd; we had not fully antic-ipated the extent to which we were meeting a need greater than the one we had identified in our own lives. Volunteers quickly appeared who expressed a willingness to help in ways that matched their strengths and interests. And perhaps most surprisingly, several folks contacted the nascent leadership of the minyan to offer unsolicited donations. Through *Kiddush* sponsorship, these donations, and prudent financial management, we were able to hold off on asking for money from the community in a formal way until the minyan had half a year under its belt and had demonstrated its viability and value as a worthwhile investment. This allowed for a membership launch in August of the first year, to coincide with our first High Holiday services.

To avoid the pitfalls listed above, we took a different approach to membership. In our e-mail to the community, after listing our accom-plishments and our goals for the upcoming year, we introduced our con-cept of membership as "an opportunity to participate in the costs of the minyan." By this point, in addition to the unsolicited donations that had flowed in, we had also received multiple inquiries from community members eager to help contribute and curious about how the minyan would stay operational without their financial support. By phrasing membership this way, we acknowledged this groundswell of support and gave people an outlet to support the minyan financially, without falling into the trap of expectations and demands. The response to this approach was overwhelmingly positive, both because of this sense that minyan participants were seeking a way to help and because this stance represented a sea change from the culture in the broader community that uses tactics of guilt and fear to raise money.

A Passive Approach

Instead, we took a rather passive stance to the fundraising process. We set the membership bar at a reasonable rate—at the time, $100—but offered full "membership" for a donation of any amount. The overwhelming response was full payment at the standard rate. This allowed us to avoid the pitfall of having to negotiate over dues. In lieu of the standard discounted membership price for programs, we ran all programs on Shabbat and holidays—including some meals—free of charge for all. This helped us avoid the awkwardness of collecting money either in advance or after the fact and allowed us to throw open participation to anyone who showed up. Once again, the investment was repaid in spades: at every free event there are inevitably new people who see the benefits of participation in the community, understand that the events cannot actually be free, and send in a donation afterward. Our approach of maturely expecting that participants will acknowledge their need to contribute has—perhaps surprisingly—been rewarded.

> Realistic expectations, combined with trust in a constituency, may be a more effective strategy than louder and more constant pleas for donations.

This particular approach may not work in all communities; we probably have more professionals and fewer full-time students than other minyanim, and as a result we may have a higher donation yield. What's more, this structure may only be able to work for organizations with smaller budgets or those that can tolerate some fluidity in the revenue that is raised. Nevertheless, there are a few useful lessons from which other minyanim might benefit.

Lessons Learned

Good financial management, honesty, and a reasonable dose of passivity in fund-raising can produce good and even unexpected results.

Realistic expectations, combined with trust in a constituency, may be a more effective strategy than louder and more constant pleas for donations.

Younger populations in independent minyanim will contribute money, but the burden sometimes is—and should be—on us to produce a product that is deserving of their money. The quick turn to fundraising for an idea erodes the benefits that can be reaped by first creating the product and making it worthy of the investment of others.

The concept of membership in and of itself is value neutral and even offers some benefit in fostering a sense of belonging. But membership goes astray and creates untenable expectations and demands on the leadership when it is assumed that members can tax their leaders in exchange for a check. Membership is not destructive, but privileges can be. A reframed membership creates a revenue stream for the community and a wide sense of belonging.

Without the privileges of membership, the line between insider and outsider disappears rather quickly. If a check in any amount makes someone a member, membership is an open door that achieves its objective—bringing revenue to the community and broadening the sphere of participation.

Meeting in a Synagogue Space at Altshul in Brooklyn, New York
By Amanda Pogany and Aaron Bisman, www.altshul.org

There are distinct pros and cons to meeting in a synagogue.

When Altshul began in September 2005, we alternated our meetings between two participants' apartments. We quickly outgrew these spaces and found ourselves in need of something larger. We faced several challenges, because we did not have a membership structure and we had never asked our participants for donations. A rental space would have cost upwards of $300 per meeting, a sum we could not afford at that stage in our community's existence.

At the same time, Rabbi Andy Bachman, rabbi of a large Reform synagogue in Park Slope, Brooklyn, invited our minyan into a conversation about forging a nonrental relationship that would entitle us to meeting space. Rabbi Bachman opened the conversation in an effort to see his wider vision for his synagogue fulfilled. His goal, in addition to building a home for his congregants as a Reform temple, is to build a strong, integrated Jewish community in our Brooklyn neighborhood. With our minyan's leadership open to a commitment to be a part of this larger community, Rabbi Bachman made rooms in the temple available to us for davening as well as lunch-and-learns, kids' events, and holiday programming—all for no charge.

This successful partnership has entailed a great deal of work on both sides. Our minyan's leadership is in constant contact with the synagogue's leadership and key members. We include the synagogue's programming on our minyan e-mails and are always looking for collaborative opportunities outside of our individual services. For Shavuot, for example, we davened *Ma'ariv* separately and came together for a *tikkun* (all-night study session) where members of both our minyan and the temple taught sessions. For Purim, the temple advertised our all-Hebrew *Megillah* reading as an alternative for its congregants. Our Friday night davening meets twice a month, in rotation with the temple's Friday night services. We participate in and support the temple's social-action project, we teach in their adult-education classes, and some of the minyan's participants teach in the temple's religious school.

Whenever possible, we seek strategic partnership with our host. Altshul needed a Torah at the same time we were looking for a way to thank and give back to the temple. We raised $3,000 to fix one of their Torahs, which we now use during our davening.

This relationship has been extremely beneficial and successful, but it is not without its challenges. Synagogues have guidelines and procedures for all their regular activities, but there are no set guidelines and procedures for our partnership. This means that every time Altshul needs or wants to do something new, it requires conversation on both sides. In addition, we do have concerns about overstaying our welcome or overstepping our bounds, and we wonder whether paying members of the temple feel as open to our use of the space as the rabbi does. Collaborative programs can also be challenging because of the distinct differences in our religious approaches.

Lessons Learned

- Being housed in a temple of a different denomination is extremely beneficial to our ongoing relationship. Our minyan does not take away members from the temple's regular services.

- Communication both with our host and with our community is of the utmost importance. Our minyan's leadership is primarily involved in conversations and relationship building with our host. It is important for us to communicate with all Altshulers the value and the nature of the relationship.

- We need to be open to unexpected collaboration. Just because we are young and doing something independent does not mean we are or should be closed off to participating in the larger Jewish community.

CHALLENGES AND OPPORTUNITIES FOR NONCOASTAL INDEPENDENT MINYANIM AT NA'ALEH IN DENVER, COLORADO

By Josh Fine and Eliana Schonberg, www.naalehdenver.org

In forging independent minyanim outside of major centers of Jewish life, organizers need to address different issues than do leaders of those starting up in urban centers.

Over a Sukkot lunch on a warm fall day in 2004, four recent arrivals to Denver were discussing what they missed about davening on the East Coast. Two of the four had grown up in Denver; the other two were New Yorkers. All four had gone to college in New England and lived and worked on the East Coast. While there, they davened with grassroots communities such as Kehilat Hadar in New York. They wanted to replicate that experience in their new (or renewed) home in Denver and, from this conversation, decided to start a new independent minyan, which later became known as Minyan Na'aleh ("We will go up").

In the five years since its founding, Na'aleh has grown into a vibrant community with monthly Shabbat services, communal meals, holiday celebrations, classes, and retreats. Not surprisingly, however, Denver is a very different city from New York or Boston, presenting both challenges and opportunities that may be helpful for other emergent communities "off the coasts."

Some of the unique features of Denver's Jewish community make it a particularly fertile site for an independent minyan. At the outset, Minyan Na'aleh benefited from the relative youth of the Denver Jewish community. A recent demographic study of the Denver Jewish community revealed that 25 percent of the Jewish population in Denver and Boulder are in their twenties and thirties. A significant portion of these younger Jews in Denver are also newcomers: 46 percent of Denver's Jews under the age of forty were born outside Colorado. These new arrivals often do not have ties to the existing community infrastructure. There is no "family shul" that they have gone to since childhood, and they fall within an age demographic that simultaneously expresses strong Jewish identity and a desire to connect to Judaism outside traditional structures. For those young new arrivals seeking a prayer community as their connection to Jewish Denver, an independent minyan is a logical choice.

> The community-building aspect of the minyan is as important, if not more important, than the actual prayer services. Every Na'aleh prayer service that does not fall on a fast day is followed by a communal meal.

However, because of this dynamic, the community-building aspect of the minyan is as important, if not more important, than the actual prayer services. Every Na'aleh prayer service that does not fall on a fast day is followed by a communal meal. The minyan publicizes the start time for both the prayer services and the meal, so that participants can come to one or both. Na'aleh also organizes nonprayer programming, such as yoga classes, a poker night, and a Tu B'Shvat outdoor service project. Whereas prayer services may be the main draw for participants in other minyanim, many Na'aleh participants are involved in the minyan despite its prayer services, which are too traditional for some and too liberal for others. Na'aleh continues to attract these participants, however, because of the community with which it allows them to connect.

Although the abundance of young newcomers has allowed Na'aleh to grow and thrive, a challenging difference between Denver and coastal communities like New York or Los Angeles is the smaller pool of laypeople with strong Jewish educations, especially in the non-Orthodox community. Although Denver has several Jewish day schools, they are smaller than their counterparts on the coasts, with only one small Jewish high school (aside from separate boys' and girls' ultra-Orthodox schools, whose graduates rarely participate in independent minyanim). Many independent minyanim on the coasts have relied on a solid core of laypeople capable of leading services, reading Torah, and teaching Jewish texts. Na'aleh certainly has participants with these capabilities, but they are few in number, and the minyan has had to plan carefully to organize a full array of programming without as deep a reservoir of leaders from whom to draw.

To avoid burnout among the small group of participants who are comfortable leading services, Na'aleh limits its prayer service offerings. For example, Na'aleh meets regularly on Friday nights but rarely on Shabbat mornings. A Shabbat morning service requires more expertise. In addition to the longer service, Shabbat morning involves Torah and Haftarah readings. When participants expressed a desire to try holding Yom Kippur services, the Na'aleh board ultimately decided to limit the offerings to *Kol Nidre*. Although this decision meant that participants had to find another place to pray communally on Yom Kippur day, it also meant that Na'aleh was able to organize a well-run *Kol Nidre* without overburdening the small group of laypeople who could lead High Holiday services.

A final difference between Denver and larger coastal cities is that although Denver has many newcomers, it is less transient than places like Cambridge, Massachusetts; Washington, D.C.; or Manhattan's Upper West Side. Unlike other urban communities with concentrated Jewish populations, students and young professionals can afford to settle and raise a family in Denver. In other cities, young professionals often move outward from the center of the city as their families grow, so that, for example, a person may move from the Upper West Side to Forest Hills (both New York City neighborhoods) and be unlikely to continue to participate in a minyan that meets on the Upper West Side. In Denver, by contrast, even after people move to accommodate a growing family they will still participate in Na'aleh. Because the city's neighborhoods are closer together, urban and suburban areas are both part of the Na'aleh community. This has provided tremendous continuity in terms of participants, but it also presents challenges because Na'aleh must decide how to address the changing needs of those participants for whom Na'aleh is their primary community affiliation.

In its five years of existence, Na'aleh has grown as its participants and founders recognized the needs that it serves for its different constituents. Although services once a month and on selected holidays provide sufficient prayer opportunities for many participants (and others choose to attend other local synagogues on non-Na'aleh weeks), the community connections did not feel strong enough to newcomers who use Na'aleh as their primary Jewish home in Denver. In response, a Na'aleh participant initiated a "meal matching" program titled "Break Bread with Jews" in which Na'aleh matches guests and hosts for Shabbat meals at people's homes on a week when Na'aleh does not meet for prayers. These meals have created a greater sense of community within Na'aleh and have helped encourage new participants to attend other Na'aleh events more frequently.

This community building has had additional far-reaching effects, as demonstrated when participants have stepped up to cook meals for parents of new babies or for a shiva. However, the relatively permanent nature of the young Denver Jewish community presents Na'aleh with challenges that we are just beginning to address. As our participants' lives evolve, Na'aleh is also evolving to accommodate a more varied demographic. Child-care and children's programming are becoming essential at nearly every Na'aleh event. At the 2009 Shavuaton (a Shavuot retreat in the Rocky Mountains that is a highlight of the Na'aleh year), substantive educational children's programming was implemented for the first time and was met with resounding praise from the twenty-six children participating and their parents. For some participants for whom Na'aleh is their primary Jewish home, and for many who see it as their closest community, the minyan will also need to begin to address life-cycle events such as births, deaths, and bnei mitzvot.

What Na'aleh's five years have demonstrated is that not only can an independent minyan endure, but it can also thrive away from the coasts, provided that minyan participants are willing and able to adapt their vision to the needs of a smaller Jewish community. We continue to discuss how Na'aleh can best expand to meet our participants' needs in the same grassroots, lay-led, pluralistic format that defines our community.

CREATING A SUPPORTIVE COMMUNITY AT SHIRA HADASHA IN JERUSALEM, ISRAEL

By Alexandra Benjamin, www.shirahadasha.org.il

Beyond prayer, some independent minyanim look to create a strong sense of community, including ongoing support services for their members.

From the beginning it has been important to us at Shira Hadasha to build a *kehilah* (community), not merely a minyan. As a prayer community in Israel, both *tefillah* and *kehilah* are part of our essence. If people aren't being cared for, our *tefillah* cannot be whole or holy.

A few years ago we decided to introduce a systemic and comprehensive approach to ensure that we were able to provide sustainable ongoing support systems. It was important to make sure that the services we offered were easily accessible and that we also enjoyed widespread involvement and awareness across the community. This process began with an assessment of need. We asked: What are the times in people's lives when they require the most support? What kinds of support do people need that they may not easily find elsewhere? What capacities do we have to provide support, and what is outside the realm of our responsibility/ability to give? Infused through this initial process was learning and study. We used traditional sources and text study, along with our own experiences and knowledge, to identify a path of action.

Our community is multigenerational, which has both advantages and challenges. We must concern ourselves with the full range of life-cycle events from birth, to illness, to elder care and bereavement. We founded Kehilah Tomechet (Supportive Community) to take a strategic approach to these challenges.

We recruited a small team to coordinate the efforts of a range of committees, each acting within a specific sphere of need. Members of the *gabbaut* (executive committee) oversaw the team. Their role was to provide both volunteer support and encouragement as well as ensure that the direction of the project continued to be consistent with the values of Shira Hadasha as a whole. In this way we constructed a large pyramid of support and activism, encompassing more than fifty volunteers.

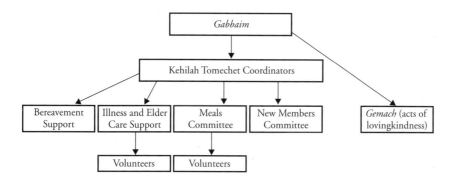

Bereavement

In Israel, much of the logistics of death and bereavement is taken care of by the state-funded *chevra kadisha* (burial society). The Va'ad Tmicha B'Aveilut (Bereavement Support Committee) identified the following functions and services necessary to mourners:

- Coordinating with the *chevra kadisha*, helping to explain and navigate the logistics of the death and burial process, and being an advocate for the bereaved;
- Providing halakhic advice and information on the topic of shiva and mourning;
- Preparing the house for shiva and providing siddurim, a *sefer Torah*, chairs, and other necessary items;
- Ensuring that there is a minyan for all services during the shiva as well as people to lead services, read Torah, and give *divrei Torah*;
- Providing support for the mourner to reenter the *kehilah* after the shiva, including *Kaddish* mentoring—pairing people who are new at saying *Kaddish* with others who have experience saying it.

Sickness and Elder Care

Tmicha B'Cholim (Support for the Sick) began with the intention of supporting ill community members, or those with ill family members, by offering hospital and home visits as well as emotional and practical (cooking, cleaning, babysitting) support. However, it quickly became clear that the greatest need in our community was for elder care. Many members of the community are caregivers for elderly relatives. The committee has tried to provide some respite support for these members as well as volunteers for regular home visits.

The transition to a focus on elder care has been very challenging because providing long-term support for ongoing need is much harder to supply than one-time care in urgent situations. The team, most of whom have had personal or professional experience in this area, coordinate home and hospital visits and offer training and support for a wider pool of volunteers.

Meals Support

Volunteers from the community provide home-cooked meals for members in need, such as in cases of illness, childbirth, and bereavement. A small team of three coordinates a larger roster of volunteers.

Gemach (Gemilut Hasadim—Acts of Lovingkindness)

Shira Hadasha has a separate *gemach* bank account for interest-free loans, made up of the donations received for this specific purpose. We raise money for the *gemach* through sales of a Shira Hadasha CD of tunes and prayers. The *gemach* account is spent on loans of up to 5,000 NIS (about $1,500) to people with specific needs, such as medical expenses or unexpected financial difficulties, in accordance with predetermined and legally governed guidelines.

Because of the particular sensitivity of this area, the *gemach* doesn't operate under the same structure as the rest of the Kehilah Tomechet. Only the four coordinators of the *gemach* (including one *gabbai*) are aware of applications and distributions of the fund.

New Members (Panim Hadashot)

A committee was created to recognize and integrate new members, introduce new people to the range of services we offer, and identify and meet the needs of this specific group of people, many of whom have only recently moved to Jerusalem from other places.

The committee's activities include:

- Social events during the year, including community meals.
- New members Shabbat, where all *kibbudim* (shul honors) and parts of the service are run by people new to the community, concluding with a special *Kiddish* to introduce people to one another.
- Ongoing connections to new members. Before major community events throughout the year, each of our new members receives a personal call from someone on the committee, checking in with her and inviting her to participate in the activity.
- The publication and distribution of the *Guide to Shira Hadasha Services*, with information and contact details.

Strengths, Challenges, and Solutions

Connecting volunteers to our meta-values. We felt it was important for all the volunteers in each specific area to be connected to the meta-values of the community and the larger goals of the Kehilah Tomechet. We also wanted to increase motivation and support for volunteers and enable them to share what they were doing with one another. We therefore created a regular Forum Kehilatiyut (Community Forum), which meets four times a year. Each meeting of the forum includes text-based Jewish learning and a presentation by one or two of the committees about the work they have been doing, during which they can also seek help and advice from others. We also hold a broader conversation about how to promote *kehilatiyut* (sense of community).

> Learning together binds us with one another.

Learning together. We believe that an important part of Kehilah Tomechet is learning together. This has many purposes. We teach ourselves to better meet our responsibilities and fulfill our tasks. We reinforce the value of Shira Hadasha as a learning community. Learning together binds us with one another. Finally, it provides a traditional Jewish underpinning to the social services we provide and connects the volunteers to a larger purpose. In addition to Forum Kehilatiyut, many of the different committees have run learning sessions for themselves or their volunteers. We have also sought to engage the community at large with our learning. For example, our *divrei Torah* connect to, and highlight, the Kehilah Tomechet work. All this contributes to drawing more people in and highlighting the holistic nature of our *kehilah*, tying together prayer, community, social action, and learning.

Working with limited resources. Unlike traditional synagogues, we do not have a rabbi or pastoral team, so we needed to create a structure based on a foundation of volunteerism and community activism. We drew from the strengths, skills, and professional experience of our members, rather than relying on paid employees. This has been a huge challenge but has also been an opportunity to get more people involved and invested in the community. The dependence on volunteers also forces us to be aware of our limitations. We must confront the realization that we can't do everything we would like to do. We must consolidate our resources to have the most effective impact.

Preventing volunteer fatigue. Managing volunteers is very complex. Some committees struggled, and early setbacks sometimes led to low motivation and inactivity. Some committees found it hard to recruit volunteers, especially for jobs that are less appealing, such as ongoing elder care. We had to contend with volunteer burnout, limited time, and competing priorities. We introduced individualized support and consultancy together with the Forum Kehilatiyut to help with these problems. They have been partially successful and we continue to seek improvement.

Balancing the need for information against confidentiality. We must constantly be sensitive when working with people at very vulnerable times in their lives. A community can easily become a place of gossip. On the other hand, we can't provide services without knowing who is in need, who is sick, and so on. We must constantly consider and monitor ourselves when discussing people and sharing information.

Creating *kehilatiyut* is an ongoing process that requires constant and consistent nurturing. Kehilah Tomechet has not always met the high standards we set for ourselves, but we have had significant, often quiet, successes. Together we have created a structure that supports people in some of the most difficult times in their lives. As a result, not only individuals but also the community as a whole has been strengthened.

Balancing Tradition and Inclusiveness at Mission Minyan in San Francisco, California

By Roger Studley, www.missionminyan.org

A prayer community where pluralism flourishes, together with traditional observance, seemed unlikely in San Francisco—until its founders figured out how to make it work. The balance isn't perfect, but striving for it keeps the independent minyan fresh and empowers all its members.

Who knew? Who knew, when David Henkin and Mickey Heimlich decided in late 2003 to host a minyan at Mickey's apartment in the Mission District of San Francisco that it would revive Jewish life in a part of the city where it had once thrived but had been absent for decades? Who knew that egalitarian and Orthodox Jews (and others who hold by *mechitza* and gender distinctions) could daven, celebrate, learn, buy a Torah, and make a community together? Who knew that serious Judaism and Jewish life could flourish without paid staff, without rabbinic leadership, without a building (or a building fund), and without membership dues?

No one knew, really. In fact, no two people present at Mission Minyan's inception had the same idea about what they were creating. There was no grand vision or mission (despite the name), just a shared desire among a handful of progressive-minded friends for spirited, traditional davening. Even one of the minyan's hallmarks—its collaboration between egalitarian and Orthodox Jews—emerged somewhat accidentally, because there simply weren't enough Orthodox Jews living in the neighborhood to form their own minyan. Describing the minyan remains challenging even today, because just as every Israelite at Sinai is said to have received the Torah differently, each of our participants has his or her own perspective on what makes the community vibrant and special. What follows, then, is my own perspective on the Mission Minyan.

As I see it, the essence of the minyan—the quality that makes it stand out even among the dozens of exciting, independent, innovative Jewish communities that have emerged in recent years—is a deep and abiding commitment to inclusiveness. Mission Minyan is not an Orthodox community trying to expand the role of women, nor is it an egalitarian community trying to accommodate the traditionally observant. It is a pluralistic community, with participants from a wide variety of Jewish backgrounds, that strives to be a place where any Jew can participate. This is, of course, impossible, because some differences in belief or practice are irreconcilable. Even some of the minyan's most committed participants do not feel completely comfortable with every aspect of its communal practice. But participants have discovered that sacrificing a little comfort for the sake of community can bring huge rewards in terms of connection, learning, growth, and our experience and understanding of Judaism.

Who Leads the Service?

Consider how Mission Minyan conducts *Kabbalat Shabbat* davening. According to traditional halakhah, the *Ma'ariv* portion of the liturgy must be led by a man, and this is indeed the practice at the minyan. If a woman were to lead *Ma'ariv*, Orthodox Jews would not feel comfortable participating. Denying women the opportunity to lead *Ma'ariv*, however, offends those who believe that women and men should have equal roles in Jewish ritual. To compensate, therefore, for the minyan's requirement that a man must lead *Ma'ariv*, the minyan also requires that *Kabbalat Shabbat*, the first part of the Friday night service, be led by a woman. (The minyan has similar requirements for Shabbat morning services.)

This solution is not entirely satisfactory. From an Orthodox perspective, it is far from universally accepted for women to lead *Kabbalat Shabbat*. From an egalitarian perspective, a role is still being denied to women (and now also to men), and the situation remains unfair because the part of the liturgy that fulfills an obligation (*Ma'ariv*) is still denied to female leaders. Nonetheless, by each accepting some discomfort, Orthodox and egalitarian Jews can daven together in the same community.

Who Counts in the Minyan?

Another principle adopted by Mission Minyan is our definition of a minyan, or prayer quorum. Traditional Judaism requires ten men for a minyan; egalitarian Judaism requires ten people, irrespective of gender. As with service leading, neither group's position is satisfactory to the other. Like some other independent minyanim, Mission Minyan addressed this problem by requiring ten men *and* ten women for a min-yan. Even if a hundred Jews of one gender and nine of the other were present, we still would not recite the prayers that require a minyan. On at least one occasion, the result was that we could not say Mourner's *Kaddish*, even though the personal minyan requirement of the person wishing to do so had been met. Doing otherwise would have meant abandoning one of the minyan's bedrock principles of inclusiveness.

Seating Issues

In an egalitarian setting, men and women sit together during prayer services. In an Orthodox setting, the two genders sit separately, with a *mechitza* (physical barrier) between the men's and women's sections. In contrast to both, Mission Minyan generally uses three separate sections: men's section on one side of the room, women's on the other, and mixed in the middle. On Shabbat morning, when our crowd tends to be more traditional, almost half the seating is mixed, and tables holding sid-durim divide the three sections. On Friday nights, almost all of the seat-ing is mixed, though small single-gender sections are available.

Seating has been the minyan's most difficult issue. From an egali-tarian perspective, some people find the availability of single-gender areas to be unacceptable segregation. From a traditional perspective, some see the availability of mixed-gender seating as an unacceptable violation of Jewish law. The minyan's three-section approach does not satisfy those who completely reject the competing perspective. Rather, it gives each group a seating option that suits its own needs, and it requires tolerance and respect for the needs of others. This is not a per-fect solution—indeed, our community continues to wrestle with the issue—but it is an inclusive compromise that allows Jews with diverse beliefs and practices to make a community together.

Each of the above practices is grounded in a careful examination of halakhah as well as the values of gender equality and respect for vari-ations in personal observance. Admittedly, the minyan's communal practice is not (and cannot be) inclusive of the practices of all Jews; the minyan tries, however, to be a place where all Jews can practice. We have, for example, high kashrut standards for communal meals to accommodate strictly observant members of our community. But we also have meal matching in which we connect Shabbat dinner guests with hosts (another inclusive practice), and we welcome all hosts, irrespective of their level of kashrut. (We do, of course, make sure that guests' dietary requirements, including kashrut, are satisfied—no small task in San Francisco.) For another example, while we have gender-specific seating to accommodate halakhic needs, we also fully respect every individual's choice of gender identification.

Membership and Governance

Mission Minyan's commitment to inclusiveness extends to membership and governance as well. The minyan has no formal membership or dues; people join simply by showing up and contributing to the life of the community. Our leadership is distributed, with most of the work done by a large (currently thirty-five-member) steering committee that makes decisions by consensus and a five-person administrative committee whose members rotate off after ten-month (staggered) terms. The non-hierarchical nature of this leadership structure is reflected in the tongue-in-cheek name of the steering committee, which is referred to with self-conscious irony as the "Machers." Although several rabbis (two Orthodox and three Conservative) are currently among the Machers, they have no more authority in minyan affairs than other leaders.

Building Community through Radical Inclusiveness

The minyan's inclusive ritual practices and organizational structure have created an engaged and growing Jewish community. With non-hierarchical leadership, enthusiasm for innovation, and respect for halakhah, a diverse group of committed volunteers has coalesced and organized weekly Shabbat services (averaging one hundred attendees every Friday night and forty every other Shabbat morning), davening on all festivals, *Megillah* readings and Purim parties, Pesach retreats, all-night Shavuot study, monthly learning events, and more. Despite having no dues, institutional sponsorship, or foundation support (not that we would mind the latter), the minyan has successfully raised funds sufficient to rent space for all of our events, commission a Torah, purchase and print siddurim, and cover a variety of administrative and other expenses. When the minyan started, there were no more than five kosher homes within walking distance of Friday night services. By 2008 there were twelve, and by mid-2009, there were about thirty. Some of this growth came from minyan participants being inspired to kasher their kitchens so that friends could eat in their homes, and some of it came from Jews moving to the Mission District to be part of this vibrant and inclusive community.

Many of the features described above are present in other communities, but Mission Minyan is unique in the constellation of practices it has adopted in its devotion to inclusiveness. This is perhaps a radical inclusiveness, one that attempts to bridge the divide between Orthodoxy and egalitarianism, adheres to tradition while pushing the boundaries of custom and comfort, and requires tolerance and respect for varied and sometimes conflicting needs. None of the people who gathered in Mickey's apartment five years ago knew exactly where their efforts were headed, but the minyan has evolved into a rich and complementary marriage of tradition and diversity, and minyan participants feel blessed to be part of the warm, Jewishly committed, and inclusive community that we have created together.

OUR SPONGES ARE PRAYING: HOW A DISH SYSTEM REFLECTS PLURALISM, ENVIRONMENTALISM, EGALITARIANISM, AND COMMUNITY AT TIKKUN LEIL SHABBAT IN WASHINGTON, D.C.

By Joelle Novey, www.tikkunleilshabbat.org

Sometimes the most mundane practices become transcendent, as the founders of Tikkun Leil Shabbat discovered when they tried to put their eco-friendly values into practice.

At Tikkun Leil Shabbat (whose name alludes to *tikkun olam*—repairing the world, and is a pun on *Tikkun Leil Shavuot*, a traditional all-night study session held during the spring holiday of Shavuot), more than 150 folks in their twenties and thirties gather regularly on Friday nights for a songful, soulful service featuring a teaching about a social justice issue—and just about all of them stick around afterward to share a vegetarian potluck dinner.

For more than four years, Tikkun Leil Shabbat (TLS) in Washington, D.C., has managed to establish a system for hosting collaborative Shabbat dinners without using disposable plates, cutlery, or napkins, while meeting the needs of people with varied practices of kashrut. People share the work of cleaning up while maintaining an atmosphere of *oneg Shabbat* (delight in Shabbat).

Honoring Diverse Dietary Practices

The "two-table" potluck system, which TLS borrowed from the independent minyan Kol Zimrah (Sound of Song) in New York (which claims it may have originated, in turn, back in DC), is designed to honor a variety of Jewish dietary practices. We have one table for vegetarian food and another table for vegetarian food that is also *hekhshered* (certified kosher) or made in a *hekhsher*-only kitchen, each with its own sets of dishes and cutlery that are washed separately. This makes it possible for the maximum number of people to eat and contribute food. By saying "vegetarian" and "*hekhshered*," rather than "not kosher" and "kosher," we make clear that TLS is not taking any position on what it means to keep kosher, but is simply setting out a logistical arrangement so that we all can share the meal.

Environmental Potluck

We've also sought to minimize waste from disposable tableware. On both potluck tables, we use lightweight reusable plates and cups from Recycline, made from recycled yogurt containers. We use a collection of previously loved forks purchased from Goodwill and donated by participants, and we wash and reuse plastic cutlery and cups. We use a colorful collection of cloth napkins we procured on Craigslist and through donations from participants—a volunteer launders them after each Shabbat. We recycle glass, plastic, and aluminum containers after TLS meals. (To keep the separateness of the *hekhsher* tableware simple, the "H-table" sports its own set of dishes, serving utensils, and sponges, all of a lime-green color, and its own dish bin that sits under the *hekhsher* table. When an "H" fork or plate finds its way into the wrong bin from time to time, it is retired.)

Everyone Cleans Up

At least thirty people end up playing a role in washing all these dishes after dinner. We have developed an extensive online spreadsheet of a dozen volunteer roles at each TLS meal, including, for example, a "Food

Monitor" who sets and refreshes the buffet tables, and two "Dish Captains," one for each potluck table. The fifteen members of the Tomchei Tikkun (Supporters of the Minyan) coordinating team play a "spreadsheet role" pretty much every time. Additionally, a group of reliable volunteers, known as the "Tachlist," gets an e-mail inviting them to sign up for these spreadsheet roles (a list of tasks for each role is included in the spreadsheet for those signing up for the first time).

Attendees are invited to volunteer for ten-minute dishwashing shifts by accepting a colorful lei necklace, which they wear while they're helping and can then bestow on someone else, until the dishes are all clean. (We like to joke that we are a "lei-led" Jewish community.) The volunteers circulating in the crowd collecting dishes with a Hawaiian necklace on add to a generally festive atmosphere, and some of the best conversations, new melodies, and personal connections at Tikkun Leil Shabbat happen around the kitchen during dishwashing.

On several different dimensions, Tikkun Lèil Shabbat's dinner system reflects our community's core values:

- It is pluralistic, because it permits people with various practices of kashrut to eat and to contribute food.

- It is egalitarian, because everyone brings food to help create the meal, and just about everyone ends up helping to clean up, through a combination of roles signed up for in advance (such as Dish Captain) or accepted in the moment (such as a lei for ten minutes of dishwashing).

- Just as important, by having named roles and physical markers of who is helping and how at a given meeting, we also help clarify who is "off the hook" this week. Naming explicitly who has signed up for particular tasks helps prevent certain conscientious souls, or women more likely to have been socialized to help with dishes, from accidentally becoming the default cleaning crew week after week.

- It is socially conscious, by being mindful of minimizing our waste from disposables and modeling a greener way of eating (vegetarian, and using reusable napkins and dishware).

- Finally, it is community building. By involving so many people, even those newly arrived, in the act of helping to feed one another and then doing the dishes, we've created an atmosphere of hands-on participation and provided the context for many conversations and connections that arise around the sinks.

Someone wrote a satirical song about TLS last year, which included the line, "You just might get your wishes, meet your soul mate washing dishes...." Although we have yet to report an incident of true love arising from dishwashing at TLS, it's not too much of a stretch to say that our dish system in all its glory is one of our community's spiritual practices.

4

Engaged Davening

How Empowered Jews Pray

Being an Empowered Jew means being unwilling to give up on the power of prayer. What are the factors that help people experience the possibility for a meaningful, spiritual prayer experience? This is, of course, a subjective question, and its answers vary even among independent minyanim. But independent minyanim as a whole have demonstrated that there is room for a reconsideration of the factors that build vibrant prayer communities. Below I will deal with elements specific to Shabbat morning davening, but they can apply to most other prayer environments as well.

PRAYER CAN UNLOCK EMOTIONS

Has a prayer service ever moved you to tears? In some ways, I think this is the ultimate goal of prayer—to unlock some of the emotional space that is cordoned off by the modern world. Talmudic wisdom had a similar conception, claiming that since the destruction of the Temple, the gates of prayer are locked, but the gates of tears remain unlocked (Babylonian Talmud, *Berakhot* 32b; *Bava Metzia* 59a). When the prayer leader and the congregation believe that it is possible to unlock deep emotions in prayer, real, powerful prayer can take place.

Our liturgy's range of emotion is vast. For instance, Yom Kippur has a range of emotions embedded in the *machzor*. At moments like the slow recitation of *Kol Nidre*, there is fear. With *Unetane Tokef*, there is introspection. But at the end of Yom Kippur, having made it through the ups and downs of the day, there is even a celebratory mood. The first Yom Kippur service we conducted at Hadar ended with people spontaneously dancing and singing "Next Year in Jerusalem." I had never encountered a Yom Kippur service that ended with joy. But the prayer leader understood the mood of the moment, and he started to sing energetically. The people in the room picked up on his lead and started to dance (instead of rushing out to eat food!). Understanding prayer as an opportunity to express a range of emotions and allowing the space for those emotions to come to the fore is a transformative way of relating to prayer.

ACOUSTICS AND INTIMACY

One of the most critical keys to the success of a davening environment is not what you would think. It's not theology, liturgy, or leadership. It is simply having good acoustics. I have walked into dozens of synagogue sanctuaries, many of them beautiful, with the knowledge that no amount of melodies training or education could ever enhance the service. The room is simply too big, the acoustics too diffuse. For prayer to be powerful, it needs to resonate in the room. It can't fall flat. This is one of the greatest advantages of the minyanim: their ability to meet in a space that is acoustically resonant. That is why davening in an apartment or a low-ceilinged basement, while perhaps not visually pleasing, allows for the possibility of "good davening."

> For prayer to be powerful, it needs to resonate in the room. It can't fall flat.

Most synagogues are built to hold the capacity crowd that comes on the High Holidays. The acoustics are often designed for those big-time events, in which a cantor with a powerful voice performs for an audience. But what works for a crowd of five hundred is often counterproductive for regular Shabbat services, when synagoguegoers (and their voices) are dwarfed in the cavernous sanctuaries.

Many shuls could improve the chances of having inspiring services if they were willing to let go of the sanctuary as the default location for prayer. They usually have a multiplicity of smaller rooms, and often one of them has good acoustics and is more appropriate for a Shabbat morning crowd. This is a thorny political issue in any synagogue ("What do you mean *my* son won't be bar mitzvahed on the bimah!"), but the costs of sticking with the main sanctuary should be clear.

I once davened at a synagogue that was forced, because of a conflicting event, to conduct services in a very small room. The room held about forty people comfortably, which was the size of the average Shabbat morning crowd. The room had no carpeting and a low ceiling, and the acoustics were resonant. Everyone commented on how inspiring the davening was and how surprised they were by that. But the next week, as soon as they could be back in the bigger space, they were.

There is something about prayer that is different from other large-crowd events. At a movie, you might hope the theater isn't crowded and there is enough breathing room around your seat. In a synagogue service, by contrast, there is value in feeling a bit crowded. By sitting near someone else, I can hear her voice in prayer and don't have to work too hard to connect my voice to hers. This intimate prayer layout is a given in Hasidic *shtiebls* (small, intimate congregations). In those communities, the premium on personal space is very low (at some personal cost), but the cumulative effect is a collective purpose and enterprise. This runs counter to our American value of staking out our own separate space.

> At Hadar we always put out fewer chairs than necessary in the beginning, so people will be drawn to sitting near others.

That's why at Hadar we always put out fewer chairs than necessary in the beginning, so people will be drawn to sitting near others. Only in the middle of the service, when people are packed in, do we add more chairs. This helps create a feeling of a robust prayer space.

INTERNAL LAYOUT

The layout of the room is critical to building a certain atmosphere of participatory and engaged prayer. The classic layout of the liberal American synagogue is one in which the clergy face the congregation from an elevated bimah, and all the davening and Torah reading take place at the front of the room. The layout of the room reinforces a feeling that this prayer service is a performance to be watched, with the actors onstage at the front and the audience dutifully listening in the rows below.

Most independent minyanim have chosen two basic types of layout, in strong contrast to the typical synagogue. The first is seen in some Sephardic congregations and is modeled, most recently, on those of the havurah movement: people sit in a circle (or concentric circles, depending on the size). The power of this layout lies in its inherent critique of the traditional hierarchical arrangement—in a circle, no one is in the front. But perhaps the biggest advantage—and drawback—of this layout is that everyone can see each other's face in prayer, fostering connection between human beings in the service of God. This is moving for some, but in my opinion, the inhibition that it causes far outweighs the benefits. Self-consciousness and an inability to let go are perhaps the biggest challenges to prayer in the modern age.

The other layout popular in independent minyanim, and the one that I advocate, is that used in many traditional Orthodox synagogues: all rows face forward, with the prayer leader stationed in the center, also facing forward. This sends a few important messages. First, everyone is facing the *aron kodesh* (the holy ark) rather than facing a leader who is davening toward (at?) the congregation. The unity of purpose is clearly reinforced by the direction of the community. Second, the charismatic role of the prayer leader is diminished—half of the congregation sits in front of the leader, while the other half sits behind her. While at first blush this may seem impersonal, it actually allows both the congregation and the leader to avoid self-consciousness, putting the focus on sound rather than sight. A third advantage is that the prayer leader experiences a different relationship to the congregation by being in their midst. She can better gauge to what extent a melody is "working" and can feel supported by the more active daveners in the congregation. She is simply closer to the entire congregation than in a standard synagogue layout, and she draws strength from that closeness.

This layout is critical not only for prayer, but also for Torah reading. Here the layout is somewhat less intuitive. After all, the Torah was meant to be read *to* the people and might require a reader facing the congregation. But to the extent that the Torah reading is meant to mimic the original revelation at Sinai, the critical feature is not seeing the reader, but listening to his voice. I have found that allowing the Torah reader to face forward—toward the *aron kodesh,* as opposed to facing the congregation—removes a critical impediment to a well-done Torah reading. When people face the congregation, all the issues of stage fright and performance anxiety become heightened. This can often lead to a shaky voice, nervous laughter, and general discomfort with the act of reading. When the reader faces the ark and allows the sound of his voice to carry from the center without experiencing the stares of the congregation, his performance anxiety lessens, and he is able to concentrate on reading the words themselves. This applies to the person who is taking an *aliyah* as well.

A Sensitive Prayer Leader

Even with the right acoustics and layout, participatory services are still only as good as the person who is leading them. We might think that a participatory service with no paid clergy would not be concerned with the qualities of the leader—after all, the prayer is carried by the entire congregation. But the leader in this type of service is just as critical as in more traditional services, only the necessary skills are different. The leader sets a tone for the service and is charged with drawing people into prayer. This is a difficult task and one that takes time to perfect. The following are some characteristics of very good prayer leaders.

A decent voice. In some ways this is obvious, but in the volunteer culture of a minyan, good voices are not always made a prerequisite to leading prayers. It is worth noting that "a good voice" is not necessarily a trained one. The optimal voice for leading prayer is one that draws people in, not one that excludes people by being overpowering, overly professional, or operatic. The overly performative leader is the flip side of the person who can't sing: he sings so well that he leaves the congregation behind. I think the most powerful davener is the one who is truly a "messenger of the community"—someone who represents the other people in the room. When members of the congregation think, "I could pray like that person," they are more likely to participate with the leader. When the leader is so far removed from the real sounds of the voices in the community—even with the best intentions—it often prevents others from joining in.

Competence in the words of the siddur. The leader needs the skills to bring others through a journey of prayer. The people are putting their confidence in the leader's ability, trusting her to lead them in a prayer experience that often skirts the cognitive. When her competence is called into question by mistakes or mispronounced words, the congregation becomes distracted from the very hard task of trying to lose themselves in the davening. For better or worse, this is true with even just a few errors in the span of a long service. I don't mean that there is no place for mistakes in prayer or that this impugns a person's character or worth. But mistakes come at a cost.

I have long thought that to be a truly competent prayer leader, a person must memorize large parts of the siddur. This is probably an unrealistic standard, but it points to a larger goal: complete comfort with the words of prayer. As Rabbi Ebn Leader, a master prayer leader, once told me regarding prayer: "An actor would never dream of taking the stage without memorizing the script. What gives me the right to get up to lead prayer without the same level of competence?"

> A good voice is one that draws people in, not one that excludes people by being overpowering or overly professional. This is often the flip side of the person who can't sing: the person who sings so well that he leaves the congregation behind.

Awareness of one's own ego. Most prayer leaders fall on the far poles of the ego spectrum. On one side are those who get stage fright, ever afraid that they will make a mistake or lead a flat davening. On the opposite pole are those with an outsized sense of self-worth. The first pole is characterized by a leader who wants the experience to be over as quickly as possible. She is afraid to lead new melodies or try something other than the "same old, same old." This leads to a timid davening. The congregation never reaches a volume louder than the leader, so someone who is nervous and quiet will engender that space for others in the room. The other pole springs from an inflated ego: "How wonderful I am! I am really leading the congregation and taking them to spiritual heights." This prayer leader often leaves the congregation behind by running on too long with a melody or drifting off into a cantorial-style flourish when the congregation simply wants to move on.

Both of these personalities detract from what I think is the only way to really be a prayer leader—directing the community's prayer to God. At the end of the day, the prayer leader is a functionary, whose role is to facilitate an experience that wouldn't happen without her: making a group entreaty to the Divine Presence. By balancing the confidence necessary to move beyond the "fear factor" side of leading davening against an overemphasis on the ego, the prayer leader offers the possibility of moving beyond herself and playing a critical role in the facilitation of a truly meaningful, spiritually uplifting prayer experience.

A sense of the meaning behind the words, and an ability to connect the words to the melody. The prayer book is not simply a string of sounds in a foreign language, but a collection of phrases, images, and allusions that can be extremely resonant. If every word is said with equal time, speed, and emphasis, then there is no topography to the prayer service. If certain phrases are recited with a bit more volume, or slower, or with force, then the words of the siddur start to strike emotional chords. We don't speak in a monotone; similarly, prayer must be said with expression.

In addition, the melodies chosen should reflect a thought-out mood that the prayer leader intends to build. Often, the leader chooses a melody only because he has heard it before, set to that prayer. But this often leads to a strange amalgam of fast and slow melodies, with no coherent arc of mood. I was once in a Jerusalem minyan that used the same Carlebach melody for *Selichot* (prayers of contrition) and Yom Ha'atzmaut (a day of celebration). Because these days have opposite religious and emotional valences, the effect was very odd. I felt that the prayer leader liked the melody and would use it no matter the context of the larger religious moment in time. A prayer leader with an understanding of the words on the page and the mood of the day will be able to select appropriate melodies.

Taking the role seriously. When a person is leading prayers, does he believe that what he is doing is important? Does he think prayer has the ability to change people's lives? Is the prayer space an opportunity for real connection with the Divine? Or is it just a plodding recitation, meant to check off a box? The prayer leader sets the tone with the attitude he brings to the prayer moment.

A commitment to improving. Very few people combine all of the above elements, and no one is the perfect prayer leader. But people can approach the role from a place of openness. Prayer leaders should have trusted partners in the minyan's leadership who can—in the right context, at the right time—offer them real feedback and opportunities for improvement. Otherwise, even the best prayer leaders remain stale and don't grow. Hearing thoughtful feedback on your performance as a prayer leader is also a reminder that you are not perfect, and being aware of this is an essential element of being a good prayer leader.

The Prayer Leader as Conductor: Empowering the Congregation to Pray

In a world of Empowered Judaism, the prayer leader is not a performer, but a conductor, helping to set the pace and emotional tone of services and to encourage the congregation's active, coordinated participation. When people come to a service expecting to be engaged in this way and are motivated to put themselves forward into the space of prayer, the worship experience can be transformative. The following are some strategies for prayer leaders seeking to conduct an inspiring, participatory, and emotionally deep prayer experience.

Inviting melodies. Some melodies are exclusionary, while others invite the congregation to join in the singing. Choose melodies that encourage other voices to join in, and refrain from those that are too complicated or too vocally challenging to invite participation.

Transformative melodies. Most people are not looking to sing just any song, regardless of its connection to the prayer or the mood. Rather, they want the melody to connect them to the words and mood of the moment. Consider the melodies you choose carefully, and use them to evoke a particular mood in the congregation—be it joy, mourning, hope, or elation.

Leaving the comfort of the familiar. If services are meant only to tread down well-traveled paths, then the "good old" melodies are perfect: predictable, no surprises, enabling the congregation to zone out. But if services are meant to jolt our consciousness so that we experience the words of the siddur in a new light, then the "good old" melodies stand in the way. Although familiarity is a great benefit for those looking for consistency, the ability of a melody to surprise or to shock participants into experiencing the words in a different way is itself a countervailing value. This is not to say every "old" melody is worthless—I think there would be a revolt if *Kol Nidre* or *Avinu Malkeinu* were done differently. But, in general, melodies offer an opportunity for surprise and renewal, because the words are experienced in a new musical context. If we stick to the same melody week in and week out, that opportunity disappears.

Going beyond Carlebach melodies. A common "solution" to the issue of old familiar melodies is to introduce a "Carlebach service." Shlomo Carlebach was the modern master of designing simple melodies that resonate with a wide range of people and are relatively easy to learn, even during the davening itself. But like anything that becomes too familiar, Carlebach melodies lose some of their power if overused. This is why it is crucial to allow for the influx of new melodies from around the Jewish world. To prevent stagnation, prayer leaders (professional or lay) must periodically take time off to see other vibrant services and bring back new melodies. (See Judith Hauptman's article, "A Conservative Jew Goes Reform," in *Jewish Week*.) The opportunity to hear and share new melodies is a critical part of reinvigorating services.

> Prayer leaders should have trusted partners who can—in the right context, at the right time—offer them real feedback and opportunities for improvement.

The power of *niggunim*. In *Man's Quest for God*, Abraham Joshua Heschel wrote that a melody is even more powerful than words. *Niggunim* (melodies without words) hold immense power. Some potential uses of *niggunim* include (1) before the beginning of davening, as a way to set the mood, (2) before the repetition of the *Amidah*, as a way to transition from silence to words, (3) at the end of a prayer that has been sung to a powerful melody, to extend the feeling of the prayer and let the pure emotion soar. People are often nervous about singing a melody without words more than one time through. But in the right moments, with the right mood, a melody repeated three or four times (or more) can have a powerful effect on the davening as a whole.

Using *nusach* appropriately. The basic form of music in Jewish prayer is not any particular melody, but a thematic musical guide known as *nusach*. The *nusach* is the musical base of the service, and it provides some signal as to what prayer is currently being said. *Nusach* is the string that ties all of the individual melodies together, and it is unique to each service: the morning service has a different *nusach* from the evening service, Shabbat is different from weekdays, and most holiday prayers have their own distinct *nusach*. Even within a given prayer service, different sections are marked by different themes and moods. It is critical not to unintentionally substitute one *nusach* for another: if you are davening Ma'ariv on a Tuesday night, then the *nusach* for Friday night will confuse the davener. Or imagine the confusion if the *nusach* of *Kol Nidre* was sung on a random Shabbat morning! The *nusach* for *Kol Nidre* transports us to the emotions particular to the evening of Yom Kippur, which are out of place at any other time. This is not to say that melodies should never be transferred. But if *nusach* is to be altered, the leader must do so on purpose with a clear goal in mind.

Cuing congregational responses. Encoded within Jewish prayer are moments for the congregation to actively respond and react to the prayer leader's recitation. The best-known opportunity for this kind of call and response is the recitation of "amen." But think of all the other places where the congregation is trained to "chime in" after a particular cue from the leader: shouting *"l'chaim"* before *Kiddush*; saying the biblical verses in the *Kedushah*; responding with *"yehei shmei rabbah"* in the *Kaddish*; the congregation's line in *aliyot* and during *Barchu* at the beginning of *Shacharit*; reciting *"baruch hu u-varuch shemo"* after each mention of God's name in the repetition of the *Amidah*; reciting *"hazak hazak venithazek"* at the end of the reading of each book of the Torah; and so on. Part of the function of the prayer leader is to cue these congregational responses. This can be done by raising your voice before the congregational response and making sure you leave enough space for the response to interrupt. The congregation participates actively in the performance of the prayer service through these responses, and in many ways, the role of the leader is to step aside and let the congregation step forward in these moments.

Elongating the end of phrases. The prayer leader signals where he is by reciting the final lines of a psalm or prayer. By slowing down at the end of these phrases, a prayer leader can invite the congregation to participate in these moments. This slowing and elongating of the phrase often allows others in the congregation to sense the pace of the prayer leader and lend additional voice to the phrase.

Praying close to the leader. In many congregations, the seats in highest demand are often the ones farthest from the prayer leader. But the leader can enhance the experience for everyone by encouraging others to join him at the *amud* (prayer leader's table), surrounding himself with the supportive voices of the congregation. I have seen this in a number of minyanim during the High Holidays. The prayer leader often needs the physical support of other voices when davening for that long, and the image of other members of the congregation standing close to the prayer leader signals that this service actively invites the participation of the people in the congregation.

BALANCING SILENCE AND SOUND

Part of the powerful rhythm of prayer is found in the shifts between cacophonous noise and silence. The Talmudic tradition encodes this into law. For instance, the *Shema* must be said aloud (*Mishnah Berakhot* 2:3), while the *Amidah* must be said silently (Babylonian Talmud, *Berakhot* 31a). The emotional power of the transition from sound to silence is extremely strong. Unfortunately, in many prayer settings, the default mode of prayer is only silence. People read the prayers in complete silence, as if they were reading a novel. But in truth, other than the *Amidah*, prayer was never meant to be silent. In the ancient world, reading was done out loud (thus the word in Hebrew for "to read"— *kara*—is the same as "to call"). Psalms describe us "contemplating" the words of Torah day and night (*ve-hagita bo yomam va-laila*)—but *hagah* really means "to pronounce in a low growl."

The aesthetic effect of this mumbling serves a dual purpose. First, the cacophony of a low mumbling davening moves the worshiper from a purely cognitive experience to a deep, emotional act. Second, it provides a contrast to the silence of the *Amidah*, which is all the more powerful when it replaces the sounds that precede it. Hannah, the mother

of the prophet Samuel, was thought to be drunk when she prayed completely silently (1 Samuel 1:13–15). Clearly the *Amidah*, which the
Talmud notes is modeled after Hannah's form of prayer, is different from
the rest of the prayer experience. The silence of an *Amidah* that begins
(with no interrupting page announcement or stage direction) right after
the mumbling of the worshipers is a contrasting silence—a silence that
makes us straighten up and pay attention to the new mode of prayer
before us.

THE NEED FOR A CRITICAL MASS OF CONGREGATIONAL DAVENERS

To have an engaged, participatory congregation, not every single person
needs to be a confident, well-versed davener. But there needs to be a
critical mass of such people to create the ambience of permission to
daven loudly and not simply rely on the voice of the prayer leader.

This critical mass is smaller than we might imagine (depending on
the acoustic resonance of the room). In a group of a hundred, it could
be as few as ten people. The confidence and passion of ten engaged
members of the congregation spill over into the rest of the people in the
room, who will take their cues from these people. When this engaged
core starts to sing a melody that the prayer leader began, others know
that the melody is not just for the prayer leader, but invites general
participation.

HEBREW AS THE BASIS FOR PRAYER

There is a strong pull, especially in a society that doesn't speak Hebrew
as its vernacular, to introduce English into the service. After all, people
understand English, and isn't the goal of prayer to express to God our
feelings and emotions in a way that can be understood? Although this
is certainly one legitimate way to view prayer, another possibility is to
consider prayer as an opportunity to step beyond the normal comfort
zone of familiar language and enter a space that calls on other areas of
the soul beyond the cognitive level.

I think English readings usually fall flat because the aesthetic experience of saying those readings is lacking on a noncognitive, performa-

tive level. We may understand everything in the English prayer, but the mystery and power of the Hebrew text is completely absent. Even for someone who does not understand Hebrew, the Hebrew prayer book can serve a valuable purpose: to transport us from a cognitive, utilitarian experience of prayer ("God, please grant me X") to a mysterious, rhythmic experience of prayer. This is not to say that we should not strive to decode the Hebrew. Indeed, perhaps the most powerful experience of prayer is through the melding of the mystery of Hebrew and its allusions/meaning (see the appendix).

> Consider prayer as an opportunity to step beyond the normal comfort zone of familiar language and enter a space that calls on other areas of the soul beyond the cognitive level.

But even a person fluent in Hebrew may not always understand the simple meaning of the psalms (a large percentage of the prayer book) and can experience the mystery and complexity of the prayer sounds themselves. For those who have no comprehension of Hebrew, the Hebrew service can still remain potent as an opportunity to transport us to a realm beyond cognition and literal meaning.

ELIMINATE "DEAD TIME"

Part of what makes a service powerful is the sense of rhythm and flow. Perhaps the biggest impediment to that flow is a sense that certain parts of the service drag on—for no good reason. I am not talking here about a lengthy *Kedushah* where the leader gets carried away, but about the transition points that can slow things down unnecessarily. A lot of the "down time" that makes services drag can be prevented with preparation.

When the Torah reading begins, has the Torah been rolled to the right place? How often does the reader lose his place between *aliyot*? How long does it take to call the name of the person taking the next *aliyah*? In a complex service, how long does it take for the *gabbaim* to announce what comes next? When the Torah is being wrapped, are people singing or just standing in awkward silence? In most of these instances, the congregation feels frustrated that the service could be moving forward but isn't. *Gabbaim* can anticipate these transition points and do the legwork in advance (checking the place in the Torah, reviewing the order of a complex service, thinking of melodies to sing in moments of delay). The total time lost in any one of these moments is minimal, but the feeling that no one is paying attention to the flow or the time can drag down a service, interfering with participants' sense of spiritual connection.

MINIMAL ANNOUNCEMENTS

Perhaps the most challenging threat to a flow of the service is the announcement section at the end. I understand that announcements are part of the shul culture, but I believe that this is worth reconsidering. I have been to services where announcements have lasted for ten to fifteen minutes (and other parts of the prayers were cut for time concerns!).

Start with this premise: no one is really paying attention to announcements in the first place. They either must be far more entertaining or should be cut down to a bare minimum. In a world of e-mail and websites, announcements are not really necessary to communicate information about upcoming events. Also, it is very hard to memorize dates, places, and times at the end of a two-hour service. There is virtually no chance that someone will remember the learning session that is to take place two weeks from Thursday. The end of services is still part of services, and I firmly believe that care paid to the announcements will spill over to other aspects of the service.

INSIDER/OUTSIDER IN RITUAL GARB

Part of the feel for a davening space is reinforced by the types of ritual garb worn by the participants. There is a clear "insider/outsider" dress code at most synagogues. The active, knowledgeable participants wear a variety of *kippot* (yarmulkes) and large and/or colorful tallitot (prayer shawls). The guests and those who don't own their own ritual garb wear black satin *kippot* and scarf tallitot that have sat on a rack for the past forty years. When there is such a difference in ritual clothing, communities send a clear signal of who belongs and who is new.

For synagogues that are interested in welcoming guests, why not break down the barriers between these dress codes? Replace the scarf tallitot with the larger tallitot that many of the "insiders" wear. Instead of the satin or rayon *kippot*, spring for a range of *kippot* that look less like a uniform—maybe crocheted or suede. Part of the real project of welcoming is to start by not "othering" people through the ritual clothes offered to them when they come to pray. A congregation that projects no "in" and "out" through its ritual clothing takes a big step toward a powerful prayer experience grounded in unity of purpose.

INDIVIDUAL EXPRESSION WITHIN GROUP PRAYER

So much of public prayer is an attempt to bring people together in coordinated worship. But there are critical moments of individual prayer embedded within the public worship. Unfortunately, these moments have sometimes been eliminated or downgraded in an attempt to shorten or streamline the service. These cuts may make sense at any given moment, but it is important to recognize the cost associated with these decisions. A few examples:

Eliminating the repetition of the Amidah. In liberal synagogues, organizers will often eliminate the repetition of the *Amidah* to save time (in truth, the repetition adds probably four or five minutes). This is accomplished by reciting the first three blessings out loud, together, and then continuing on silently. However, this prevents the individual from reciting those blessings on her own. Those who have different practices concerning adding words to those blessings (such as the *imahot*) are now submitting to the practice of the shul (or the prayer leader).

Pressuring participants to finish by sitting following the Amidah. In many synagogues, it is the practice to sit down when you are finished reciting the *Amidah*. But this practice puts added pressure on each individual. Often the worshiper who is slowly making her way through the words will feel that "time is up" when the majority of the congregation sits down and will either rush to finish or just give up entirely and stop davening. A culture in which all participants continue to stand, even when they are finished with the *Amidah*, allows the individual to continue davening without the added peer pressure that results from the race to "be seated."

Tachanun: a lost moment of individual reflection. *Tachanun* is a set of prayers that is recited on most weekdays following the *Amidah*.

Originally, these prayers were open-ended—a point in the service designed for individuals to cry out to God—but in the past few hundred years, a liturgy has been standardized for this spot in the service, and many liberal congregations omit it altogether. But *Tachanun* does not need to be abandoned. In fact, *Tachanun* is the appropriate place in public prayer for a moment of real individual crying out. I learned this lesson well from a student at Yeshivat Hadar, who once gave a *dvar Torah* pointing out that *Tachanun* was the only time she felt she could finally talk to God, unfettered by the required words of the rest of the liturgy. Whenever it was canceled, she felt a deep loss of opportunity. The liturgists understood the need for this moment of personal reflection and plaintive prayer—why cheer when it is canceled?

To announce page numbers or not? Announcing page numbers is often seen as an unmitigated good—helping people who don't know where the prayer leader is in the service. But there is also a cost in announcing page numbers. Besides interrupting the flow of the service and the rhythm of the emotional arc, a page number announcement sends a clear message that (1) everyone should be on that page and (2) there is one siddur to use (the one with the page number being announced). In truth, public prayer allows for individual pace and expression much more than a page announcement might imply. For instance, the entire section of *Pesukei Dezimrah* is often experienced as a guided march through certain psalms, but it can easily be davened at a worshiper's own pace, irrespective of the leader's. Announcing the page number may cut off that individual experience of the pace of prayer and implicitly criticize anyone who is not on the accepted page (such as those who arrive late and are working to catch up at their own pace).

Finally, announcing pages every week assumes that the congregation will always depend on an announcement to know where the leader is. This gives very little sense of empowerment to the worshiper, even one new to the davening. At what point is he able to find his own way through the service, without the repeated guidance of a page announcement? A prayer leader may decide to announce pages for any number of reasons (new people each week, a group of guests who are unfamiliar with the service, a complicated service that confuses even familiar daveners). It is worth noting, however, that announcing page numbers as a rule diminishes personal engagement with the prayer service and should at least be considered to have costs as well as benefits.

This chapter represents my belief that the Jewish people is not yet ready to give up on prayer. Prayer can be inspirational, meaningful, and important. It can shape community, and it can change people's lives. Prayer is mystery, but improving prayer is not mysterious. If Empowered Jews continue to take prayer seriously, the impact will be felt not only in independent minyanim, but also in diverse Jewish communities around the world.

5

Yeshivat Hadar

Fostering a Generation of Empowered Jews

To make a true sea change in American Jewish life, we need to foster an entire generation of Empowered Jews. Independent minyanim are one example of what a group of Empowered Jews can accomplish, but it is a mistake to think that independent minyanim are the *only* expression of Empowered Judaism. Jews who are deeply engaged in traditional language and practice, knowledgeable in their textual heritage, and open to the wider world have the power to alter the course of contemporary Jewish life. They may never *be* the majority in the Jewish community, but they have the potential to *engage* the majority of Jews in a deep way. Some will join traditional synagogues and enliven those communities. Some will form new entities that will involve Jews in ways we can't even predict. Empowered Jews—wherever they go—will have a significant impact on Jewish life in America.

The question is: how can the American Jewish community foster more Empowered Jews?

The answer is, quite simply, education. Not just skills and knowledge, but also experience in a community that grapples with deep issues of meaning and holds certain values dear. The rise of the independent minyanim phenomenon relied on a number of Empowered Jews who, through somewhat haphazard journeys across Jewish communities and institutions, ended up with the skills, passion, and energy to put forth

their vision of engaged Jewish life. I had a winding empowerment journey, picking up valuable lessons as I passed through a variety of schools
and communities in America and Israel. But even though each experience was valuable, none of these places really represented my ideal
empowerment learning community. I always found myself checking a
part of my self—intellect, passion, sincerity, egalitarianism, commitment to mitzvot, connection with God—at the door. After years at
Kehilat Hadar, where I started living out my Jewish identity to its
fullest, I began to think about the next logical step: what would it take
to build the ideal learning community—one that fostered Empowered
Jews in an environment where they didn't need to compromise a core
part of their identity?

Fortunately, I was not alone in asking this question. Two of my
closest (and most talented) friends—Rabbis Shai Held and Ethan
Tucker—were starting to dream along the same lines at the same time.
Shai had spent years as a rabbinic advisor at Harvard Hillel while working on his PhD at Harvard on Abraham Joshua Heschel. He moved to
New York City in 2003 and became the scholar-in-residence at Kehilat
Hadar, anchoring the weekly learning sessions run at the JCC, speaking
on High Holidays, teaching at the Shavuot retreat, and serving as an
informal pastor to the community. Although Kehilat Hadar never had
a rabbi in the style of the American pulpit rabbi, Shai served as a model
and an inspirational teacher of Torah—a rabbinic role perfect for an
independent minyan. Shai also taught rabbinical students at The Jewish
Theological Seminary and laypeople through Me'ah and Wexner, but
he always had a dream of an intensive, passionate Torah environment
for laypeople. He wanted to foster a community that engaged in the
deepest theological questions and that would build a world where, in his
words, "human dignity is real and the presence of God is manifest." Shai
and I had been friends since college, and he shared these dreams with
me over the years.

Living thousands of miles away at Yeshivat Maale Gilboa, Ethan
also shared this vision. Since co-founding Kehilat Hadar with me in
2001, Ethan had moved to Washington, D.C., helping to found DC
Minyan, another independent minyan, and then decided to study for
rabbinical ordination through the chief rabbinate in Israel. Yeshivat
Maale Gilboa offered a fresh—and distinctively Israeli—approach to

what it meant to build intensive community engaged with critical Torah study in a passionate and religious atmosphere. Ethan spent three years on this mountaintop yeshiva, taking rabbinical exams and pondering how to bring his vision of an empowered community infused with Torah and mitzvot—with equal engagement for men and women—into reality.

When Ethan visited New York in 2005, the three of us sat down and started to put words to our collective dreams. We realized that the moment was right to experiment with one of the oldest forms of Jewish empowerment education—the yeshiva. In our vision of a yeshiva, the students—adult men and women—would learn *how* to learn Jewish texts. We would build a community, together with our students, that would practice the rhythms of Jewish life and grapple with the values-based debates in Jewish tradition. We would energize and train these students to become a new type of lay leader—change agents who could go back to their home communities and engage their peers in experiencing Jewish heritage from a place of knowledge, substance, and confidence.

> We are reclaiming the cultural valence of the term *yeshiva*—an intellectual and spiritual center where Torah radiates forth into the broader community, and the community feeds back into the yeshiva.

Friends since college in the mid-1990s, we committed to launch this venture together. In June 2006, we received our first outside funding—a four-year grant from Bikkurim, an investor in early-stage Jewish start-ups. We recruited two rising-star teachers—Shoshana Cohen and Sara Labaton—and during 2006–7, the five of us built a yeshiva from scratch. We decided to start in 2007 with an eight-week intensive summer program (fifty people applied for eighteen spots), and in 2009 we rolled out a yearlong program intended to model and teach *how* to become an Empowered Jew. We agreed to call it Yeshivat Hadar, drawing on the vision and inspiration of Kehilat Hadar and intentionally using the traditional word *yeshiva*.

Yeshivat Hadar is the first egalitarian yeshiva in the Western Hemisphere. Why is this significant? Because a yeshiva is perhaps one of the most powerful tools for fostering Empowered Jews. But the word *yeshiva* often conjures up images of boys in black hats learning by rote, or rabbinical schools preparing professional clergy. Yeshivat Hadar is not focused on ordaining rabbis—it is building an empowered laity. It is not limited to one gender, but open to men and women. We are calling it a yeshiva to reclaim the cultural valence of the term—an intellectual and spiritual center where Torah radiates forth into the broader community, and the community feeds back into the yeshiva.

A yeshiva is different from an independent minyan. Independent minyanim are communities formed by Empowered Jews; Yeshivat Hadar is a community that models and teaches *how* to become an Empowered Jew. That can be done best in an intentional community centered around God and Torah with a specific religious vision. At our opening event in 2007, Shai expressed the vision of the kind of world, in microcosm, that we aimed to create at Yeshivat Hadar:

> We have all spent a lot of our lives dreaming of a Jewish community and a Jewish institution that we never had the opportunity to live in.
>
> A community that, first of all, loves God and Torah, and wants to immerse itself in the latter in order to become closer to the former.
>
> A community that is committed to a vision of traditional Jewish practice as a spiritual path and as a means of personal growth.
>
> A community that understands halakhah as a language that expresses values, and not just rules, but believes that the language is a path for living out the will of God in the world.
>
> A community that is committed to building other communities that embody the ideals of *ahavat Hashem*, the love of God, and *ahavat Israel*, the love of the Jewish people, and *ahavat ha-briyot*, the love of humanity, and *ahavat ha-olam*, the love of the world.
>
> A community that understands that true religious living means that we are more connected rather than less connected to the world as a whole.

A community that takes the authority of tradition seriously, and at the same time affirms what is most noble and ennobling about the modern world.

A community that learns from and is enriched by academic Jewish studies, but never for one moment confuses that with Torah.

A community that asks all Jews—women and men—to take hold of Torah and make it a part of their life, to shape and be shaped by it.

A community that understands that the Torah was not given to ministering angels, but rather to human beings who are asked to embody it in their very flesh-and-blood lives in this very flesh-and-blood world.

A community that asks us to cultivate mind and soul and heart in the service of God.

A community that understands Judaism as a journey, a path, a road toward greater wholeness and greater holiness and deeper connection to God and to each other, and ultimately to ourselves as vehicles of God.

A community that values individual spiritual journeys, even as it affirms that true Judaism takes place in community.

And finally, a community that believes—but I mean really, really believes—that Torah has a contribution to make to the redemption of the world, and that ultimately the world will not be redeemed without Torah.

That, in other words, is the dream within the dream, the dream of our covenantal life, as we aspire to embody God's larger dream: a world in which human dignity is real, and the presence of God is manifest.

Over the years, hundreds of young Jews have been drawn in by this dream of Jewish community and have applied to study at Yeshivat Hadar. They have come from all across the United States (forty-seven cities) as well as from Israel, Europe, and Canada. They include people like Raffi, a brilliant religious skeptic studying English at Yale; Neria, a religious woman from Efrat who had never studied Torah with men;

Nate, a University of Southern California business school student who had never studied Jewish texts in the original; and Rebecca, a Birthright Israel alumna who is a community organizer and up-and-coming leader in her start-up shul in Philadelphia.

These students come to Yeshivat Hadar to be inspired, to immerse themselves in Jewish study, to form community with peers, and to challenge their values. Most important, they come because they envision a more robust Jewish society and they see themselves as co-creators of that world. They come to become empowered.

In building Yeshivat Hadar, we had a number of positive models to draw from (the Drisha Institute, the Pardes Institute of Jewish Studies, Yeshivat Maale Gilboa, Northwoods Kollel), but we also had a distinctive vision of how we would be different from anything that came before. To enact the bold vision that Shai expressed above and to create an environment conducive to empowerment, we made several critical early decisions that make Yeshivat Hadar unique.

Our mission: Torah, *avodah*, *gemilut hasadim*. In many respects, Yeshivat Hadar is not new at all. It is the continuation of the centuries-old mission statement of the Jewish people, expressed by Shimon Ha-Tzaddik (*Pirke Avot* 1:2): "The world stands on three things: Torah study, worship/service, and acts of lovingkindness." We recognized the critical aspect of each of these in building a yeshiva. Torah study is the backbone of the schedule. We do not limit that Torah study to Talmud and Jewish law, but include Jewish thought, Bible, midrash, liturgy, *mussar*, Hasidut, and spiritual practice. But a yeshiva is more than Torah study alone. To unleash the full power of the Jewish tradition, there must be the opportunity to live out this Torah with a community in real time. Daily egalitarian davening—service/worship—is a core feature of the schedule. Regular engagement with *hesed*—lovingkindness—is also critical and has ranged from visiting the sick and elderly to tutoring Jewish high school students to working with government programs like Head Start. It is extremely powerful to daven next to the person you learn with, next to the person you volunteer with. We designed Yeshivat Hadar with the conviction that this centuries-old, holistic mission statement is the guiding light for what it means to empower Jews in the twenty-first century.

Diversity and openness, not pluralism. Shai, Ethan, and I had all participated in a number of pluralistic Jewish communities before co-founding Yeshivat Hadar. Harvard Hillel was a robust center with a variety of Shabbat minyanim and other expressions of Jewish life. The Wexner Graduate Fellowship—of which we are all alumni—prized pluralistic cohorts in which people had honest discussions about their different approaches to Judaism and lived out these parallel approaches in multiple minyanim and subgroups. But we actively decided not to make Yeshivat Hadar a pluralistic environment. For instance, all the full-time students are expected to daven together in a single service that is egalitarian and traditional. Students must also commit to living a life engaged with Torah and mitzvot. All of the faculty we hired also support this form of prayer and commitment.

This is not to say that Yeshivat Hadar is closed to debate or values discussions about various approaches to Jewish practice—quite the contrary: our schedule builds in plenty of group time in which students hash out these questions. And our students themselves come from a variety of Jewish backgrounds and identities. But there are certain baseline givens that are not up for debate at Yeshivat Hadar, and counting women in a minyan and the centrality of mitzvot are two of them. Pluralism has made important, critical contributions to American Jewish life, but a group striving to live out a common religious vision and goal—especially as it relates to Torah, mitzvot, and gender egalitarianism—is a rare and powerful innovation. We believe that students are better pluralists in the long run when they are more confident in their particular identity. Yeshivat Hadar offers the opportunity to build and reflect on that identity with a broad, reflective, and engaged group of peers.

A new approach to halakhah. One of our goals at Yeshivat Hadar is to transform the discourse around what halakhah means. Halakhah is usually taken to mean Jewish law. You look it up in a code or ask a rabbi and get a straight yes-or-no answer. It may or may not be correlated to twenty-first-century moral sensibilities. Ethan, working with his own teachers from Yeshivat Maale Gilboa, has attempted to redefine halakhah in this way:

> Halakhah, as we understand it, is the Jewish normative vocabulary for answering religious questions that seek a thoughtful, thorough, and authentically Jewish response.

We want to refract contemporary situations and religious decisions through the lens of Jewish normative sources that span history and geography. Halakhah is a discourse that can include multiple conclusions within the same conversation, but in which all Jews can speak the same language to say different things.

This means that questions like "Can you play musical instruments on Shabbat?" do not have a simple yes-or-no answer. Rather, the values you might assign to either outcome ("music enhances Shabbat" or "loud music is detrimental to Shabbat") find expression in the halakhic literature. Yeshivat Hadar cares most about the *search* for this values debate within classical sources, as opposed to the usual approach, which draws a clear line between Jewish normative texts and modern values.

Immersive education. One of the most distinctive elements of Yeshivat Hadar is the intensive schedule. For our eight-week summer program—our most intense schedule—we designed a core day that starts with *Shacharit* (morning services) at 7:30 a.m. and ends with *Arvit* (evening services) at 9:00 p.m.

Why the long day? Because immersion is one of the most effective ways to transform people. Sleepaway summer camp is a great example: it allows children and teenagers to form community and social bonds from the moment they wake up to the moment they fall asleep. By demanding a full engagement from the students, we created our own immersive bubble within New York City. Students are able to throw themselves into the learning and community, without time (for better and worse) for many outside engagements. In a culture that demands multitasking, this presents a countermodel of deep and focused engagement.

Face-to-face encounter as the "new" technology. Much has been made about the power of online social networking to transform Jewish community. But at Yeshivat Hadar, we have declined virtual community in favor of face-to-face community. Students and faculty eat breakfast and lunch together at round tables that foster wide-ranging conversation every day of the program. Interestingly, our *beit midrash* has naturally become a computer-free zone. Although every one of our

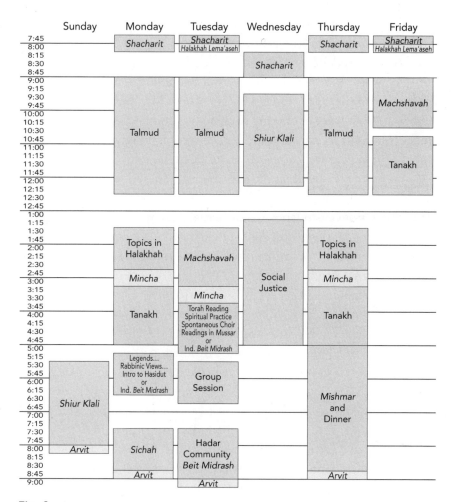

Fig. 2.

Schedule of summer programming at Yeshivat Hadar. Courtesy of Mechon Hadar.

students has access to a laptop, and although we don't have a specific policy forbidding computers, almost none of the students brings a computer to the yeshiva. Instead, they learn from books, make notes with pencils, and talk to their study partners across the table. The yeshiva has allowed them to rehearse the dying art of building community without the aid of technology, and many of the students comment that they have been looking for a way to "unplug."

Fellows, not just students. Anyone can take a class at Yeshivat Hadar, and the *beit midrash* is filled with part-time and evening students. But full-time students are fellows of the program—recipients of a competitive award that includes full tuition and a living stipend, meant to cover some of the costs of living in New York City. In the beginning, we were somewhat wary of offering students stipends. After all, why should students be paid to learn Torah? But we have found over the years that making the program a competitive, funded fellowship builds a tremendous amount of goodwill and loyalty among a student body that is committing to spending up to fourteen hours a day at Yeshivat Hadar. In attracting top-level students, we are actually competing with prestigious secular jobs and fellowships. As a statement that the Jewish community values empowerment learning, it was critical for us to style the full-time program as a selective fellowship.

Selective admissions for full-time students. Given the demands of the schedule, the particular religious approach of the yeshiva, and the goal of developing Empowered Jews, we decided to be extremely selective in our admissions program. Although part of me always wants to fling open the doors to anyone who is interested (How can we say no to people looking for Torah?), my experience in other intensive communities has taught me that just one or two people who aren't right for the program can negatively impact the atmosphere for everyone. So we take great pains to make sure the yeshiva is a good fit for the full-time students. Applicants complete a seven-essay application and submit a written recommendation. Then three people (two of them faculty at the yeshiva) interview the finalists. We look for students who have the drive to keep up with the schedule, the emotional intelligence to be strong members of a social group, and the leadership potential to engage others in substantive Jewish projects when they finish the program.

Multiple skill levels. So often, Jewish educational institutions segregate people with different backgrounds. Those with advanced skills do not encounter beginners, and beginners never see that learning continues even among those with extensive backgrounds. Part of our stated goal was to combine the diverse backgrounds of the Jews drawn to our program—to teach at the highest levels for those with significant skills (and this level is often underserved by the egalitarian world) and to welcome in those who are beginners to traditional Jewish texts. By providing appropriate venues for those students to encounter each other at different levels, we foster the types of conversations that neither advanced nor beginner students would have if they were limited to interactions with those at their own skill level.

Empowerment education. All the study at Yeshivat Hadar is done with a focus on empowerment and skills. Fellows learn how to lead davening, give a *dvar Torah*, talk about belief in God, and build a religious community. This commitment to empowerment leads to clear educational choices. For instance, we teach Talmud using the original Vilna Shas, allowing students to understand what it means to engage with the core text of Jewish heritage without mediation. For many students, this is their first encounter with a traditional Talmud. The very act of connecting to a physical book that has so often remained the domain of male-only centers of learning is a critical step in empowering the students' learning journey. But empowerment is not limited to beginners. Ethan leads a session titled "Tour of the Vilna Shas" that opens up the myriad commentaries in the back and explains their purpose and function—a critical form of empowerment for fellows with higher-level backgrounds. The students learn the texts in the original language without skipping over the difficult sections. We even test students on their reading skills to make sure they are making progress in taking hold of these texts on their own.

> Part of our stated goal was to combine the diverse backgrounds of the Jews drawn to our program—to teach at the highest levels for those with significant skills and to welcome in those who are beginners to traditional Jewish texts.

Faculty engagement beyond the classroom. Yeshivat Hadar is not a university. Faculty serve in ways that extend beyond the typical "professor" role. Faculty eat with the students every day, facilitate processing groups where students and teachers share their religious journeys, daven together, and spend Shabbat together. Being a teacher at Yeshivat Hadar means not only guiding students through a text but also modeling a religious life of study, prayer, and action. The faculty understand their role as not only to empower students with skills but also to open them up to the major struggles and questions of a religious life. In turn, faculty members challenge each other and explore their own assumptions and questions about their religious choices.

Faculty as model students. Some of the most powerful moments at Yeshivat Hadar occur when faculty learn Torah with each other. During *havruta* time, when students learn on their own in pairs, the faculty engage in their own *havrutot* in the same room as the students. They argue over the texts and raise their voices in excitement when they hit upon a new interpretation. This allows the students to experience the faculty as students also. I remember one time when Ethan was vexed for days about a particular difficulty in a Talmudic passage. One morning, as I was sitting with a student struggling through the text, Ethan banged his hand on the table and shouted, "I figured it out!" He came rushing over to explain it to me. All the students stopped to watch Ethan's excitement at his learning and his desire to share it with me, his learning partner. The faculty model for the students what it means to learn in *havruta*, to be surprised and challenged by the text, and to create relationships with peers through study.

Empowerment with a goal. At Yeshivat Hadar, we create a community of diverse, committed students who spend fourteen hours a day engaging with Torah. But we also have a vision of how these students will contribute once they leave the yeshiva. Although learning for its own sake is critical (and a value given much lip service but very little real support in modern Jewish culture), we have also designed the program to prompt students to make real change in their local communities. Yeshivat Hadar empowers students not only by bolstering their skills at learning Jewish texts but also by strengthening their own self-perception as individuals who can make a difference in community.

As a required part of the program, students propose a project to implement in their hometown communities to enliven Jewish engagement there. These have included a peer-led Jewish philosophy class at Middlebury College, a *beit midrash* program for campers in California, a girls' Talmud program at a high school in Efrat, Israel, and new egalitarian minyanim in Toronto and New Orleans. But even more important than these specific projects, the students start to shift their views of themselves from consumers of Jewish life to active producers of Jewish community. They adopt the identity—and the responsibility—of what it means to be an Empowered Jew.

THE REAL GOAL: MANY MODELS

Yeshivat Hadar is just starting to evolve from its pilot phase and will surely continue to change and grow. We are starting to experiment with other models of training Empowered Jews, not just those with a summer or a year to devote, and not just Jews in their twenties and thirties. We have a winter-break program for college students, a monthly learning program for people in the greater New York City area, podcasts that reach people across the world, lecture series that are open to the community, and day-long learning seminars. I have no doubt we will adjust our methods, but our vision will remain singular: creating a world of Empowered Judaism.

Still, Yeshivat Hadar cannot be the only solution to the lack of Jewish empowerment education available to American Jews in the twenty-first century. In fact, if Yeshivat Hadar remains the only new institution in this field in the next five years, we will have failed to achieve our broader vision. American Judaism will thrive when it offers the most active and energetic demographic in the Jewish community—those in the post-college decade—a range of opportunities to meet the demand for substantive connection to a heritage that is full of wisdom and challenge. Only through a host of new centers of education and empowerment will the next generation of Jews really begin to own the holy heritage of the Jewish people.

6

Empowerment and Meaning

A New Frame for Jewish Life

What impact can Empowered Judaism have on the wider American Jewish community? This is not a new philosophy, denomination, or set of institutions waiting to take over old ones. At its core, Empowered Judaism is an engaged approach to what it means to live life as a Jew. The real potency of this approach is that it has the potential to reframe the discourse of American Jewish life—something that will ultimately have more of an impact than any new set of institutions. Fundamentally, this means shifting the operative frame of the American Jewish experience from one of institutional preservation to one of communal empowerment. Below I explore some of the implications of that shift.

WHY ENGAGE YOUNG JEWS?

Jews of all ages are looking for ways to engage with the substance and power of Jewish life. Yet the vast majority of Jews who have engaged in the past decade with independent minyanim and other forms of Empowered Judaism are in their twenties and thirties. The fact that this approach has so captivated this demographic has the potential to offer a new model for how the larger Jewish community can relate to the next generation.

In the past decade, the focus on engaging people in their twenties and thirties hit a fever pitch, when many Jewish family foundations and federations spent millions of dollars in attempts to lure this demographic into the Jewish fold. Jewish programs that have attracted twenty- and thirtysomethings to their events are lauded and almost obsessed over by large Jewish institutions ("How did they bring in those young adults, and how can we do it?").

What lies behind this focus on Jews in their twenties and thirties? In a framework that lauds institutional preservation, young adults are seen only for their potential contributions to the institution. ("We must engage young Jews so that our synagogue, JCC, etc., will survive another generation.") Without these young Jews as members, the future of the institution—and, the argument goes, of Judaism as a whole—is in danger. This perspective does not often stop to ask: "Why are we preserving this institution in the first place? What is so essential about it, and are there new institutions that could do a better job at the same goal?"

When it comes to those in their twenties and thirties, the institutional framework is often supplemented by the survival framework. Here, the goal is not to further any given institution, but to engage young Jews in order to combat the demographic crisis of intermarriage and assimilation. In this framework, success occurs when one Jew marries another, thus continuing the Jewish bloodline (or, in some views, success means convincing a mixed-religion couple to raise their child within the Jewish faith). The survival framework's view of Jews in their twenties and thirties has led to any number of programs that explicitly encourage intermarriage, including JDate, singles events, and parties.

But there is little focus on the content of the programs that draw in this demographic—after all, this framework is not interested in the substance of Judaism per se as much as in continuity ("If juggling flaming torches draws Jews to date and marry each other, let's fund the flaming torches"). The program content is simply a means to a demographic end.

An Empowered Judaism framework takes a very different approach. Although completely in favor of the continued preservation of the Jewish people, the focus of Empowered Judaism is discovering what kind of substantive Jewish community we can build and engaging stakeholders to make it happen. In other words, a Jewish race preserved for its own sake, without any deeper connection to Torah, culture, Israel, or practice, is not on the Jewish empowerment agenda.

Through the lens of Empowered Judaism, why is it critical to engage twenty- and thirtysomethings? They are the demographic that is most available to innovate, create, and invest time and effort in building community. Because they delay marriage and children longer than ever before, and because they are interested in seeking the roots of their Jewish identity, Jews in their first two decades of adulthood have tremendous potential to spend time and energy building meaningful, engaged Jewish communities. The independent minyanim are just one example of what this age demographic can accomplish. They may also help revitalize existing institutional communities. In an Empowered Judaism framework, it is not the particular institution (independent minyan, synagogue, or other Jewish start-up) that is significant; rather, it is the substance of the Jewish community expressed by the institution that is critical. Engaging young Jews is a means to an end: not institutional preservation or survival, but furthering a meaningful, substantive Jewish life.

BETTER LABELS—MOVING BEYOND BIG DENOMINATIONAL CATEGORIES

An institutional lens on Jewish life puts a lot of stock in the big three denominations: Conservative, Orthodox, and Reform. In this framework, they are the barometers of the health of American Jewish life—the more people who affiliate with them, the more robust American Jewry is perceived to be. The Jewish news media cover them like American political parties: if one denomination is on the rise, the others must be sinking. Other denominations such as Renewal and Reconstructionist are usually ignored, even though they offer cogent philosophical approaches to Jewish life, because their relatively low membership makes them institutionally insignificant.

But the vast majority of Empowered Jews—for instance, the thousands of young Jews who attend independent minyanim—do not claim a particular denominational identity. When asked, they respond, "I don't want to label myself," or "Denominations don't represent who I am." Why is that and what does it mean?

By definition, the big three denominational labels are broad. After all, they are trying to distill the wildly diverse practice and theological terrain of all of American Judaism into just three categories. But the more Jews become empowered to define their own Jewish identity, the less likely it is that they will be satisfied by a broad label. We can see this in the hybrid labels that emerged in the decade before the independent minyanim (Conservadox, Centrist Orthodox, Traditional Reform, and Open Orthodox, to name a few). This past decade has seen a new trend: a marked shift away from sub-labels to a disinclination to categorize at all. No broad label works to identify people who are true to their own complex Jewish journey. That is why "nondenominational" is the fastest rising group in the taxonomy of Jewish denominations. If you claim to be "nondenominational," people can't make assumptions about your Jewish identity as easily as if you claim a traditional denominational label. Instead, you have to explain *what* about Judaism you connect to—forming the baseline of a robust Jewish conversation.

In addition, because of the increased mobility of young Jews as well as a thriving pluralistic Jewish culture on college campuses, Jewish identity is much more complex than any one denominational label can represent. By the time they graduate from college, many young Jews have experienced a host of Jewish communities across different denominations. I see this in the applications to enroll in Yeshivat Hadar. How would you characterize someone with the following hybrid brew of Jewish influences: she grew up with one Reform and one Conservative parent, went to a Reform synagogue's Hebrew school, then at age sixteen spent the summer in Israel and got turned on by fervent Orthodoxy. In college she was active in the pluralistic minyan on campus (the only one available). In the decade since graduating, she has never joined a synagogue, but studies Torah on the Internet. Which denomination is she? Bottom line: it is extremely hard to classify young people today.

The Internet age has created a general culture in which people feel empowered to differentiate themselves more than ever before. Why tune in to the network newscasts when there are hundreds of informed blogs and independent media websites that speak more specifically to your worldview? Chris Anderson's book *The Long Tail* spells this out: with more niche options available, people gravitate away from the big catchall websites. So too with denominations.

We might suspect this means that young Jews are not willing to locate themselves on the existing spectrum of Jewish life. Perhaps they are "transdenominational"—melding practices across the spectrum—because they no longer see distinctions between Jews. Overall, I have not found this to be the case. It is true that Empowered Jews may have connected to a range of Jewish communities throughout their lives, but they often feel most comfortable within a specific band of Jewish practice—it just may change over time and is not easily described by existing broad categories.

This difficulty of fitting into a denominational box is also a hallmark of the independent minyanim, not just of individuals. How best to define Kehilat Hadar—a minyan that was co-founded by an openly gay woman and has a Gay Pride *Kiddush* (complete with rainbow-colored M&Ms) yet preserves the traditional Jewish hierarchy by reserving the first and second *aliyot* for Kohanim and Levites only? How about the Mission Minyan—where only men can lead *Ma'ariv*, but only women can lead *Kabbalat Shabbat*? Or DC Minyan—where a quorum is twenty (ten of each gender) rather than ten people? These minyanim do not fit into preexisting boxes and therefore claim no labels. As a result, people of a wide variety of backgrounds feel welcome.

In the institutional framework, this phenomenon is seen as a threat to denominations and to organized Judaism as a whole. After all, if young Jews are less likely to identify with a denomination, this must mean trouble for the future of Judaism. Many current leaders fear that the denominational institutions—synagogues, camps, rabbinical schools—will suffer or collapse if denominational affiliation rates wither.

But an Empowered Judaism framework has an entirely different take on this phenomenon. That Jews are increasingly unwilling to settle for a broad definition is positive. Why? Because someone can no longer get away with telling you "I am Orthodox" and assume that you understand what kind of Jew she is. Instead, people are forced to explain *why* they practice in a particular way or *what*, specifically, they believe in. A world without convenient categories is a world that calls on people to take more ownership of the type of Judaism they want to practice in the world. This frame—with all its messy complexity—may frustrate those wishing to tell a simple story about American Jewish life. But it is a major step forward because it leads to a rich discussion about what being Jewish means in our richly textured, highly individualized, twenty-first-century lives.

Although seen as a threat to denominational institutions, this form of Jewish identity will likely improve the nature of Jewish institutional life. Currently, denominations need a host of affiliated institutions to claim broad demographic appeal. But this necessity incentivizes the denominations to protect their affiliates even when those institutions are no longer effectively or adequately promoting the best possible expression of Jewish life and community. If the reasons to support institutions are cast entirely in denominational terms ("We support this Reform school because we believe in the Reform movement"), then people end up debating whether the denomination is worth supporting.

If, however, people can transition to supporting institutions not out of loyalty to a denomination but to further a particular vision of Jewish life ("We support this school because we believe in its expression of Jewish practice and values"), then we begin to make room for productive development and evolution. If the school is not living up to parents' expectations, they will do what they can to improve it. If that means some schools (or synagogues, or camps) survive and others don't, that is a positive outcome: the institutions that are successful and serving their constituents will grow, and those that can't adjust will go out of business. This is ultimately a healthier expression of Jewish institutional life.

THE STABILITY OF INSTABILITY

In an institutional framework, the ultimate metric of success is the duration of an institution. But in an Empowered Judaism framework, institutional longevity is of questionable value, because the stability of an institution may actually *prevent* the most efficient furthering of its original founding purpose.

A look at the structure of independent minyanim reveals that they are quite unstable. Because none of them owns its own building, they are always one irate landlord away from losing their facility. Because their populations are highly mobile, they don't have many people who feel a long-term investment in the continuation of the minyan. Moreover, the minyanim, run entirely by volunteers, are always threatened by a potential dearth of motivated leadership.

Yet I would argue that these forms of instability are actually a plus when we are interested in furthering Empowered Judaism, rather than in furthering institutions—old or new. Independent minyanim know that they survive on the energy of volunteer leaders, and most leaders only run the minyan (together with a core group of volunteers) for a one- to two-year term. So the minyan is designed to constantly scout for fresh leadership from the people who are moving into the community.

Although this offers a certain measure of instability (what is more stable than the president of a shul who has held that position for fifteen years?), it also forces a minyan to constantly solicit direct buy-in from new community members. This, in turn, allows the minyan not to ossify in the image of the founders but to grow organically as the volunteer leadership turns over.

> The stability of an institution may actually *prevent* the most efficient furthering of its original founding purpose.

The financial structure of minyanim is often cited as a liability. No independent minyan has an endowment, a capital campaign, or a building fund. Very few have a secure cash flow extending more than a few months forward. However, the financial model of the minyanim is in some ways extremely stable and sustainable, despite those factors. The minyanim are not bankrolled by a few *machers*, without whom the minyan would collapse. Most distribute the financial burden quite evenly throughout the community. When a budget is only a few thousand dollars, a gift of any size has a significant impact. This balanced financial responsibility spills over to the culture of the minyan leadership as well. Volunteers are valued for their ability to get things done and carry out the vision of the community, not for their ability to write a check. This ultimately allows a broad path to leadership—anyone with time and skill can contribute to the minyan leadership; financial resources alone are not a deciding factor.

Even the lack of a regular meeting space—physical instability—can be a plus. When Kehilat Hadar first met in an apartment, sixty people came, spilling out into the hallway. Two years later, two hundred people were coming to Hadar, jamming into a basement gym. If Hadar had started in a space big enough to hold two hundred, the sixty people who came would not have felt nearly as enthusiastic about the enterprise as they did in that cramped apartment. At each stage of Hadar's growth, the community has met in a space that just barely accommodates—and thus seems to embrace—attendees. This was inherently unstable (and believe me, the minyan leadership was relieved to find a more permanent home), but it allowed for a prayer experience that engaged the worshipers without making them feel dwarfed by a cavernous space and empty chairs. Contrast this with the typical synagogue: nothing says stability like a six-hundred-person sanctuary, but when only a hundred people come to daven, the benefits of stability are subsumed by the lack of intimacy.

> The minyanim are not bankrolled by a few *machers*, without whom the minyan would collapse. Most distribute the financial burden quite evenly throughout the community.

A critical plus to the instability of an independent minyan is the relative ease with which it can go out of business if it ceases to become the best vehicle for expressing the meaning and value of Jewish prayer and community. When a minyan folds, no one loses his or her job, and no debts need to be paid off. This allows people to have an honest discussion about whether a minyan is serving the need to which it was originally founded to respond, whether it can be altered, or whether it should simply stop meeting. There is no shame in the dissolution of a minyan. The people who started it and were active in it go on to other communities and perhaps start a different minyan with a different focus. Or people who were peripheral to one minyan may take on the leadership of the next start-up. The ideal, of course, is for a minyan to evolve without going out of business—after all, there are a lot of start-up costs to getting a minyan off the ground. But when people are focused on the purpose behind a minyan, rather than the continuation of the minyan as an institution, then that minyan has a better chance of furthering its underlying goals.

All too often, however, an institution's stability is in tension with the stability of the idea that gave birth to it. When the institution itself becomes the ultimate goal, and the preservation of that institution impedes the furthering of an idea, then stability becomes a negative.

Minyanim are just unstable enough to allow the idea to burst forth and recombine and reconfigure in new forms decades later. This gives the real core values of Judaism a chance to grow and flourish.

JEWISH EDUCATION—THE POSSIBILITY OF BEING CHALLENGED

Empowered Judaism offers a completely new frame for what it means to engage with Jewish education as an adult. Jewish text study has made a significant comeback in the wider American Jewish world in the past thirty years. However, there is almost no adult Jewish education with the underlying goal of empowerment—reading, understanding, and owning the texts yourself. Sure, you can take an adult education class in most synagogues, and you might learn something interesting, meaning-ful, and important. But you will not learn *how* to study Jewish texts. You will always have to rely on an expert to decode the tradition, to cherry-pick the quotations that speak to an issue you want to address. You will never have the experience of reading a text just to see what emerges.

But that is where the deep power of learning Jewish texts actually lies—in the possibility that something unexpected will emerge. You will be challenged, you will be surprised, and your way of thinking will be questioned by the sources of wisdom from our ancestors. The experience of simply reading a text, without knowing what it might say or how it might affect you, is one of the great joys of study—not all the answers are foregone conclusions. The American Jewish community has for-feited this sacred investigation, ironically right at a time in the general culture when people are standing up and saying, "I do not want experi-ences translated for me; I want to encounter things directly."

Imagine the parallel in secular education. What if you were pre-sented with the top five issues raised in today's *New York Times*, but were not able to read the paper itself? You would see the world through the eyes of the sifter, not through the original text, and you would forgo the experience of surprise that takes hold when you read the newspaper. What if every great work of literature in the American canon were sim-ply boiled down and summarized for you? You could never experience firsthand what it feels like to read *The Grapes of Wrath* or, for that mat-ter, *The Cat in the Hat*.

Survival or Literacy?

Outside of Orthodoxy, an institutional framework has always viewed Jewish education chiefly as a pawn in the battle for continuity, without a real need to foster deep Jewish learning. The 1990 National Jewish Population Survey and its discovery of a reported intermarriage rate of 52 percent cast the raison d'être of every major Jewish endeavor since then like this: strengthen Jewish identity in order to preserve the Jewish people. Jewish education was no exception—it became a means to a survivalist end. This is evident in a quick tour of large central educational institutions that serve a population outside of Orthodoxy. They justify Jewish education through a demographic/identity framework rather than an empowerment/meaning framework. One such mission statement reads: "Motivate, strengthen, and increase Jewish identity and commitment to the Jewish people through educational services and acculturation programs in New York." And another states: "If we care about Jewish continuity, then we must act to strengthen and enhance Jewish education on all levels. Period."

But in an Empowered Judaism framework, Jewish education is about much more than Jewish demographic continuity. It is about fostering literacy in your own culture and heritage. The cure for illiteracy is not summaries of great ideas; it is not about providing pat answers or affirming what you already know. Simply put, it is about teaching people *how* to read. It is about giving them the tools to act as their own filter of Jewish text and tradition. Literacy gives people the confidence and desire to create and contribute to Jewish culture and to the larger society. A Jewish world in which more people have the tools for the conversation means the conversation is more robust, more opinions are expressed, and a more dynamic society is created.

Torah Study as Spiritual Practice

In my own journey with Jewish study as an adult, I have come to appreciate the ways in which an unfiltered encounter with Jewish texts is a form of spiritual practice. As I became an Empowered Jewish learner, I spent many hours talking about this with my teachers. The following thoughts are inspired mainly by my teacher Dr. Devora Steinmetz, a senior faculty member at Yeshivat Hadar.

Torah study opens us up to the notion that there is something larger than ourselves in the universe. Part of the daunting task of learning Torah is recognizing just how much there is to learn. The more we learn, the more we feel there is to learn: we cannot know it all; we cannot control it all; there will always be worlds we have no access to. This is a serious corrective to a contemporary culture that makes claims to being able to access every scrap of information. The Internet confers the illusion that everything is knowable, that it is all available for searching. But Torah study is a regular exercise in humility, a reminder that we are not able to grasp the overwhelming complexity of God's world.

> Torah study is a regular exercise in humility, a reminder that we are not able to grasp the overwhelming complexity of God's world.

Torah study opens us up to the possibility of meaningful mystery in the world. It is a literature that is mysterious by nature, and thus meant to be interpreted and reflected on. This is in stark contrast to an American culture where everything is exposed and nothing is left to the imagination. Studying Torah is not like reading Facebook updates. Torah study allows us to connect to an otherworldliness, a sense of divinity that is represented by mystery.

Torah study is also about encounters with concepts that are foreign and sometimes disturbing. A surface-level connection to Torah is fully affirming ("Look how nicely Torah correlates with my Western values of justice!"). But a real engagement with Torah is much more complex. It involves confronting the difficult and alienating passages rather than writing them off as artifacts of a culture long gone. The difficult parts of Torah are most often hidden from the American Jewish community—who would want to listen to a sermon that doesn't end with a nice moral generally applicable to today's world? But this shortchanges Torah, and it shortchanges the person engaging with it. In a world with no clear answers, what better way to reflect on the assumptions by which we live our lives than to encounter the sometimes foreign and unfamiliar values inherent in our tradition and let ourselves be surprised, shocked, and challenged by them? If a reflective life is meant to be more than just affirming our existing beliefs, then Torah provides the opportunity to engage with life more fully.

Torah study offers a way to approach the other. The fundamental method of Talmud study is to examine each sage's opinion, open it to challenge, and then try to defend it. Taken as a value, this is a form of engagement with the other in which he is not automatically wrong or automatically right. His is a valid opinion that must be grappled with. Ideas are weighed on their merits, not because of the status of the rabbi behind them. Although everything is in some ways up for debate, everything is also given the opportunity to be relevant and meaningful, even opinions that at face value seem absurd. This is a true spiritual practice. It enables us to inhabit a world in which the opinions of others are evaluated based on their merits, where people feel comfortable enough to both challenge and protect the ideas in the marketplace that are not their own or do not speak to their values. Because Torah study is often done with a partner, this exercise of "approaching the other" is not limited to the characters in the text, but also played out with the people learning Torah together.

WHO WILL FOSTER EMPOWERED JUDAISM? A NEW BLUEPRINT FOR AMERICAN RABBIS

In a world of Empowered Judaism, every Jewish adult has the possibility of taking ownership of Jewish text and practice. This can only be accomplished by an array of educators—elementary and high school teachers, youth group leaders, and Hillel executives. It will require a renewed energy and focus on teaching the Hebrew language in America. But most important, a world of Empowered Judaism demands a different kind of rabbi—one who is steeped in the Jewish tradition and is able to offer people the ability to encounter its meaning on their own. In this model, rabbis are no less crucial to the Jewish ecosystem, but their training has a different focus. They must be the highest-caliber leaders and facilitators; they must understand how to read Jewish texts fluently (at a much higher level than the average contemporary American rabbi); and they must be able to transmit the power of these texts to students in meaningful ways. This means offering their students both the tools to learn on their own and the ability to interpret and delve for meaning in the ancient texts.

American rabbis have too often ceded the high-level understanding of Jewish texts to a small cadre of Orthodox rabbinic scholars or to the realm of academics (who, by nature of their profession's culture, have very little incentive to transmit the meaning and passion behind these texts to their university students). Liberal rabbis often become sacred social workers, mainly focused on pastoral and life-cycle moments in their communities. I do not wish to dismiss the holy work of acting as pastor to families in joy or need. But this cannot be the only role or training for rabbis. Jews in America are yearning for someone to show them the way into the meaning and deeper beauty of our tradition. They need teachers to guide them in how to open up the world of Torah study for themselves. Empowered Judaism has opened up new possibilities of what it could mean to be a rabbi in America.

DEMAND FOR EMPOWERED JUDAISM IS STRONG

Among American Jews, there is a significant demand for meaningful, engaged Jewish life. There is a temptation to assume that Jews—especially young adults—are only interested in surface-level engagement with Jewish culture: jokes, bagels, singles events. Anything challenging, deep, or smacking of religion might scare people away. This is simply not the case. Jews are in search of meaning and engagement, and they are interested in the wisdom of their own heritage. They may not find that engagement in existing institutions, but that does not mean they aren't looking for it. They are looking for more than a class; they want to build real community. They want substance, and they want the skills to own their Jewish lives.

Demand for Empowered Judaism spans the Jewish spectrum. Some young Jews are just beginning to deepen their journeys. They were drawn in by any number of experiences: a trip to Israel, a college course in Jewish studies, an engaging *dvar Torah*. They are finally ready to move to the next level of engagement. Some led engaged Jewish lives as teenagers—at camp, with Hillel, in youth groups—but could not find that community in their twenties. Some came from a strong textual background but had no experience with communities that treated men and women as equals, drew on academic tools to study Torah, or deeply cared about the wider world. The demand for an engaged, empowered community is not limited to people in their twenties and thirties—it spans the demographic continuum of Jewish life.

But although demand is strong, supply is very weak. Essentially, the American Jewish institutional landscape offers Jews looking to become empowered the following options:

- Become a rabbi
- Learn in a gender-segregated institution
- Earn a PhD in Jewish studies
- Take a mishmash of adult education evening classes
- Move to Israel

Although these choices may be right for some Jews, the total range of options is simply too narrow for the dream of fostering a generation of Empowered Jews. An Empowered Judaism framework recognizes that demand is strong among the general population and responds to that demand by building communities and institutions that offer direct engagement with Jewish life. Responding to this demand is the real challenge of our time.

7

Pathways Forward

The Real Crisis in
American Judaism

A merican Judaism is in crisis. But it isn't the crisis that mainstream American Jewish leaders would have you believe. It is at once much better and much worse. The false crisis—declining Jewish continuity, caused by assimilation and an intermarriage rate of 52 percent—has become the rallying cry of institutional Judaism. But fundamentally, it is a red herring. The real crisis is one of meaning and engagement. For the first time in centuries, two Jews can marry each other and have Jewish children without any connection to Jewish heritage, wisdom, or tradition.

Part of the problem is that there are very few places that offer Jews an opportunity to experience the power and mystery of Jewish tradition firsthand. Even people who are intermarried by and large have little connection to Torah, Jewish practice, and values. They are dependent on others to translate Judaism for them, and they trudge to High Holiday services to receive the requisite "be good!" sermons, only to return to their lives unchallenged and unchanged. They have been sold a world in which Judaism is a bunch of platitudes, at best matching their existing modern liberal values (but adding nothing beyond what they already know), and at worst completely irrelevant to the struggles they experience day to day. Who can blame these Jews for disengaging with Judaism?

This is the legacy of American Judaism in the twenty-first century— a Judaism that has been undersold and watered down. It is a Judaism where those who know its beauty are often unable or unwilling to connect to the larger Jewish community, and those on the front lines of the welcome wagon to Judaism have little skill or facility with Jewish texts to elucidate their beauty to others. People want deep meaning and connection, but they move through life thinking of Judaism's contribution to the world as *Seinfeld* and guilt. Many would be shocked to find out that Judaism has vigorous debates about the most central existential problems facing people today.

WITHOUT SUBSTANCE, JEWISH ENGAGEMENT FADES

The tragedy is that although there is a very weak supply side to the equation of Jewish meaning, there is very strong demand. Take young Jews returning from Birthright Israel. After a ten-day trip, they have been opened to the possibility that there is real substance in Judaism. But upon returning home, they have no clear educational option. They want to learn Hebrew, but there are not enough high-quality Hebrew classes. They are interested in basic Jewish knowledge but are unable to connect to synagogues. The Jewish community does not have the teachers and the leaders who can step forward to meet this need. So what do Birthright alumni do? They get funded to have beer nights, ski trips, and at best a Shabbat dinner (with no intellectual or traditional content necessary or encouraged). Because their enthusiasm for deeper Jewish engagement has no substantial outlet, it eventually fades away. This is just one example among many. There is simply no coordinated effort to educate the Jewish people in a way that empowers them.

> It is time for us to start meeting the demand for meaning and substance.

It is time to stop short-selling Judaism. It is time for us to start meeting the demand for meaning and substance. What does that look like? The strategy is straightforward.

Invest in empowerment education. We do not have the luxury of assuming that Jews will feel engaged in the Jewish tradition just by experiencing a few inspiring programs. Jews of all ages, but especially those in the time-abundant years following college, must become self-directed translators of the Jewish tradition—for themselves and their peers. This means less focus on "experiences" and more focus on the building blocks of educational discovery. This is not about religious indoctrination. This is unlocking the power of Jewish heritage.

American culture supports so many forms of creativity and experimentation—but this rarely extends to Judaism. We believe that an education must include Shakespeare, Joyce, and knowledge of the Civil War, yet not the Mishnah or Psalms. What would it take to promote a deep engagement with the building blocks of the Jewish tradition and to make this pursuit an acceptable pre- or post-college endeavor?

Educate toward meaning. Education cannot only be about grammar and technical skills. It must have an eye toward translation into meaning. But meaning is not just an affirmation of our existing values. Rather, it is the belief that these texts can both challenge us and bring us closer to the divine will. Part of the difficulty of supporting Jewish empowerment is the legitimate fear many of us have of feeling ignorant in our own heritage ("How can I advocate for Jewish empowerment education if I myself can't live up to these standards?"). But this is not a way forward; it is a recipe for stasis. Those engaged in a life of study know that the consummate orientation to the Jewish tradition is one in which you will never know enough. This should not, however, prevent us from challenging ourselves and our peers to start down the road of learning how to learn.

I am not advocating for everyone to become a scholar. But we have to create more pathways for people to access the tradition on their own terms. Part of living in the twenty-first century is engaging with data firsthand—the unfiltered access to information that is the gift of the Internet. Judaism cannot survive without real engagement by masses of Jews in the substance of the tradition itself.

Create the pathways to support empowerment. So many Jews have been turned on to the tradition of Judaism but have no path to become empowered. The options are these: become an academic, a rabbi, or Orthodox. There are tiny blips of improvement on the landscape, but nothing that would provide the sea change in meeting the demand of Jewish engagement. Yet the infrastructure is in place—we have synagogues in every city and town that often stand empty during the nine-to-five workday. Imagine a world in which those synagogues were hothouses of learning for people who had time to invest in their Jewish heritage. Imagine if all our post-college students spent six months or a year immersing themselves in Jewish texts and traditions, gaining the skills to become Empowered Jews.

Train better rabbis, but don't rely on them to do everything. We need rabbis who are prepared to lead the supply-side response to the demand for high-level Jewish engagement. The focus of rabbinical-school training has often been on how we can attract more Jews to Judaism. But the secret is this: Jews *are* attracted to Judaism—the unadulterated, complex and nuanced, powerful Jewish tradition. We just don't have enough teachers out there who can speak their language and transmit the beauty and intricacy of Jewish tradition to those hungry for some meaning in their lives. We have been working so hard to pull people back from complete repudiation of Judaism—or worse, apathy—that we don't know how to meet the demand of those finally interested in the conversation and looking to own it themselves.

But even if we train the rabbis who can teach people beyond Judaism 101, the ultimate theory of change must extend beyond the professionals. There will never be enough professional clergy to reach the numbers of Jews who demand serious engagement with a tradition that can speak to them. The answer has to lie in peer engagement—through hosted meals, through study classes and pairings, through grassroots communities and learning circles. Rabbis can train some, but those some must fan out and connect to others. In this world of social networks and mobility, our only chance for real engagement involves an empowered, educated corps of peers who have not devoted their lives to becoming Jewish professionals, but who can live out a rich Jewish culture and heritage and connect others to that experience.

Focus on the substance, not the institution. We must find new ways to unlock the power of Judaism in a contemporary context. But we miss the point by categorizing every innovation in Jewish communal life as a threat or an opportunity for co-opting by existing Jewish institutions. If institutions are performing their mission well and their mission is still relevant, they will thrive. If either of these is not the case, let's not put them on life support. American Judaism is in need of revival now, and it behooves us to look to whatever energy is coming forward and encourage it without the constant check on how it will or won't support an existing institution.

Accept that there is no new "big idea." The Jewish community is obsessed with the "next big idea." There are conferences and panels organized every year to investigate what magic bullet could solve all of our woes in the decades to come. There are prizes offered for innovation and for "thinking big." But the crisis is not one of theory—the power of Judaism is clear to those truly engaged in its complex struggles and searchings for truth and divinity. Instead of focusing on new ideas, the Jewish community would be better served by connecting to the original "big ideas" of our heritage: Torah, *avodah,* and *gemilut hasadim,* for instance. To put it another way: there is no new "big idea"; there is just investment in the old, but in a serious, meaningful, and thoughtful way.

> The secret is this: Jews *are* attracted to Judaism—the unadulterated, complex and nuanced, powerful Jewish tradition. We just don't have enough teachers out there who can speak their language and transmit the beauty and intricacy of Jewish tradition to those hungry for some meaning in their lives.

Recognize that a new Jewish world is possible. The biggest challenge before us is one of imagination and vision. Do we really believe that Judaism has something to teach? Are we prepared to articulate *why* it is important to be Jewish? Can we move beyond a mission to survive as a people to a deep engagement with the power of our heritage?

As we entered the twenty-first century, the independent minyanim gave us a glimpse of a world of Empowered Judaism. But the real legacy of the independent minyanim extends beyond these local communities. In fact, the independent minyanim are ultimately important because they make a bold claim: a different kind of community is possible, and we are capable of building that community. Our task now is to think beyond the scale of individual minyanim: to imagine a world of Empowered Judaism, where every Jew has the potential to take hold of the gift of Jewish heritage. Imagining that world is the first step to building it.

An Empowered Judaism Approach to Understanding Prayer

W hat would it mean to look at the words of the traditional siddur from the perspective of Empowered Judaism? This means not only understanding the prayers in a literal sense, but also looking beyond the surface to uncover the deeper meaning. In this appendix, we will look at the beginning of the *Amidah,* one of the most basic Jewish prayers, and draw from it a sense of how this ancient prayer relates to twenty-first-century life.[1]

A FOCUS ON TRADITIONAL HEBREW PRAYER

One of the most surprising aspects of the independent minyanim is their allegiance to traditional Hebrew prayer. Who could have predicted that one of the most vibrant sectors of Judaism at the beginning of the twenty-first century would center around such a difficult enterprise? In my travels to various Jewish communities across the country, including many independent minyanim, I have heard dozens of objections to traditional Hebrew prayer:

- "I don't understand what the words mean because I can't understand Hebrew."
- "The pace of davening is too fast for me to keep up."
- "I never know when to stand up or sit down."
- "There is so much repetition."
- "Why do we have to recite so many forms of praise for God—does God really need to hear that?"

But perhaps the sharpest objection—and the most oft-repeated one—is this:

- "I understand perfectly what the words mean, and I don't agree with them."

This objection has animated most of the alterations to the prayer book in many Jewish communities during the past two centuries. Mordecai Kaplan, founder of Reconstructionist Judaism, writing in 1945, expressed the dilemma this way: "People expect a Jewish prayer book to express what a Jew should believe about God, Israel and the Torah, and about the meaning of human life and the destiny of mankind. We must not disappoint them in that expectation. But unless we eliminate from the traditional text statements of beliefs that are untenable and of desires which we do not or should not cherish, we mislead the simple and alienate the sophisticated."[2]

Kaplan viewed prayer as an expression of dogma: say what you mean, and mean what you say. But the great theologian Abraham Joshua Heschel, writing in the same period as Kaplan, pointed out the difficulties with Kaplan's proposed solution of radical editing: "True, the text of the prayer book presents difficulties to many people. But the crisis of prayer is not a problem of the text. It is a problem of the soul. The Siddur must not be used as a scapegoat. A revision of the prayer book will not solve the crisis of prayer. What we need is a revision of the soul, a new heart rather than a new text.... What we need is a *sympathetic prayer book exegesis*."[3]

Although Heschel never fully articulated what a "sympathetic prayer book exegesis" might look like, I want to offer one possibility grounded in the most basic Rabbinic prayer in the siddur: the *Amidah*.

Multiplicity of Interpretations through Intertextuality: An Analysis of the First Blessing of the *Amidah*

There is a Rabbinic debate concerning how much intentionality—*kavannah*—a worshiper needs when saying the *Amidah*. The Rabbinic consensus is that we only need critical focus (*kavannah*) for the first blessing of the *Amidah* (*Shulchan Arukh, Orach Haim* 101:1). This is perhaps another way of saying that the essence of the *Amidah* itself can be found in the first blessing—if we do not have *kavannah* for that blessing, it is as if we have not said the *Amidah*.

The difficulty of that conclusion for many modern Jews is this: the content of that blessing is often difficult to relate to at best, and objectionable at worst. Let's examine the language closely (I have numbered the lines in the text for ease of reference).

The First Blessing of the *Amidah*

[1]Blessed are You, YHVH, our God and God of our ancestors

בָּרוּךְ אַתָּה יְיָ אֱלֹהֵינוּ וֵאלֹהֵי אֲבוֹתֵינוּ ¹

[2]The God of Abraham, the God of Isaac, and the God of Jacob

אֱלֹהֵי אַבְרָהָם אֱלֹהֵי יִצְחָק וֵאלֹהֵי יַעֲקֹב ²

[3]The great, mighty, and awesome God

הָאֵל הַגָּדוֹל הַגִּבּוֹר וְהַנּוֹרָא ³

[4]God Most High

אֵל עֶלְיוֹן ⁴

[5]Who performs acts of lovingkindness

גּוֹמֵל חֲסָדִים טוֹבִים ⁵

[6]And Creator of all

וְקוֹנֵה הַכֹּל ⁶

[7]And remembers the lovingkindness of our ancestors

וְזוֹכֵר חַסְדֵי אָבוֹת ⁷

[8]And brings a redeemer to their children's children for His name's sake, with love.

וּמֵבִיא גוֹאֵל לִבְנֵי בְנֵיהֶם לְמַעַן שְׁמוֹ בְּאַהֲבָה. ⁸

[9]Helping, saving, and shielding king!

מֶלֶךְ עוֹזֵר וּמוֹשִׁיעַ וּמָגֵן. ⁹

[10]Blessed are You, YHVH, shield of Abraham.

בָּרוּךְ אַתָּה יְיָ מָגֵן אַבְרָהָם. ¹⁰

Taken on its own, the blessing seems to focus on two goals: first, praising God for various benevolent acts, past and future, and second, defining the relationship to God through the lens of three patriarchs. The most common objections I have encountered in dozens of conversations with people about this prayer are as follows:

- Many people, including all women, are excluded from this prayer (see line 2).

- Why do I need to state over and over again the ways God is cosmically transcendent (see line 3)?

- This prayer claims God is a benevolent actor (line 5), but I look outside my window and I see tremendous suffering.

In dealing with these very serious forms of disconnect from the core blessing of the most essential Rabbinic prayer, let me state my approach upfront: prayer is not meant to be seen as a flat statement of belief. It is a literary creation with all the power, nuance, and complexity of literary creations. As Rabbi Jeremy Kalmanofsky has written: "Prayer had better be poetry, not prose; it had better be mythic poetry at that, correlating the mortal human heart and the eternal divine spirit."[4]

One of the ways in which poetry is different from prose is the multiple allusions within the poetic text. A poem is not meant to be considered only on its own plane, but also on the plane of the allusion. Reuven Kimelman, professor of classical rabbinic literature at Brandeis, writes about prayer: "[T]he meaning of the liturgy exists not so much in the liturgical text per se as in the interaction between the liturgical text and the biblical intertext. Meaning, in the mind of the reader, takes place between texts rather than within them."[5]

Kimelman argues here that every prayer is in dialogue with a biblical text. By unlocking the biblical allusions in the liturgical text, meaning emerges. Although this method can be employed for almost any line of prayer, as an example I will focus on a few lines of the first blessing of the *Amidah*.

"God of our ancestors, the God of Abraham, the God of Isaac, and the God of Jacob" (lines 1–2). To a modern ear, this line glaringly ignores the corresponding matriarchs. Kaplan's solution to this sort of dilemma would be to rewrite the prayer so that it matches the belief and values system of the modern worshiper. And indeed, this prayer has been rewritten to include the four matriarchs (see chapter 3 in Samuel Freedman, *Jew vs. Jew*). But this line of prayer, and indeed the entire blessing, excludes so many more people than just the four matriarchs! For instance, there is no mention of Moses, perhaps the leading model of effective Jewish prayer (who makes no appearance in the *Amidah* at all). It goes without saying that there is no mention of non-Jews (more on this below).

What might a "sympathetic prayer book exegesis" of this line look like? Using Kimelman's methodology,[6] let's examine the biblical intertext behind this line (which the midrash in *Mekhilta Pisha* 16 clearly connects to the *Amidah*). It is the scene of Moses the shepherd standing at the "burning bush": "[God] said, 'Do not come closer. Remove your shoes from your feet, for the place on which you stand is holy ground.' He said, 'I am **the God of your father, the God of Abraham, the God of Isaac, and the God of Jacob.**' Moses hid his face, for he was afraid to look at God" (Exodus 3:5–6).

This intertext opens up this line of prayer for interpretation. First, it is clear that the main character in this line is not one of the patriarchs, but Moses (one of the figures we noticed was strangely missing from the *Amidah*). But more important, this is Moses at the beginning of his relationship with God. He is alienated from God and is wandering about in a land far removed from his people. He is so disconnected from the Divine that God has to basically make an introduction to Moses by stating how his ancestors worshiped God. The Moses in this scene is not the leader we know from the rest of the Torah, but a reluctant shepherd who is about to receive the mission and purpose of his life: to redeem the people of Israel from Egypt and lead them to the promised land. Significantly, Moses does not jump at this offer, but instead "hides his face."

Reading this biblical text back into the prayer, new layers of meaning arise for this section of the blessing. First, this line signals the beginning of a Divine-human relationship. It is the very first communication between God and Moses. Perhaps in choosing this biblical allusion for the very prayer that is said most often in Judaism, the author invites the worshiper to see his or her relationship with God as if it were still "the very first time." Perhaps in recognition of the difficulty of repeating the same blessing (at least) three times a day every day, the author of the prayer consciously reminds us of the original inspiration of prayer: the heady beginnings of the personal-Divine relationship. In addition, the Moses portrayed in this biblical scene is perhaps more akin to the modern-day worshiper who objects to this line in the first place: a person completely disconnected from Jewish heritage and alienated from a deep relationship with God.

Second, we see how this line is in fact not (merely) a description of God by us, but a *quotation from* God to a human being. Prayer is not only about us trying to open communication with God but also about listening to the ways in which God is speaking to us. What is the message of God's speech? It is an invitation to ponder the mission of your life. Indeed, Moses's first verbal response to God is: "Who am I?" (Exodus 3:11). Although we certainly don't have the same mission as Moses, we do have some purpose, and the quotation from the burning bush scene offers worshipers an opportunity to think about who they really are and what the deeper mission of their life may be.

Moses's physical reaction to God at the burning bush is most powerful: he hides his face. If the *Amidah* were meant to mirror the biblical scene perfectly, we would expect Jewish prayer to take place with the worshiper lying flat on the ground (as much of biblical prayer and even Second Temple–era prayer was performed). But this line, and the entire *Amidah*, is said standing. Even the parts of the blessing in which we bow are severely constrained, and one is not allowed to bow more than what is prescribed (Tosefta, *Berakhot* 1:8 [11]). Perhaps most surprisingly, the Babylonian Talmud (*Berakhot* 12a) is clear that we must not bend over when reciting God's name in the *Amidah*, but must stand tall. Unlike Moses's visceral reaction to his encounter with God, the worshiper is called on to stand before God. The meaning of the standing position takes on more significance when we see the alternative—lying prostrate on the ground. This ruling begs the questions: How is your relationship with God different if you stand before God as opposed to lying prostrate? What is that position meant to symbolize? The interplay between the biblical text and the prayer text opens up new possibilities for interpretation.

This method of searching for a biblical intertext bears fruit through the rest of the *Amidah* blessing as well. Take line 3: "The great, mighty, and awesome God." To the modern ear, this line feels typical of Jewish prayer: a (somewhat random) piling of adjectives in an attempt to describe God. But these are not just any adjectives, as made clear from the following story, drawn from Babylonian Talmud, *Megillah* 25a:

> There was once one who prayed (the Amidah) before Rabbi Haninah and said: "The great, mighty, awesome, powerful, strong, courageous God." [The prayer leader added three additional adjectives—powerful, strong, and courageous—to those that are in the standard Amidah.]
>
> Rabbi Haninah said to him: "Have you exhausted all the possible praise of your Master? Were it not that they were written by Moses in the Torah and affixed by the Men of the Great Assembly, we would not even dare to utter those *three* [descriptions]! But you go on adding all of these?! It may be compared to a human king who had thousands upon thousands of gold coins, and people praised him for owning silver. Isn't that a terrible degradation of him?"[7]

Here Rabbi Haninah is pointing to the futility of the project to describe God in human terms. Any attempt is doomed to fail, because that is the nature of the infinite Divine. Indeed, this line offers the only adjectives in the blessing (all the other descriptions of God are actually forms of verbs—it is much easier to say what God does than to say what God is). What is the reason we are able to use the three sanctioned adjectives? Because they are written in the Torah (here is Talmudic support for Kimelman's biblical intertext theory). This is the full context of the biblical quotation used in this line of the Amidah:

> For YHVH your God is the God of gods and the Lord of lords. The **great, mighty, and awesome God** who shows no favor and takes no bribe; who does justice for the orphan and widow, and loves the stranger, providing him with food and clothing. You too must love the stranger, for you were strangers in the Land of Egypt.
>
> *Deuteronomy 10:17–19*

Here the biblical context of this line in prayer makes clear that this is not simply a random collection of cosmic adjectives. What does it mean for God to be "great, mighty, and awesome" in the Bible? It means being just and ethical and protecting the most vulnerable members of society (widows and orphans). It involves concrete acts of kindness: providing food and clothing. And in case there is any doubt, the biblical context makes clear that this behavior is not simply the purview of God: "you too must love the stranger, for you were strangers in the Land of Egypt."

Again, a line that seemed to be a human attempt to describe God becomes—when seen in its biblical context—an ethical charge for how humans should treat other humans. If line 2 was about pondering the mission of your life, then line 3 is a moral demand as the animation of your life.

But what if we look out the window and question the claims made about God in this biblical paragraph? How can God be said to perform acts of lovingkindness when we see so many people scorned and downtrodden in this world? It may be well and good that the biblical allusion of "great, mighty, and awesome" refers to a God who protects the widow and the orphan, but where is that protecting God in our current reality?

Here, too, the parallel texts in the Bible are instructive, especially as woven together by the Rabbis of the Talmud:

> Rabbi Simon said in the name of Rabbi Yehoshua ben Levi: "Why were they called the Men of the Great Assembly? Because they returned greatness to its earlier place."
>
> Rabbi Pinhas said: "Moses established the form of the *Amidah*: The great, mighty, and awesome God" (Deuteronomy 10:17).
>
> Jeremiah (32:18) said: "The great and mighty God," but did not say "awesome."
>
> Why did he say "mighty"? One who can watch the destruction of His house and be quiet is fittingly called mighty.
>
> And why didn't he say "awesome"?
>
> Because only the Temple is awesome, as it says (Psalm 68:36): "Awesome is God from His Sanctuary."
>
> Daniel (9:4) said: "The great, awesome God," but did not say "mighty." His sons have been captured and imprisoned, so where is His might?
>
> Why did he say "awesome"? For the awesome things He did for us in the fiery furnace, He is fittingly called awesome.
>
> When the Men of the Great Assembly arose, they returned greatness to its earlier place: The great, mighty, awesome God.
>
> *Jerusalem Talmud*, Berakhot 7:3; 11c

Rabbi Yehoshua ben Levi noticed something in the later books of the Bible: the phrase "great, mighty, and awesome God" is not fully quoted. Jeremiah cut out the word *awesome*, and Daniel cut out the word *mighty*. Rabbi Yehoshua ben Levi then wove those facts into a sharp midrash about the presence of God in our current world. Jeremiah, who witnessed the destruction of the Temple and Jerusalem, could not bring himself to say *awesome*. Daniel, who lived in the pain of exile, could not bring himself to say *mighty*. Even more severe, the adjective that Jeremiah uses to modify *mighty* no longer has the protective connotation as in Deuteronomy. Rather, God is "mighty" because only a God who stands by silently during destruction can be called "mighty." This can be seen as a subtle but sharp critique of God: how mighty is God if God can't step in and rescue God's children in their hour of need?

This Rabbinic interpretation of the other biblical allusions occasioned by the line in our *Amidah* offers the modern reader yet another strategy for grappling with a text that may not reflect contemporary reality. If the modern worshiper is concerned about misdescribing God, she is in good company: Jeremiah and Daniel also cut down their praise of God to reflect their realities. Even though the full phrase is restored ultimately by the Men of the Great Assembly, the implied critique remains. By using a biblical quotation that hearkens back to other biblical verses with diminished descriptions of God, the liturgist embeds a form of protest within the *Amidah* itself. Liberal editors of the siddur were not the first to cut words from the *Amidah*; Jeremiah and Daniel preceded them. It is a powerful theological statement to reject those critiques of Jeremiah and Daniel and return to the full, original phrase. Nevertheless, the echoes of Jeremiah and Daniel's complaints remain in the text of the *Amidah*. God is sometimes "mighty" only as a reflection of God's inaction. This is a subversive, but Rabbinically authentic, understanding of "great, mighty, and awesome" that acknowledges in some way the disconnect between the active God of Moses's phrase and the hidden God in our current world.

There is another embedded biblical quotation in the next line (line 4) of the *Amidah*: "God Most High." Although this phrase is not clearly a biblical reference, a closer look at the line as well as the lines following it reveal an obvious biblical quotation. The full lines read:

"God most high / Who performs acts of lovingkindness / And Creator of all" (lines 4–6). But another version of this blessing, sung in Ashkenazic prayer on Friday night, preceding the text of *Magen Avot*, words the blessing this way:

אֵל עֶלְיוֹן קוֹנֵה שָׁמַיִם וָאָרֶץ

God Most High, Creator of heaven and earth

This wording is actually an ancient form of the *Amidah* that was preserved in the Cairo Genizah (a storehouse of Jewish manuscripts, some dating back to the ninth century), discovered more than a hundred years ago and published by Solomon Schechter. The full blessing is as follows:

The First Blessing of the *Amidah*—Alternate Version

[1]Blessed are You, YHVH, our God and God of our ancestors

בָּרוּךְ אַתָּה יְיָ אֱלֹהֵינוּ וֵאלֹהֵי אֲבוֹתֵינוּ

[2]The God of Abraham, the God of Isaac, and the God of Jacob

אֱלֹהֵי אַבְרָהָם אֱלֹהֵי יִצְחָק וֵאלֹהֵי יַעֲקֹב

[3]The great, mighty, and awesome God

הָאֵל הַגָּדוֹל הַגִּבּוֹר וְהַנּוֹרָא

[4]God Most High, Creator of heaven and earth

אֵל עֶלְיוֹן קוֹנֵה שָׁמַיִם וָאָרֶץ

[5]Our shield, the shield of our ancestors

מָגִנֵּנוּ מָגֵן אֲבוֹתֵינוּ

[6]Our security in every generation

מִבְטַחֵינוּ בְּכָל דּוֹר וָדוֹר

[7]Blessed are You, YHVH, shield of Abraham.[8]

בָּרוּךְ אַתָּה יְיָ מָגֵן אַבְרָהָם:

It is clear from this version of the *Amidah* that the original line 4 was one in which a full line of the Bible is quoted: Genesis 14:19. (For an interesting theory about why this quotation was edited in the standard version of the *Amidah*, see Naphtali Wieder, *The Formation of Jewish Liturgy in the East and the West*, vol. 1, pp. 65–93. He claims that the קוֹנֵה שָׁמַיִם וָאָרֶץ section of the verse is midrashically understood [*Genesis Rabbah* 43:7] to refer to Abraham, and therefore an editor changed the quotation to obviate any misunderstanding about who created the world [God alone, not Abraham with God].)

Having discovered the biblical intertext, let's look at the context of the biblical quotation. Below is the full story (Genesis 14:17–20):

> When (Abram) returned from defeating Chedarlaomer, and the kings with him, the king of Sodom came out to meet him in the Valley of Shaveh, which is the Valley of the King. And Malki-Zedek, king of Shalem, brought out bread and wine; he was a priest of **God Most High [El Elyon].**
>
> He blessed him, saying: "Blessed be Abram to **God Most High, Creator of heaven and earth.** And blessed be **God Most High,** who has delivered your foes into your hand."

In this story, Abraham (then known as Abram) had just returned from rescuing his nephew Lot from captivity, and he is about to refuse to take money from the king of Sodom (whose kingdom later symbolized the utmost of evil). But interrupting this story is a brief interaction with a character named Malki-Zedek, king of Shalem. While we don't know much about him, we have a sense that he is a favorable character simply by his name (literally, "righteous king") and the name of his kingdom ("wholeness/peace," which the Rabbis later interpreted as Jerusalem). All we know of Malki-Zedek is his profession—he is a priest to *El Elyon*, God Most High. Because Abram and Sarai are the only Jews at this point, whoever *El Elyon* is, it cannot be the Jewish God, YHVH. Yet Abram is blessed by this non-Jewish priest.

The story continues:

> Then the king of Sodom said to Abram, "Give me the people, and take the possessions for yourself." But Abram said to the king of Sodom: "I swear to **YHVH, God Most High, Creator of heaven and earth:** I will not take so much as a thread or a sandal strap of what is yours. You shall not say: 'It is I who made Abram rich.'"

Here Abram reclaims the expression *God Most High* and applies it as a modifier to YHVH. Abram's co-opting of a turn of phrase from a pagan priest is a fitting end to the biblical scene: YHVH becomes God Most High.

But what is striking about the use of this biblical intertext in the *Amidah* is that it does *not* quote Abram; rather, it quotes Malki-Zedek, the pagan priest (if the *Amidah* were quoting Abram, it would have mentioned YHVH at the beginning of line 4). Although the simple reading of the *Amidah* seems to exclude everyone but the three patriarchs, the biblical intertexts bring in missing characters, including Malki-Zedek, someone who is a clergy member of another religion! The biblical intertexts can open us up to any number of surprising conclusions, including one in which a non-Jew is quoted in the middle of the classic Jewish prayer.

The fundamental theme of any blessing is often found in the final words of the blessing, following "Blessed are You, YHVH." Here, those words are simply "shield of Abraham." A common objection I have heard to this is the exclusion concern—where is the matriarch? Where are the other biblical characters? Why only Abraham? Of less concern is the word *shield*, but a fundamental question is this: in what way is God a shield for Abraham? God is a shield for Abraham in one story, that of Genesis 15 (the continuation of the above passage with Malki-Zedek). It reads:

> After those things, the word of YHVH came to Abram in a vision, saying: "Don't fear, Abraham, I am a **shield** for you. Your reward will be very great." But Abram said: "Lord, YHVH, what can You give me, seeing that I shall die childless and the one in charge of my household is

Damesek Eliezer?" Abram said: "Since You have granted me no offspring, my steward will be my heir."

The word of *YHVH* came to him, saying: "That one shall not be your heir; none but your very own issue shall be your heir".... Then He said to him: "I am *YHVH* who brought you out from Ur Casdim to assign this land to you as a possession." And he said: "Lord, *YHVH*, how shall I know that I am to possess it?" (Genesis 15:1–8, based on New Jewish Publication Society translation)

The foundation of the relationship between God and Abraham is based on two promises: Abraham will have many offspring, and he will inherit the land of Canaan. When God encountered Abraham in Genesis 12, these promises were made outright. But here in Genesis 15, Abraham is afraid that God will not make good on these promises. Abraham questions God—where is my child? God does not get angry but simply reiterates the promise that children are on the way. But when God renews the promise of the land, Abraham does not fundamentally believe. He asks: "Lord, *YHVH*, how shall I know?" This verse is viewed in early Jewish tradition as the classic expression of doubt in the mouth of Abraham (see further, Babylonian Talmud, *Nedarim* 32a).

We often think of Abraham as the "knight of faith," the one who was willing to sacrifice his beloved son on the altar to fulfill God's word. However, the *Amidah* chose to reflect a very different Abraham—the one who is plagued by doubts. In many ways this is the crux of the blessing, which is the foundation of the *Amidah*. Read with the biblical intertext, the prayer can be saying: don't worry about your doubts. Even Abraham was filled with doubt, and he had a direct relationship with God. The project of prayer, this blessing could say, is that of holding your doubt and grappling with it, but not letting that be a reason to drop out of relationship with God.

Whether or not these particular interpretations speak to you, the larger point is that an interpretive approach to prayer yields a tremendous amount of nuance to an enterprise that, on the surface, may feel like a piling on of praise after praise for God. The experience of prayer is greatly enhanced if the siddur is treated like so many other texts in Jewish heritage, as a starting point for interpretation rather than a surface statement of dogma. We have the tendency to run through the words of the siddur and make a mental list of the phrases that do and—more significantly—don't speak to us.

But just as we engage in interpretation of Torah, so too can we hold the siddur in the same light. Seen as a book of poetry, with myriad allusions waiting to be unlocked, the question of "How can I pray what I don't believe?" becomes somewhat misplaced. We have not even begun to unlock the words of the siddur, so perhaps the real question is: "How can I interpret what I am praying?"

Acknowledgments

One of the core values of the independent minyanim, as well as Yeshivat Hadar, is the cultivation of the *middah* (character trait) of gratitude. I am filled with gratitude to so many people, not only for making this book a reality, but also for fostering the approach to Jewish life that I call Empowered Judaism.

My parents, Rabbi Alvan and Marcia Kaunfer, educators and social entrepreneurs (before the term was in vogue), gave me the backbone of my Jewish identity. Their passion for meaningful Jewish education, which I was able to experience firsthand in our home and at the school they started, taught me to demand a certain level of excellence from Jewish communities. My brother Oren showed me time and again what it means to bring a full heart to davening—as well as what it means to have fun in life. My in-laws, Jake and Emma Exler, and extended family, including many enterprising rabbis and educators, have served as inspirational role models.

Harvard Hillel in the mid-1990s was my training ground for building grassroots Jewish community. In addition to connecting with talented student leaders, I had the privilege of working with Bernie Steinberg, executive director, in his first year at Harvard Hillel, while I served as student president. His gentle guidance, willingness to remain in touch in the years following, and belief in Hadar, from the first he heard of it, served as significant support to me.

I am the graduate of two life-changing fellowship programs, the Dorot Fellowship in Israel and the Wexner Graduate Fellowship program. Their willingness to invest in me and provide a social network of some of the most talented and motivated peers in the Jewish world is a gift I can never repay. In addition, the Avi Chai Fellowship allowed me to connect to an astounding group of colleagues invested in literacy, religious purposefulness, and peoplehood. Their award gave me the opportunity and confidence to expand Yeshivat Hadar to a full-year program.

I have been blessed with gifted teachers over the years, in Jewish and secular studies. I would not call myself an educator without the guidance of Edward Adler, Aaron Amit, Moshe Benovitz, Neil Danzig, Eliezer Diamond, Israel Francus, Marshall Ganz, Stephen Geller, Dudi Goshen, Judith Hauptman, Judy Klitsner, Danny Landes, Ebn Leader, Debra Reed Blank, Leah Rosenthal, Joel Roth, Menahem Schmelzer, Avigdor Shinan, and Mychal Springer. Special thanks to Devora Steinmetz, my teacher and also my vision mentor in so many aspects of the Hadar enterprise.

Mara Benjamin and Rabbi Ethan Tucker were my original partners in founding Kehilat Hadar. Without their vision, tenacity, and innate sense of what needed to be done to succeed, this minyan would have remained just a good idea. Rabbi Shai Held—my original peer role model from Harvard Hillel—served as the scholar-in-residence at Kehilat Hadar for years, shaping the learning, providing big-picture vision, and stepping into a pastoral role when needed.

The *gabbaim*, or organizers, of Kehilat Hadar are a unique type of Jewish leader. The vast majority of them are not Jewish professionals and have committed thousands of hours to bringing a community to life and pushing it to the next level. Week after week, I was privileged to work with these loving, egoless leaders, planning and executing the details of the community: Tammy Arnow, Debbi Bohnen, Rachel Forster, Deena Fox, Josh Greenfield, Debbie Kaufman, Jill Levy, Jessica Lissy, Emily (Michal) Michelson, and Adam Wall. Kehilat Hadar continues to be run entirely by volunteers, led to new heights by *gabbaim* who followed my own time as a *gabbai* at the minyan (which ended in 2005): Talya Bock, Andrea Brustein, Yael Buechler, Farell Diamond, Lisa Exler, Aaron Kasman, Ashira Konigsburg, Adam Levine, Marc Melzer, Charlie Schwartz, Danny Serviansky, and Rebecca Zeidel. Julia Andelman was critical to many of the successes at Hadar, particularly in the creation of the CD of melodies and in leading memorable High Holiday services.

The spirit and organizing model of the independent minyanim eschews single leaders, and readers of this book should know that these minyanim could only happen with the tireless investments of time and energy of scores of people. I have unending gratitude to the hundreds of volunteers who make up the core of the independent minyanim, thank-fully too numerous to list here.

Mechon Hadar is the organization I feel privileged every day to work for. It is the engine of the dream of Empowered Judaism, and it succeeds because of the dedication of its founders and staff. Rabbi Shai Held and Rabbi Ethan Tucker are more than partners or colleagues. They are my teachers. I have the honor of learning from them and being inspired by them on a regular basis. They give vision, voice, structure, and substance to the world of Empowered Judaism. They each read sections of this book and made crucial suggestions. My Talmud *havruta*, Avital Campbell Hochstein, is a perfect completion to this founding trio. She has added immeasurable insight to the growth of Yeshivat Hadar. Avital is my teacher in Torah and in *menschlichkeit* (being a good person).

In 2006–7, Shai, Ethan, and I laid out the details of Yeshivat Hadar in a series of Skype phone calls with two gifted teachers and partners-in-crime: Sara Labaton and Shoshana Cohen. Sara and Shoshana brought their entire beings to the founding of this fourteen-hour-a-day place of Torah; their energy and passion still infuse the culture of the *beit midrash*, despite each of them moving to the next stage of their careers, in Israel. Jaclyn Rubin, a 2007 fellow at Yeshivat Hadar and later "employee number 1," has modeled what it means to be a start-up employee and served as the glue that kept the operation together. She leads the next generation of Torah scholars, and I am overjoyed that she has managed to reduce her organizing work to focus on Torah study. The rest of the full-time Mechon Hadar staff works tirelessly to bring about a world of Empowered Judaism: Aryeh Bernstein, Alyssa Frank, Avram Sand, Devora Steinmetz, and Miriam-Simma Walfish. Thanks also to the many part-time faculty members who teach students in a wide variety of subject areas and bring their full selves to the yeshiva experience.

Yeshivat Hadar is nothing without its full-time students (hundreds more attend part-time classes and listen to podcasts). At this writing, there are close to a hundred alumni of three summer programs and eighteen brave students at the first-ever yearlong egalitarian yeshiva in North America. The students—from so many diverse backgrounds—are united in their drive to learn Torah, connect to God, and empower themselves and others to connect to Judaism in a new way. They are my inspirations, and I am privileged to be their teacher.

We could not build the dream of Mechon Hadar without the vision and support of an extraordinary board of directors: Talya Bock,

Debbi Bohnen, Alisa Doctoroff, Eric Fisher, and Jon Lopatin. Ariela Dubler, the inaugural president of the board, has been an incredible leader and fellow traveler on this adventure.

As a professional not-for-profit executive director, I appreciate the importance of funders—large and small—in bringing an idea to life more than I ever could have imagined. Thankfully, our financial supporters are too numerous to mention. I also have particular gratitude for the foundation supporters of this dream—major philanthropists who were willing to take a gamble on an idea. Particularly, the Jim Joseph Foundation has invested more than $1.5 million in the endeavor, and without their support, we simply could not grow. I am especially grateful to those foundations that committed dollars when the vision of an egalitarian yeshiva was just an idea: Dorot Foundation, Jewish Funders Network, Natan, Alan B. Slifka Foundation, and UJA-Federation of New York (which also funded Kehilat Hadar's learning program for four years). The Nathan Cummings Foundation funded our first national minyan conference in 2006, and the Samuel Bronfman Foundation funded our second one in 2008. The Covenant Foundation has generously funded our work with Yeshivat Hadar alumni, and the Berrie Foundation Fellows funded our first work with lay leaders in northern New Jersey. Finally, Bikkurim, an incubator for Jewish start-ups, provided Mechon Hadar with its first grant and also provided funding for Kehilat Hadar. Martin Kaminer, Nina Bruder, and Aliza Mazor at Bikkurim provided critical advice over the years.

Special thanks also for the support, encouragement, and advice from Elka Abrahamson, Vicki and Bill Abrams, Mimi Alperin, David Arnow, Noah Arnow, Marc Baker, Yael Bendat-Appell, Steve Bursey, Josh Cahan, Cindy Chazan, Steven and Marion Lev Cohen, Michael Colton, Paula Dagen, Abi Dauber-Sterne, Ben Dreyfus, Adina Dubin, Aliza Dzik, Arnie Eisen, Steven Exler, Joel Fleishman, Jeff Fox, Rachel Friedrichs, Sarah Gershman, Laura Gold, Nathan Goldberg, Sharna Goldseker, Eli Gottlieb, Lee Hendler, Felicia Herman, Jeremy Hockenstein, Larry Hoffman, Jill Jacobs, James Jacobson-Maisels, Amy Kalmanofsky, Nadine Kochavi, Lori Koffman, Yehuda Kurtzer, J. Shawn Landres, Jessica Liebowitz, Dov Linzer, Jenny Lyss, Atara Margolies, Larry Moses, Karen Naimer, Rachel Nussbaum, Lila Pahl, Dan Pekarsky, Noam Pianko, Amanda Pogany, Yossi Prager, Riv-Ellen Prell, Micha'el

Rosenberg, David Rosenn, Jason Rubenstein, Adene Sacks, Liz Kessler Sacks, Joanna Samuels, Jonathan Sarna, Moshe Sayer, Meir Schecter, Rob Scheinberg, Jeffrey Schwarz, Michelle Shain, Len Sharzer, David Silber, Ben Skydell, David Starr, David Stone, Rebecca Stone, Adam Szubin, Diane Troderman, Skip Vichness, Ruthie Warshenbrot, Molly Weingrod, Melissa Weintraub, Joey Weisenberg, and Mishael Zion.

Stuart M. Matlins, publisher of Jewish Lights, patiently convinced me to write this book and guided me through the process, and his capable team of editors, led by Emily Wichland and Lauren Hill, made this book a reality. Rae Janvey, my talented mentor, Erica Brown, and Leah Kaplan Robins read the entire manuscript and offered critical revisions.

My partner in this book and in life is Lisa Exler. I met Lisa at that magical first Hadar Shavuot retreat, and my life has been blessed ever since our first e-mail exchanges. A former *gabbai* of Kehilat Hadar (after my time), she encourages me every single day and models for me what it means to act on the values of the Jewish tradition. Lisa challenges me in the most wonderful ways and is a real co-conspirator in bringing the vision of Empowered Judaism to fruition. Not only did Lisa read and edit the entire manuscript (some chapters more than once), but she also made space in our family life to allow this book to be written. I am privileged to build a home and a family together with her, and with our daughter, Maytal.

Finally, I give thanks to God, the source of all real empowerment, inspiration, and vision.

Notes

FOREWORD

1. Jonathan Sarna, *American Judaism: A History* (New Haven: Yale University Press, 2005), 56.
2. Ibid., 136.
3. Ibid., 234.
4. Ibid., 268.
5. Ibid., 319.

CHAPTER 2—INDEPENDENT MINYANIM NATIONWIDE: SIGNIFICANCE AND IMPACT

1. See Steven Cohen, J. Shawn Landres, Elie Kaunfer, and Michelle Shain, "Emergent Jewish Communities and Their Participants" (Synagogue 3000 Synagogue Studies Institute and Mechon Hadar, November 2007), www.mechonhadar.org/2007scstudy.
2. See note 1 for the 2007 study. For information about the 2008 independent minyanim conference, see www.mechonhadar.org/imconference.
3. See note 1. All subsequent references to the 2007 study also refer to note 1.

APPENDIX—AN EMPOWERED JUDAISM APPROACH TO UNDERSTANDING PRAYER

1. I owe the insights of this method to Reuven Kimelman, "The Shema' Liturgy," *Kenishta: Studies of the Synagogue World* 1 (2001): 9–105; and Reuven Kimelman, "The Daily *Amidah* and the Rhetoric of Redemption," *Jewish Quarterly Review* 79 (1989): 165–197.
2. Mordecai Kaplan, *Shabbat Prayer Book* (New York: Jewish Reconstructionist Foundation, 1945), xxiii.
3. Abraham Joshua Heschel, *Man's Quest for God: Studies in Prayer and Symbolism* (Santa Fe, NM: Aurora Press, 1998), 83.
4. Jeremy Kalmanofsky, "Accepting Ishei Yisrael with Love," *Conservative Judaism* 57/4 (Summer 2005): 54.
5. Kimelman, "The Shema' Liturgy," 28.

6. Although Kimelman developed this into a full-blown methodology, medieval siddur commentators engaged in the same project. See one early example in *Perush Ha-Tefilot Ve-Ha Berachot Le-Rabbenu Yehudah b. R. Yakar*, ed. Shmuel Yerushalmi (Jerusalem: Meorei Yisrael, 1979), 35–36.
7. Adapted from Reuven Hammer, *Entering Jewish Prayer* (New York: Schocken, 1995), 96.
8. Solomon Schechter, "Genizah Specimens," *Jewish Quarterly Review* (Old Series) 10 (1898): 656.

GLOSSARY

1. Adapted from Jonathan Sarna, *American Judaism: A History* (New Haven: Yale University Press, 2004).

Glossary

Adon Olam (pronounced ah-DOHN oh-LAHM): An early-morning prayer of unknown authorship, but dating from medieval times, and possibly originally intended as a nighttime prayer, because it praises God for watching over our souls while we sleep. Nowadays, it is also used as a concluding prayer.

Al Hanisim (pronounced ahl ha-NEE-seem): Special prayer inserted into the *Amidah* and the blessing after food to mark special occasions of salvation in Jewish history—specifically Purim and Hanukkah.

Aleinu (pronounced ah-LAY-noo): The first word and, therefore, the title of a major prayer as part of the New Year (Rosh Hashanah) service, but from about the fourteenth century on, used also as part of the concluding section of every daily service. *Aleinu* means "it is incumbent upon us" and introduces the prayer's theme: our duty to praise God.

aliyah (pronounced ah-lee-YAH; plural: *aliyot*; pronounced ah-lee-YOHT): Ritual call to perform a blessing before and after a selection of reading from the *sefer Torah*. Literally, "going up."

Amidah (pronounced ah-mee-DAH or, commonly, ah-MEE-dah): One of three commonly used titles for the second of two central units in the worship service, the first being the *Shema* and Its Blessings. It is composed of a series of blessings. *Amidah* means "standing" and refers to the fact that the prayer is said standing up.

aron kodesh (pronounced ah-ROHN KOH-desh): Holy ark, or sacred storage vessel for the *sefer Torah*.

Arvit (pronounced ahr-VEET or, commonly, AHR-veet): From the Hebrew word *erev* (pronounced EH-rev), meaning "evening." One of two titles used for the evening worship service (also called Ma'ariv).

Ashrei (pronounced ahsh-RAY or, commonly, AHSH-ray): The first word and, therefore, the title of a prayer said three times each day, composed primarily of Psalm 145. *Ashrei* means "happy" and introduces the phrase "Happy are they who dwell in Your [God's] house."

Avinu Malkeinu (pronounced ah-VEE-noo mal-KAY-noo): Litany requesting forgiveness recited on days of penitence, especially Yom Kippur. Literally, "our Father, our King."

Avodah (pronounced ah-voe-DAH): Literally, "sacrificial service," a reference to the sacrificial cult practiced in the ancient Temple until its destruction by the Romans in the year 70 CE; on Yom Kippur, the sacrifices for the day are reenacted poetically by the prayer leader.

Barchu (pronounced bah-r'-KHOO or, commonly, BOH-r'-khoo): The first word and, therefore, the title of the formal call to prayer with which the section called the *Shema* and Its Blessings begins. *Barchu* means "praise," and it introduces the invitation to the assembled congregation to praise God.

beit midrash (pronounced beit mee-DRASH): Place of study.

bimah (pronounced BEE-mah): A raised platform common in many synagogues from which the ritual services (prayer leading, Torah reading) are performed. In many American synagogues, this platform is located in the front of the synagogue.

chevra kadisha (pronounced KHEV-ra ka-DEE-sha): Burial society traditionally responsible for carrying out every detail from death to burial.

daven (pronounced DAH-ven): Yiddish for "pray."

Dorot (pronounced doh-ROHT): Yearlong leadership program that funds recent post-college graduates for a year of study and volunteering in Israel. See www.dorot.org.

dvar Torah (pronounced de-var TOH-rah; plural: *divrei Torah*; pronounced DEE-vray TOH-rah): Literally, "a word of teaching." Traditional teaching offered on the weekly Torah portion.

Ein Keloheinu (pronounced ayn kay-loh-HAY-noo): Literally, "There is none like our God," a concluding prayer of the Shabbat *Musaf* service.

Etz Chaim Hi (pronounced aytz kha-yeem HEE): Conclusion of litany of verses recited upon returning the *sefer Torah* to the ark.

gabbai (pronounced GAH-bai; plural: *gabbaim*; pronounced gah-ba-IM): Originally the collector of communal funds (from the Hebrew word "to collect"), here used as organizer/leader of a minyan.

Genizah (pronounced g'-NEE-zah): A cache of documents, in particular the one discovered at the turn of the twentieth century in an old synagogue in Cairo; the source of our knowledge about how Jews prayed in the Land of Israel and vicinity prior to the twelfth century. From a word meaning "to store or hide away," "to archive."

hachnasat orchim (pronounced hach-nah-SAHT or-CHEEM): Welcoming guests.

Haftarah (pronounced hahf-tah-RAH or, commonly, hahf-TOH-rah): The section of scripture taken from the prophets and read publicly as part of Shabbat and holiday worship services. From a word meaning "to conclude," because it is the "concluding reading," that is, it follows a reading from the Torah (the Five Books of Moses).

hagbahah (pronounced hag-BAH-hah): The ritual lifting of the Torah scroll.

hakafah (pronounced hah-kah-FAH; plural: *hakafot*; pronounced hah-kah-FOHT): Literally, "going around [the room]," a procession in which the Torah is taken from the ark and carried to the bimah during the introductory prayers. On Simchat Torah, this is performed seven times.

halakhah (pronounced ha-LA-khah): Normative direction emerging from Rabbinic sources. "The halakhah follows so-and-so" means that so-and-so's ruling is accepted as the normative position. Halakhah also signifies the Jewish legal discourse in its entirety.

hametz (pronounced khah-MAYTZ): Leavened products forbidden to be consumed on Passover.

Hamotzi (pronounced hah-moh-TZEE): Blessing said over bread.

Hasidut (pronounced khah-see-DOOT): Also known as Hasidism. The doctrine generally traced to an eighteenth-century Polish Jewish mystic and spiritual leader known as the Ba'al Shem Tov. Followers are called Hasidim (pronounced khah-see-DEEM or khah-SIH-dim; singular: Hasid, pronounced khah-SEED or, commonly, KHA-sid), from the Hebrew word *hesed* (pronounced KHEH-sed), meaning "lovingkindness" or "piety."

Hattan/Kallat Torah (pronounced chah-TAHN/kah-LAHT toh-RAH): Final *aliyah* given in the yearly Torah cycle, concluding the book of Deuteronomy.

havruta (pronounced kha-VROO-tah): Study partner. From the Hebrew *haver*, meaning "friend" or "colleague."

havurah (pronounced khah-voo-RAH; plural: havurot; pronounced khah-voo-ROHT): A term originally appropriated by the Reconstructionist movement in the early 1960s to foster small "fellowship circles," later used by more politically active and liberal students to form communities concerned with "the quality of Jewish living and the desire for an integrated lifestyle." Havurot adopted '60s-era ideals, including egalitarianism, informality, cohesive community, active participatory prayer, group discussion, and unconventional forms of governance. Participants met weekly, biweekly, or monthly; sat in circles; dressed casually; took turns leading worship and study; ate, talked, and celebrated together; and participated in the happy and sad moments of one another's lives.[1]

hekhsher (pronounced hech-SHER): Kosher certification.

hesed (pronounced CHEH-sed): Covenantal lovingkindness.

Hinei Mah Tov (pronounced hee-nay mah-TOV): Selection from Psalm 133:1, literally: "Behold, how good is it...."

Hoshanot (pronounced ho-SHAH-noht): Litany recited on Sukkot asking for salvation.

imahot (pronounced ee-mah-HOHT): The four biblical matriarchs: Sarah, Rebekah, Rachel, and Leah.

Kabbalat Shabbat (pronounced kah-bah-LAHT shah-BAHT): Literally, "Welcoming Shabbat." The preamble to the evening synagogue service (*Ma'ariv*) for Friday night, climaxing in the mystical poem *L'khah Dodi*.

Kaddish (pronounced kah-DEESH or, commonly, KAH-d'sh): One of several prayers from a Hebrew word meaning "holy," and therefore the name given to a prayer affirming God's holiness. This prayer was composed in the first century but later found its way into the service in several forms, including one known as the Mourner's *Kaddish*.

kahal (pronounced kah-HAHL): Gathering, specifically a congregation in worship.

kavannah (pronounced kah-vah-NAH): From a word meaning "to direct," and therefore used technically to denote the state of directing our words and thoughts sincerely to God, as opposed to the rote recitation of prayer.

Kedushah (pronounced k'-doo-SHAH or, commonly, k'-DOO-shah): From the Hebrew word meaning "holy," and therefore one of several prayers from the first or second century occurring in several places and versions, all of which have in common the citing of Isaiah 6:3: "Kadosh, kadosh, kadosh...." ("Holy, holy, holy is the Lord of hosts. The whole earth is full of His glory").

kehilah (pronounced keh-hee-LAH): See *kahal*.

kehilatiyut (pronounced keh-hee-lah-tee-YOOT): Sense of community.

Ki Mi'tzion (pronounced kee mee-tzee-YON): Selection from Isaiah 2:3 and Micah 4:2 recited upon removing the *sefer Torah* from the ark.

Kiddush (pronounced kee-DOOSH but, commonly, KIH-d'sh): Literally, "sanctification," in this case, the prayer for the eve of Shabbat and holidays, intended to announce the arrival of sacred time, and accompanied by the blessing over wine. Also refers to a reception following services.

kippah (pronounced kee-PAH; plural: *kippot*; pronounced kee-POHT): Traditional head covering worn by Jews.

Kohen (pronounced koh-HAYN or KOH-hayn; plural: Kohanim; pronounced koh-hah-NEEM or koh-HAH-neem): Descendants of Aaron the high priest, who traditionally receive the first *aliyah* in a Torah service.

Kol Nidre (pronounced kohl nee-DRAY): Post-Talmudic-era formula recited at the beginning of Yom Kippur, meant to annul vows.

Levi (pronounced lay-VEE or LAY-vee; plural: Levite; pronounced LEE-vite): Descendants of Levi, who traditionally receive the second *aliyah* in a Torah service.

leyn (pronounced LAYN): Yiddish for "read"—specifically, read publicly from the *sefer Torah*.

Ma'ariv (pronounced mah-ah-REEV or, commonly, MAH-ah-reev): From the Hebrew word *erev* (pronounced EH-rev), meaning "evening"; one of two titles used for the evening worship service (also called *Arvit*).

macher (pronounced MAH-kher): Yiddish for "big shot" (literally, "maker").

machzor (pronounced MAKH-zohr): Prayer book used for holidays, specifically High Holidays.

Magen Avot (pronounced mah-GAYN ah-VOHT): Poetic abbreviated recitation of the *Amidah* for Shabbat, recited on Friday nights following the silent recitation of the *Amidah*.

Mah Tovu (pronounced mah TOH-voo): Technically, the prayer to be said upon approaching or entering a synagogue; in practice, the first prayer of *Birkhot Hashachar*, the morning blessings.

mechitza (pronounced me-KHEE-tzah): Traditional barrier separating men and women in prayer.

Megillah (pronounced me-GIH-lah): Scroll of the book of Esther, read on Purim.

Mekhilta (pronounced me-KHIL-tah): Earliest stratum of Rabbinic exegesis on the book of Exodus.

middah (pronounced mee-DAH or MEE-dah): Character trait.

Mincha (pronounced meen-CHAH or, commonly, MIN-chah): Originally the name of a type of sacrifice, then the word for a sacrifice offered during the afternoon, and now the name for the afternoon synagogue service.

minyan (pronounced meen-YAHN, or, commonly, MIN-y'n; plural: minyanim; pronounced meen-yahn-IM): A quorum, the minimum number of people required for certain prayers. Minyan comes from the Hebrew word meaning "to count." In this book, it also means a community of people who come together to pray (not limited to ten people).

mitzvah (pronounced meetz-VAH, or, commonly, MITZ-vah; plural: mitzvot; pronounced meetz-VOHT): A Hebrew word denoting any commandment from God.

Modeh/ah Ani (pronounced moh-DEH ah-NEE [for women, moh-DAH ah-NEE]): Literally, "I gratefully acknowledge [... that You have returned my soul to me]"—therefore, the standard prayer to be said upon awakening.

Musaf (pronounced moo-SAHF or, commonly, MOO-sahf): The Hebrew word meaning "extra" or "added," and therefore the title of the additional sacrifice that was offered in the Temple on Shabbat and holy days. It is now the name given to an added service of worship appended to the morning service on those days.

mussar (pronounced moo-SAHR): From Proverbs 1:2, literally meaning "discipline" or "conduct."

niggun (pronounced NIH-guhn; plural: *niggunim;* plural: nih-guhn-IM): Wordless melody, often written in Hasidic circles.

nusach (pronounced NOO-sakh): Traditional musical mode in which prayers are chanted.

parsha (pronounced PAHR-shah): Torah portion of the week.

Pesukei Dezimrah (pronounced p'-soo-KAY d'-zeem-RAH or, commonly, p'-SOO-kay d'-ZIM-rah): Literally, "verses of song," and the title of a lengthy set of opening morning prayers that contain psalms and songs and serve as spiritual preparation prior to the official call to prayer.

petichah (pronounced peh-TEE-khah): Opening the ark that contains the *sefer Torah.* Literally, "opening."

Rashi (pronounced RAH-shee): Solomon ben Isaac (1040–1105), one of the most significant Jewish exegetes and commentators.

sefer Torah (pronounced SAY-fer TOH-rah): Torah scroll.

Selichot (pronounced seh-lee-KHOT): Collection of biblical verses and poems recited in the days or weeks leading up to Yom Kippur.

Shacharit (pronounced shah-khah-REET): Traditional morning service, from the Hebrew word meaning "dawn."

Shavuot (pronounced shah-voo-OHT): One of three biblical pilgrimage festivals, Rabbinically associated with the giving of the Torah on Mt. Sinai.

Shekhinah (pronounced she-khee-NAH): Presence or dwelling of God, associated by kabbalists with God's most immanent and feminine incarnation.

Shema (pronounced sh'-MAH): The central prayer in the first of the two main units in the worship service, the second being the *Amidah*. The *Shema* comprises three citations from the Bible, and the larger unit in which it is embedded (called the *Shema* and Its Blessings) is composed of a formal call to prayer (see *Barchu*) and a series of blessings on the theological themes that, together with the *Shema*, constitute a liturgical creed of faith. *Shema*, meaning "hear," is the first word of the first line of the first biblical citation, "Hear, O Israel: Adonai is our God; Adonai is One," which is the paradigmatic statement of Jewish faith, the Jews' absolute commitment to the presence of a single and unique God in time and space.

shiva (pronounced SHIH-vah): Period of seven days of mourning following the death of an immediate relative.

shul (pronounced SHOOL): Yiddish for "synagogue."

Shulchan Arukh (pronounced shool-KHAN ah-ROOKH or, commonly, SHOOL-khan AH-rookh): The name given to the best-known code of Jewish law, compiled by Joseph Caro in the Land of Israel and published in 1565. *Shulchan Arukh* means "The Set Table" and refers to the ease with which the various laws are set forth—like a table prepared with food ready for consumption.

siddur (pronounced see-DOOR or, commonly, SIH-d'r): From the Hebrew word *seder*, meaning "order," and, by extension, the name given to the "order of prayers," or prayer book.

Simchat Torah (pronounced seem-KHAHT toh-RAH or, commonly, SIM-khaht TOH-rah): Holiday that celebrates the completion of the yearly Torah reading cycle.

spiel (pronounced SHPEEL): Yiddish for "play"—especially performed on Purim.

sukkah (pronounced soo-KAH or, commonly, SUH-kah): Temporary dwelling Jews are commanded to use during the pilgrimage festival of Sukkot.

Sukkot (pronounced soo-KOHT): One of three biblical pilgrimage festivals, marking God's love for the Jewish people as God led them through the desert.

Tachanun (pronounced TAH-khah-noon): A Hebrew word meaning "supplications," and, by extension, the title of the large unit of prayer that follows the *Amidah*, which is largely supplicatory in character.

tallit: (pronounced tah-LEET; plural: tallitot; pronounced tah-lee-TOHT): The prayer shawl equipped with tassels (*tzitzit*) on each corner.

Talmud (pronounced tahl-MOOD or, commonly, TAHL-m'd): The name given to each of two great compendia of Jewish law and lore compiled over several centuries and, ever since, the literary core of the Rabbinic heritage. The Talmud Yerushalmi (pronounced y'-roo-SHAHL-mee), the "Jerusalem Talmud," is earlier, a product of the Land of Israel generally dated about 400 CE. The better-known Talmud Bavli (pronounced BAHV-lee), or "Babylonian Talmud," took shape in Babylonia (present-day Iraq) and is traditionally dated about 500 CE. Talmud means "teaching."

tefillah (pronounced teh-fee-LAH; plural: *tefillot;* pronounced teh-fee-LOHT): Prayer.

Tikkun Leil Shavuot (pronounced tee-KOON layl shah-voo-OHT): A liturgy composed mostly of study passages, designed to be read throughout the night of Shavuot. Now refers to the practice of staying up all night and studying on Shavuot.

tisch (pronounced TISH): Yiddish for "table," originally associated with the Hasidic practice of the rebbe leading a gathering marked by Torah and singing *niggunim.*

Tisha B'Av (pronounced tee-SHAH b'AV): Ninth day of the month of Av. Traditional day of mourning for the destruction of the Temple in Jerusalem and other national Jewish tragedies.

Tosefta (pronounced toh-SEF-tah): Early rabbinic work of law and exegesis contemporary with the Mishnah (ca. 200 CE). From the Hebrew word meaning "extra," denoting texts that were not included in the canonical Mishnah.

tsaraat (pronounced tza-RAH-aht): A physical manifestation of a spiritual impurity, described in Leviticus 13 and 14.

Unetane Tokef (pronounced oo-n'-TAH-neh TOH-kehf): A *piyyut* (liturgical poem) for the High Holidays emphasizing the awesome nature of these days when we stand before God for judgment.

Vilna Shas (pronounced VIL-nah SHAHS): Traditional printing and layout of the Talmud, published in 1870s in Vilna. Shas is an abbreviation for Shisha Sedarim—the six orders of the Mishnah.

Wexner: Jewish professional leadership training program and fellowship run by the Wexner Foundation. See www.wexnerfoundation.org.

Yom Ha'atzmaut (pronounced YOHM ha-AHTZ-mah-oot): Modern holiday marking the founding of the State of Israel.

Suggestions for Further Reading

In the past eight years, there have been scores of newspaper articles about independent minyanim in the print media. For a full listing, see www.mechonhadar.org/news-archive, and for those specifically about Kehilat Hadar, see www.kehilathadar.org/node/10. Many of the other articles are available at www.bjpa.org. In addition, audio from the 2008 National Independent Minyan Conference is online at www.mechonhadar.org/imconference.

Below are some suggested readings of particular note.

Anderson, Chris. *The Long Tail: How Endless Choice Is Creating Unlimited Demand*. New York: Random House Business, 2006.

Aron, Isa. *Becoming a Congregation of Learners: Learning as a Key to Revitalizing Congregational Life*. Woodstock, Vt.: Jewish Lights, 2000.

———. *The Self-Renewing Congregation: Organizational Strategies for Revitalizing Congregational Life*. Woodstock, Vt.: Jewish Lights, 2002.

Banerjee, Neela. "Challenging Tradition, Young Jews Worship on Their Own Terms." *New York Times*, November 28, 2007.

Belzer, Tobin. "The Independent Minyan and Havurah Phenomena." *My Jewish Learning*, 2009. www.myjewishlearning.com/practices/Ritual/Prayer/Synagogue_and_Religious_Leaders/independent-minyan.shtml.

Bossidy, Larry, and Ram Charan. *Execution: The Discipline of Getting Things Done*. New York: Crown Business, 2002.

Bronfman, Edgar. "A Time to Innovate." JTA, March 13, 2009. www.jta.org/news/article/2009/03/13/1003706/op-ed-a-time-to-innovate.

Bronfman, Edgar, and Beth Zasloff. *Hope, Not Fear: A Path to Jewish Renaissance*. New York: St. Martins Press, 2008.

Brown, Erica. *Inspired Jewish Leadership: Practical Approaches to Building Strong Communities*. Woodstock, Vt.: Jewish Lights, 2008.

Bronznick, Shifra. "DIY Judaism: A Roundtable on the Independent Minyan Phenomenon." *Zeek*, January 2008. www.zeek.net/801roundtable.

Burton, Jeremy. "What Defines the New Minyan Movement?" JSpot.org, November 28, 2007. www.jspot.org/showDiary.do?diaryId=1546.

Cohen, Deborah Nussbaum. "The New Gen-X Judaism." *Jewish Week*, August 2, 2002.

Cohen, Steven, and Ari Kelman. "Cultural Events and Jewish Identities: Young Adult Jews in New York." UJA-Federation of New York, 2005. www.bjpa.org/Publications/details.cfm?PublicationID=2911&Keyword=cultural%20events.

———. "Uncoupled: How Our Singles Are Reshaping Jewish Engagement." Jewish Identity Project of Reboot, 2008. www.bjpa.org/Publications/details.cfm?PublicationID=332&Keyword=uncoupled.

Cohen, Steven, J. Shawn Landres, Elie Kaunfer, and Michelle Shain. "Emergent Jewish Communities and Their Participants." Synagogue 3000 Synagogue Studies Institute and Mechon Hadar, November 2007. www.mechonhadar.org/2007scstudy.

Cohen, Steven, Jeffrey Solomon, Ari Kelman, and Roger Bennett. "The Continuity of Discontinuity: How Young Jews Are Connecting, Creating, and Organizing Their Own Jewish Lives." 21/64, 2007. www.bjpa.org/Publications/details.cfm?PublicationID=327&Keyword=continuity%20of%20discontinuity.

Dreyfus, Ben. "Portrait of an Unaffiliated Jew." *Jewish Education News*, Spring 2005.

Fishkoff, Sue. "Minyan Study: Jews Pray on Own Terms." JTA, November 30, 2007. www.jta.org/news/article/2007/11/30/105614/studyminyans.

———. "Turned Off by Traditional Services, Young Jews Form New Prayer Groups." JTA, September 11, 2006. www.mechonhadar.org/news-archive/JTA_9-11-06.

Fox, Seymour, Israel Scheffler, and Daniel Marom. *Visions of Jewish Education.* New York: Cambridge University Press, 2003.

Freedman, Samuel G. *Jew vs. Jew: The Struggle for the Soul of American Jewry.* New York: Simon & Schuster, 2001.

Gladwell, Malcolm. *The Tipping Point: How Little Things Can Make a Big Difference.* Boston: Back Bay, 2002.

Hammer, Reuven. *Entering Jewish Prayer: A Guide to Personal Devotion and the Worship Service.* New York: Schocken, 1995.

Harris, Ben. "Independent Minyanim Growing Rapidly, and the Jewish World Is Noticing." JTA, November 13, 2008. www.jta.org/news/article-ambush/2008/11/11/1000894/minyanim-growing.

Hauptman, Judith. "A Conservative Jew Goes Reform." *The Jewish Week,* December 23, 2008.

Heilmen, Uriel. "Beyond Dogma." *Jerusalem Post,* February 11, 2005.

Herman, Felicia. "Funding Innovation." *Journal of Jewish Communal Service* 84, no. 1/2 (2009): 45–61.

Heschel, Abraham Joshua. *Man's Quest for God: Studies in Prayer and Symbolism.* Santa Fe: Aurora Press, 1998.

Hoffman, Lawrence A. *The Art of Public Prayer: Not for Clergy Only.* 2nd ed. Woodstock, Vt.: SkyLight Paths, 1999.

———. *Beyond the Text: A Holistic Approach to Liturgy.* Bloomington: Indiana University Press, 1987.

———, ed. *My People's Prayer Book: Traditional Prayers, Modern Commentaries.* 10 vols. Woodstock, Vt.: Jewish Lights, 1997–2007.

———. *Rethinking Synagogues: A New Vocabulary for Congregational Life.* Woodstock, Vt.: Jewish Lights, 2006.

———. *The Way Into Jewish Prayer.* Woodstock, Vt.: Jewish Lights, 2004.

———, ed. *Who by Fire, Who by Water—Un'taneh Tokef.* Woodstock, Vt.: Jewish Lights, 2010.

Jarvis, Jeff. *What Would Google Do?* New York: Collins Business, 2009.

Kalmanofsky, Jeremy. "Accepting Ishei Yisrael with Love." *Conservative Judaism* 57/4 (Summer 2005).

Kaplan, Mordecai. *Shabbat Prayer Book.* New York: Jewish Reconstructionist Foundation, 1945.

Kaplowitz, William. "Partnership Minyanim in the United States: Planning Theory in Action." MA thesis, University of Michigan, 2008.

Kaunfer, Elie. "Attracting Young People to Jewish Life: Lessons Learned from Kehilat Hadar." *Jewish Education News,* Spring 2005.

———. "Conservative Judaism at a Crossroads." *Forward,* August 31, 2007.

———. "Prayer Education: A Plan for Revitalization." *Jewish Education News,* Spring 2006. www.mechonhadar.org/news-archive/caje-06.

Kaunfer, Elie, in Daniel Gordis, et al. "Dear Chancellor: Letters of Welcome, Words of Advice." *Conservative Judaism* 59/1 (Spring 2007): 12–16.

Kimelman, Reuven. "The Daily *Amidah* and the Rhetoric of Redemption." *Jewish Quarterly Review* 79 (1989): 165–97.

———. "The Shema' Liturgy; from Covenant Ceremony to Coronation." *Kenishta: Studies of the Synagogue World* 1 (2001): 9–105.

Landres, J. Shawn. "The Emerging Spiritual Paradigm." *Sh'ma: An Online Journal of Jewish Responsibility* (June 2006).

Lewis, Miriam. "Emergence and Rebirth: Independent Minyanim in Contemporary American Society." Senior essay, Yale University, 2009.

Lipman, Steve. "Not Your Grandfather's Beit Midrash." *Jewish Week,* October 10, 2009.

———. "'Wake-Up Call' for the Denominations." *Jewish Week,* December 5, 2007.

Musleah, Rahel. "Individualism and Community." *Hadassah Magazine* 91, no. 1 (August/September 2009). www.hadassah.org/news/content/per_hadassah/archive/2009/09_Sep/feature_2.asp.

Prell, Riv-Ellen. "Independent Minyanim and Prayer Groups of the 1970s: Historical and Sociological Perspectives." *Zeek*, January 2008. www.zeek.net/ 801prell.

———. *Prayer and Community: The Havurah in American Judaism*. Detroit: Wayne State University Press, 1989.

Ratner, Lizzy. "Passionate Prayer." *New York Observer*, October 13, 2003.

Samuel, Nicole. "The Evolving Edah: The Influence of Social Trends and the Creation of Innovative Minyanim." MA thesis, Brandeis University, 2005.

Sarna, Jonathan. *American Judaism: A History*. New Haven: Yale University Press, 2004.

Schwarz, Sidney. *Finding a Spiritual Home: How a New Generation of Jews Can Transform the American Synagogue*. Woodstock, Vt.: Jewish Lights, 2003.

Sege, Irene. "A 'Radical Position': Orthodox Judaism Meets Feminism at Minyan Tehillah." *Boston Globe*, April 19, 2005.

Shain, Michelle. "Against the Tide? An Empirical Analysis of Independent Minyan Members." MA thesis, Hebrew University of Jerusalem, 2008.

Shirky, Clay. *Here Comes Everybody: The Power of Organizing without Organizations*. New York: Penguin, 2009.

Simon, Charles. *Building a Successful Volunteer Culture: Finding Meaning in Service in the Jewish Community*. Woodstock, Vt.: Jewish Lights, 2009.

Slutsky, Carolyn. "Minyanim Grow Up, Turn Inward." *Jewish Week*, November 25, 2008.

Spence, Rebecca. "Leaders of Indie Prayer Groups Get Grants, Become Mainstream Darlings." *The Jewish Daily Forward*, October 17, 2008.

Tucker, Ethan. "What Independent Minyanim Teach Us About the Next Generation of Jewish Communities." *Zeek*, Spring 2007. www.zeek.net/ 801tucker.

Tucker, Gordon. "On Independent Jewish Communities and the Movements." In *Synagogues in a Time of Change*, edited by Zachary Heller, 225–234. Herndon, Va.: Alban Institute, 2009.

Ukeles, Jack, Ron Miller, and Pearl Beck. "Young Jewish Adults in the United States Today." American Jewish Committee, September 2006. www.bjpa.org/Publications/details.cfm?PublicationID=143&Keyword=ukeles.

Wertheimer, Jack. "All Quiet on the Religious Front? Jewish Unity, Denominationalism, and Postdenominationalism in the United States." American Jewish Committee, 2005.

Wieder, Naphtali. *The Formation of Jewish Liturgy in the East and West*. Jerusalem: Yad Ben Zvi, 1998.

Wuthnow, Robert. *After the Baby Boomers: How Twenty- and Thirty-Somethings Are Shaping the Future of American Religion*. Princeton: Princeton University Press, 2007.

Bar/Bat Mitzvah

The JGirl's Guide: TheYoung Jewish Woman's Handbook for Coming of Age
By Penina Adelman, Ali Feldman, and Shulamit Reinharz This inspirational, interactive
guidebook helps pre-teen Jewish girls address the many issues surrounding coming
of age. 6 x 9, 240 pp, Quality PB, 978-1-58023-215-9 **$14.99** *For ages 11 & up*
  Also Available: **The JGirl's Teacher's and Parent's Guide**
  8½ x 11, 56 pp, PB, 978-1-58023-225-8 **$8.99**
Bar/Bat Mitzvah Basics, 2nd Edition: A Practical Family Guide to Coming of Age
  Together *Edited by Cantor Helen Leneman* 6 x 9, 240 pp, Quality PB, 978-1-58023-151-0 **$18.95**
The Bar/Bat Mitzvah Memory Book, 2nd Edition: An Album for Treasuring the
  Spiritual Celebration *By Rabbi Jeffrey K. Salkin and Nina Salkin*
  8 x 10, 48 pp, 2-color text, Deluxe HC, ribbon marker, 978-1-58023-263-0 **$19.99**
For Kids—Putting God on Your Guest List, 2nd Edition: How to Claim the
  Spiritual Meaning of Your Bar or Bat Mitzvah *By Rabbi Jeffrey K. Salkin*
  6 x 9, 144 pp, Quality PB, 978-1-58023-308-8 **$15.99** *For ages 11–13*
Putting God on the Guest List, 3rd Edition: How to Reclaim the Spiritual
  Meaning of Your Child's Bar or Bat Mitzvah *By Rabbi Jeffrey K. Salkin*
  6 x 9, 224 pp, Quality PB, 978-1-58023-222-7 **$16.99**; HC, 978-1-58023-260-9 **$24.99**
  Also Available: **Putting God on the Guest List Teacher's Guide**
  8½ x 11, 48 pp, PB, 978-1-58023-226-5 **$8.99**
Tough Questions Jews Ask: A Young Adult's Guide to Building a Jewish Life
  By Rabbi Edward Feinstein 6 x 9, 160 pp, Quality PB, 978-1-58023-139-8 **$14.99** *For ages 11 & up*
  Also Available: **Tough Questions Jews Ask Teacher's Guide**
  8½ x 11, 72 pp, PB, 978-1-58023-187-9 **$8.95**

Bible Study/Midrash

The Modern Men's Torah Commentary: New Insights from Jewish
Men on the 54 Weekly Torah Portions *Edited by Rabbi Jeffrey K. Salkin*
A major contribution to modern biblical commentary. Addresses the most important concerns of modern men by opening them up to the life of Torah.
6 x 9, 368 pp, HC, 978-1-58023-395-8 **$24.99**

The Genesis of Leadership: What the Bible Teaches Us aboutVision,
Values and Leading Change *By Rabbi Nathan Laufer; Foreword by Senator Joseph I. Lieberman*
Unlike other books on leadership, this one is rooted in the stories of the Bible.
6 x 9, 288 pp, Quality PB, 978-1-58023-352-1 **$18.99**

Hineini in Our Lives: Learning How to Respond to Others through 14 BiblicalTexts and
Personal Stories *By Rabbi Norman J. Cohen, PhD* 6 x 9, 240 pp, Quality PB, 978-1-58023-274-6 **$16.99**
Moses and the Journey to Leadership: Timeless Lessons of Effective Management from
the Bible and Today's Leaders *By Rabbi Norman J. Cohen, PhD*
  6 x 9, 240 pp, Quality PB, 978-1-58023-351-4 **$18.99**; HC, 978-1-58023-227-2 **$21.99**
Self, Struggle & Change: Family Conflict Stories in Genesis and Their Healing Insights for
Our Lives *By Rabbi Norman J. Cohen, PhD* 6 x 9, 224 pp, Quality PB, 978-1-879045-66-8 **$18.99**
The Triumph of Eve & Other Subversive Bible Tales *By Matt Biers-Ariel*
5½ x 8½, 192 pp, Quality PB, 978-1-59473-176-1 **$14.99**
(A book from SkyLight Paths, Jewish Lights' sister imprint)

The Wisdom of Judaism: An Introduction to theValues of the Talmud
By Rabbi Dov Peretz Elkins Explores the essence of Judaism through reflections on
the words of the rabbinic sages. 6 x 9, 192 pp, Quality PB, 978-1-58023-327-9 **$16.99**
  Also Available: **The Wisdom of Judaism Teacher's Guide**
  8½ x 11, 18 pp, PB, 978-1-58023-350-7 **$8.99**

Or phone, fax, mail or e-mail to: **JEWISH LIGHTS Publishing**
Sunset Farm Offices, Route 4 • P.O. Box 237 • Woodstock, Vermont 05091
Tel: (802) 457-4000 • Fax: (802) 457-4004 • www.jewishlights.com
Credit card orders: **(800) 962-4544** (8:30AM–5:30PM ET Monday–Friday)
Generous discounts on quantity orders. SATISFACTION GUARANTEED. Prices subject to change.

Congregation Resources

Empowered Judaism: What Independent Minyanim Can Teach Us about Building Vibrant Jewish Communities
By Rabbi Elie Kaunfer; Foreword by Prof. Jonathan Sarna
Examines the independent minyan movement and what lessons these grassroots communities can provide. 6 x 9, 224 pp, Quality PB, 978-1-58023-412-2 **$18.99**

Spiritual Boredom: Rediscovering the Wonder of Judaism *By Dr. Erica Brown*
Breaks through the surface of spiritual boredom to find the reservoir of meaning within. 6 x 9, 208 pp, HC, 978-1-58023-405-4 **$21.99**

Building a Successful Volunteer Culture
Finding Meaning in Service in the Jewish Community
By Rabbi Charles Simon; Foreword by Shelley Lindauer; Preface by Dr. Ron Wolfson
Shows you how to develop and maintain the volunteers who are essential to the vitality of your organization and community. 6 x 9, 192 pp, Quality PB, 978-1-58023-408-5 **$16.99**

The Case for Jewish Peoplehood: Can We Be One?
By Dr. Erica Brown and Dr. Misha Galperin; Foreword by Rabbi Joseph Telushkin
6 x 9, 224 pp, HC, 978-1-58023-401-6 **$21.99**

Inspired Jewish Leadership: Practical Approaches to Building Strong Communities
By Dr. Erica Brown 6 x 9, 256 pp, HC, 978-1-58023-361-3 **$24.99**

Jewish Pastoral Care, 2nd Edition: A Practical Handbook from Traditional & Contemporary Sources *Edited by Rabbi Dayle A. Friedman, MSW, MAJCS, BCC*
6 x 9, 528 pp, Quality PB, 978-1-58023-427-6 **$30.00**; HC, 978-1-58023-221-0 **$40.00**

Rethinking Synagogues: A New Vocabulary for Congregational Life
By Rabbi Lawrence A. Hoffman 6 x 9, 240 pp, Quality PB, 978-1-58023-248-7 **$19.99**

The Spirituality of Welcoming: How to Transform Your Congregation into a Sacred Community *By Dr. Ron Wolfson* 6 x 9, 224 pp, Quality PB, 978-1-58023-244-9 **$19.99**

Children's Books

What You Will See Inside a Synagogue
By Rabbi Lawrence A. Hoffman, PhD, and Dr. Ron Wolfson; Full-color photos by Bill Aron
A colorful, fun-to-read introduction that explains the ways and whys of Jewish worship and religious life. 8½ x 10½, 32 pp, Full-color photos, Quality PB, 978-1-59473-256-0 **$8.99**
For ages 6 & up (A book from SkyLight Paths, Jewish Lights' sister imprint)

Because Nothing Looks Like God
By Lawrence Kushner and Karen Kushner Introduces children to the possibilities of spiritual life. 11 x 8½, 32 pp, Full-color illus., HC, 978-1-58023-092-6 **$17.99** *For ages 4 & up*
Board Book Companions to *Because Nothing Looks Like God*
5 x 5, 24 pp, Full-color illus., SkyLight Paths Board Books *For ages 0–4*
What Does God Look Like? 978-1-893361-23-2 **$7.99**
How Does God Make Things Happen? 978-1-893361-24-9 **$7.95**
Where Is God? 978-1-893361-17-1 **$7.99**

The Book of Miracles: A Young Person's Guide to Jewish Spiritual Awareness
Written and illus. by Lawrence Kushner
6 x 9, 96 pp, 2-color illus., HC, 978-1-879045-78-1 **$16.95** *For ages 9 & up*

In God's Hands
By Lawrence Kushner and Gary Schmidt 9 x 12, 32 pp, HC, 978-1-58023-224-1 **$16.99**

In Our Image: God's First Creatures *By Nancy Sohn Swartz*
9 x 12, 32 pp, Full-color illus., HC, 978-1-879045-99-6 **$16.95** *For ages 4 & up*

Also Available as a Board Book: **How Did the Animals Help God?**
5 x 5, 24 pp, Full-color illus., Board Book, 978-1-59473-044-3 **$7.99** *For ages 0–4*
(A book from SkyLight Paths, Jewish Lights' sister imprint)

The Kids' Fun Book of Jewish Time
By Emily Sper 9 x 7½, 24 pp, Full-color illus., HC, 978-1-58023-311-8 **$16.99**

What Makes Someone a Jew? *By Lauren Seidman*
Reflects the changing face of American Judaism.
10 x 8½, 32 pp, Full-color photos, Quality PB, 978-1-58023-321-7 **$8.99** *For ages 3–6*

Judaism / Christianity / Interfaith

How to Do Good and Avoid Evil: A Global Ethic from the Sources of Judaism *By Hans Küng and Rabbi Walter Homolka* Explores how the principles of Judaism provide the ethical norms for all religions to work together toward a more peaceful humankind. 6 x 9, 224 pp, HC, 978-1-59473-255-3 **$19.99** *

Getting to the Heart of Interfaith: The Eye-Opening, Hope-Filled Friendship of a Pastor, a Rabbi and a Sheikh
By Rabbi Ted Falcon, Pastor Don Mackenzie and Sheikh Jamal Rahman
Present ways we can work together to transcend the differences that have divided us historically. 6 x 9, 192 pp, Quality PB, 978-1-59473-263-8 **$16.99** *

Claiming Earth as Common Ground: The Ecological Crisis through the Lens of Faith *By Rabbi Andrea Cohen-Kiener; Foreword by Rev. Sally Bingham*
Inspires us to work across denominational lines in order to fulfill our sacred imperative to care for God's creation. 6 x 9, 192 pp, Quality PB, 978-1-59473-261-4 **$16.99** *

Talking about God: Exploring the Meaning of Religious Life with Kierkegaard, Buber, Tillich and Heschel *By Daniel F. Polish, PhD* 6 x 9, 160 pp, Quality PB, 978-1-59473-272-0 **$16.99**
HC, 978-1-59473-230-0 **$21.99** *

InterActive Faith: The Essential Interreligious Community-Building Handbook
Edited by Rev. Bud Heckman with Rori Picker Neiss
6 x 9, 320 pp, Quality PB, 978-1-59473-273-7 **$16.99**; HC, 978-1-59473-237-9 **$29.99** *

The Jewish Approach to Repairing the World (*Tikkun Olam*)
A Brief Introduction for Christians *By Rabbi Elliot N. Dorff, PhD, with Rev. Cory Willson*
5½ x 8½, 256 pp, Quality PB, 978-1-58023-349-1 **$16.99**

Modern Jews Engage the New Testament: Enhancing Jewish Well-Being in a Christian Environment *By Rabbi Michael J. Cook, PhD*
A look at the dynamics of the New Testament.
6 x 9, 416 pp, HC, 978-1-58023-313-2 **$29.99**

Disaster Spiritual Care: Practical Clergy Responses to Community, Regional and National Tragedy *Edited by Rabbi Stephen B. Roberts, BCJC, and Rev. Willard W. C. Ashley Sr., DMin, DH*
6 x 9, 384 pp, HC, 978-1-59473-240-9 **$40.00** *

The Changing Christian World: A Brief Introduction for Jews
By Rabbi Leonard A. Schoolman 5½ x 8½, 176 pp, Quality PB, 978-1-58023-344-6 **$16.99**

Christians and Jews in Dialogue: Learning in the Presence of the Other
By Mary C. Boys and Sara S. Lee; Foreword by Dorothy C. Bass
6 x 9, 240 pp, Quality PB, 978-1-59473-254-6 **$18.99**; HC, 978-1-59473-144-0 **$21.99** *

Healing the Jewish-Christian Rift: Growing Beyond Our Wounded History
By Ron Miller and Laura Bernstein; Foreword by Dr. Beatrice Bruteau
6 x 9, 288 pp, Quality PB, 978-1-59473-139-6 **$18.99** *

Introducing My Faith and My Community
The Jewish Outreach Institute Guide for the Christian in a Jewish Interfaith Relationship
By Rabbi Kerry M. Olitzky 6 x 9, 176 pp, Quality PB, 978-1-58023-192-3 **$16.99**

The Jewish Approach to God: A Brief Introduction for Christians
By Rabbi Neil Gillman 5½ x 8½, 192 pp, Quality PB, 978-1-58023-190-9 **$16.95**

The Jewish Connection to Israel, the Promised Land: A Brief Introduction for Christians *By Rabbi Eugene Korn, PhD* 5½ x 8½, 192 pp, Quality PB, 978-1-58023-318-7 **$14.99**

Jewish Holidays: A Brief Introduction for Christians *By Rabbi Kerry M. Olitzky and Rabbi Daniel Judson* 5½ x 8½, 176 pp, Quality PB, 978-1-58023-302-6 **$16.99**

Jewish Ritual: A Brief Introduction for Christians *By Rabbi Kerry M. Olitzky and Rabbi Daniel Judson* 5½ x 8½, 144 pp, Quality PB, 978-1-58023-210-4 **$14.99**

Jewish Spirituality: A Brief Introduction for Christians *By Rabbi Lawrence Kushner*
5½ x 8½, 112 pp, Quality PB, 978-1-58023-150-3 **$12.95**

A Jewish Understanding of the New Testament *By Rabbi Samuel Sandmel;*
Preface by Rabbi David Sandmel 5½ x 8½, 368 pp, Quality PB, 978-1-59473-048-1 **$19.99***

We Jews and Jesus: Exploring Theological Differences for Mutual Understanding
By Rabbi Samuel Sandmel; Preface by Rabbi David Sandmel
6 x 9, 192 pp, Quality PB, 978-1-59473-208-9 **$16.99**

*(A book from SkyLight Paths, Jewish Lights' sister imprint)

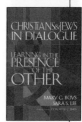

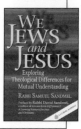

Current Events/History

Hannah Senesh: Her Life and Diary, the First Complete Edition
By Hannah Senesh; Foreword by Marge Piercy; Preface by Eitan Senesh; Afterword by Roberta Grossman
6 x 9, 368 pp, b/w photos, Quality PB, 978-1-58023-342-2 **$19.99**

Ecology/Environment

A Wild Faith: Jewish Ways into Wilderness, Wilderness Ways into Judaism
By Rabbi Mike Comins; Foreword by Nigel Savage 6 x 9, 240 pp, Quality PB, 978-1-58023-316-3 **$16.99**

Ecology & the Jewish Spirit: Where Nature & the Sacred Meet
Edited by Ellen Bernstein 6 x 9, 288 pp, Quality PB, 978-1-58023-082-7 **$18.99**

Torah of the Earth: Exploring 4,000 Years of Ecology in Jewish Thought
Vol. 1: Biblical Israel & Rabbinic Judaism; Vol. 2: Zionism & Eco-Judaism
Edited by Rabbi Arthur Waskow Vol. 1: 6 x 9, 272 pp, Quality PB, 978-1-58023-086-5 **$19.95**
Vol. 2: 6 x 9, 336 pp, Quality PB, 978-1-58023-087-2 **$19.95**

The Way Into Judaism and the Environment *By Jeremy Benstein, PhD*
6 x 9, 288 pp, Quality PB, 978-1-58023-368-2 **$18.99**; HC, 978-1-58023-268-5 **$24.99**

Graphic Novels/History

The Adventures of Rabbi Harvey: A Graphic Novel of Jewish Wisdom and Wit in the
Wild West *By Steve Sheinkin* 6 x 9, 144 pp, Full-color illus., Quality PB, 978-1-58023-310-1 **$16.99**

Rabbi Harvey Rides Again: A Graphic Novel of Jewish Folktales Let Loose in the
Wild West *By Steve Sheinkin* 6 x 9, 144 pp, Full-color illus., Quality PB, 978-1-58023-347-7 **$16.99**

Rabbi Harvey vs. the Wisdom Kid: A Graphic Novel of Dueling
Jewish Folktales in the Wild West *By Steve Sheinkin*
Rabbi Harvey's first book-length adventure—and toughest challenge.
6 x 9, 144 pp, Full-color illus., Quality PB, 978-1-58023-422-1 **$16.99**

The Story of the Jews: A 4,000-Year Adventure—A Graphic History Book
By Stan Mack 6 x 9, 288 pp, illus., Quality PB, 978-1-58023-155-8 **$16.99**

Grief/Healing

Facing Illness, Finding God: How Judaism Can Help You and Caregivers
Cope When Body or Spirit Fails *By Rabbi Joseph B. Meszler*
Helps you deal with the difficulties of disease when you are questioning where
God is when we get sick. 6 x 9, 208 pp, Quality PB, 978-1-58023-423-8 **$16.99**

Midrash and Medicine: Healing Body and Soul in the Jewish Interpretive
Tradition *Edited by Rabbi William Cutter, PhD*
Explores how Midrash can help you see beyond the physical aspects of healing to
tune in to your spiritual source. 6 x 9, 240 pp (est), HC, 978-1-58023-428-3 **$24.99**

Healing and the Jewish Imagination: Spiritual and Practical Perspectives on
Judaism and Health *Edited by Rabbi William Cutter, PhD*
6 x 9, 240 pp, Quality PB, 978-1-58023-373-6 **$19.99**; HC, 978-1-58023-314-9 **$24.99**

Grief in Our Seasons: A Mourner's Kaddish Companion *By Rabbi Kerry M. Olitzky*
4½ x 6½, 448 pp, Quality PB, 978-1-879045-55-2 **$15.95**

Healing of Soul, Healing of Body: Spiritual Leaders Unfold the Strength & Solace
in Psalms *Edited by Rabbi Simkha Y. Weintraub, CSW*
6 x 9, 128 pp, 2-color illus. text, Quality PB, 978-1-879045-31-6 **$16.99**

Mourning & Mitzvah, 2nd Edition: A Guided Journal for Walking the Mourner's
Path through Grief to Healing *By Anne Brener, LCSW*
7½ x 9, 304 pp, Quality PB, 978-1-58023-113-8 **$19.99**

Tears of Sorrow, Seeds of Hope, 2nd Edition: A Jewish Spiritual Companion for
Infertility and Pregnancy Loss *By Rabbi Nina Beth Cardin*
6 x 9, 208 pp, Quality PB, 978-1-58023-233-3 **$18.99**

A Time to Mourn, a Time to Comfort, 2nd Edition: A Guide to Jewish
Bereavement *By Dr. Ron Wolfson; Preface by Rabbi David J. Wolpe*
7 x 9, 384 pp, Quality PB, 978-1-58023-253-1 **$19.99**

When a Grandparent Dies: A Kid's Own Remembering Workbook for Dealing
with Shiva and the Year Beyond *By Nechama Liss-Levinson, PhD*
8 x 10, 48 pp, 2-color text, HC, 978-1-879045-44-6 **$15.95** *For ages 7–13*

Social Justice

There Shall Be No Needy
Pursuing Social Justice through Jewish Law and Tradition
By Rabbi Jill Jacobs; Foreword by Rabbi Elliot N. Dorff, PhD; Preface by Simon Greer
Confronts the most pressing issues of twenty-first-century America from a deeply
Jewish perspective.
6 x 9, 288 pp, Quality PB, 978-1-58023-425-2 **$16.99**; HC, 978-1-58023-394-1 **$21.99**

Conscience: The Duty to Obey and the Duty to Disobey
By Rabbi Harold M. Schulweis
This clarion call to rethink our moral and political behavior examines the idea of
conscience and the role conscience plays in our relationships to governments, law,
ethics, religion, human nature, God—and to each other.
6 x 9, 160 pp, Quality PB, 978-1-58023-419-1 **$16.99**; HC, 978-1-58023-375-0 **$19.99**

Judaism and Justice: The Jewish Passion to Repair the World
By Rabbi Sidney Schwarz; Foreword by Ruth Messinger
Explores the relationship between Judaism, social justice and the Jewish identity
of American Jews.
6 x 9, 352 pp, Quality PB, 978-1-58023-353-8 **$19.99**; HC, 978-1-58023-312-5 **$24.99**

Spiritual Activism: A Jewish Guide to Leadership and Repairing the World
By Rabbi Avraham Weiss; Foreword by Alan M. Dershowitz
6 x 9, 224 pp, Quality PB, 978-1-58023-418-4 **$16.99**; HC, 978-1-58023-355-2 **$24.99**

Righteous Indignation: A Jewish Call for Justice
Edited by Rabbi Or N. Rose, Jo Ellen Green Kaiser and Margie Klein; Foreword by Rabbi David Ellenson
Leading progressive Jewish activists explore meaningful intellectual and spiritual
foundations for their social justice work.
6 x 9, 384 pp, Quality PB, 978-1-58023-414-6 **$19.99**; HC, 978-1-58023-336-1 **$24.99**

Spirituality/Women's Interest

New Jewish Feminism: Probing the Past, Forging the Future
Edited by Rabbi Elyse Goldstein; Foreword by Anita Diamant
Looks at the growth and accomplishments of Jewish feminism and what they
mean for Jewish women today and tomorrow.
6 x 9, 480 pp, HC, 978-1-58023-359-0 **$24.99**

The Quotable Jewish Woman: Wisdom, Inspiration & Humor from the Mind & Heart
Edited by Elaine Bernstein Partnow
6 x 9, 496 pp, Quality PB, 978-1-58023-236-4 **$19.99**

The Divine Feminine in Biblical Wisdom Literature
Selections Annotated & Explained
Translated and Annotated by Rabbi Rami Shapiro
5½ x 8½, 240 pp, Quality PB, 978-1-59473-109-9 **$16.99**
(A book from SkyLight Paths, Jewish Lights' sister imprint)

The Women's Haftarah Commentary: New Insights from Women
Rabbis on the 54 Weekly Haftarah Portions, the 5 Megillot & Special Shabbatot
Edited by Rabbi Elyse Goldstein
Illuminates the historical significance of female portrayals in the Haftarah and the
Five Megillot.
6 x 9, 560 pp, Quality PB, 978-1-58023-371-2 **$19.99**; HC, 978-1-58023-133-6 **$39.99**

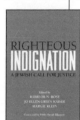

The Women's Torah Commentary: New Insights from Women
Rabbis on the 54 Weekly Torah Portions
Edited by Rabbi Elyse Goldstein
Over fifty women rabbis offer inspiring insights on the Torah, in a week-by-week format.
6 x 9, 496 pp, Quality PB, 978-1-58023-370-5 **$19.99**; HC, 978-1-58023-076-6 **$34.95**

See Passover for *The Women's Passover Companion: Women's Reflections on
the Festival of Freedom* and *The Women's Seder Sourcebook: Rituals &
Readings for Use at the Passover Seder.*

Holidays/Holy Days

Who By Fire, Who By Water—Un'taneh Tokef
Edited by Rabbi Lawrence A. Hoffman, PhD
Examines the prayer's theology, authorship and poetry through a set of lively essays, all written in accessible language.
6 x 9, 304 pp (est), HC, 978-1-58023-424-5 **$24.99**

Rosh Hashanah Readings: Inspiration, Information and Contemplation
Yom Kippur Readings: Inspiration, Information and Contemplation
Edited by Rabbi Dov Peretz Elkins; Section Introductions from Arthur Green's These Are the Words
An extraordinary collection of readings, prayers and insights that will enable you to enter into the spirit of the High Holy Days in a personal and powerful way, permitting the meaning of the Jewish New Year to enter the heart.
Rosh Hashanah: 6 x 9, 400 pp, HC, 978-1-58023-239-5 **$24.99**
Yom Kippur: 6 x 9, 368 pp, HC, 978-1-58023-271-5 **$24.99**

Jewish Holidays: A Brief Introduction for Christians
By Rabbi Kerry M. Olitzky and Rabbi Daniel Judson
5½ x 8½, 176 pp, Quality PB, 978-1-58023-302-6 **$16.99**

Reclaiming Judaism as a Spiritual Practice: Holy Days and Shabbat
By Rabbi Goldie Milgram 7 x 9, 272 pp, Quality PB, 978-1-58023-205-0 **$19.99**

7th Heaven: Celebrating Shabbat with Rebbe Nachman of Breslov
By Moshe Mykoff with the Breslov Research Institute
5⅛ x 8¼, 224 pp, Deluxe PB w/ flaps, 978-1-58023-175-6 **$18.95**

Shabbat, 2nd Edition: The Family Guide to Preparing for and Celebrating the Sabbath *By Dr. Ron Wolfson*
7 x 9, 320 pp, illus., Quality PB, 978-1-58023-164-0 **$19.99**

Hanukkah, 2nd Edition: The Family Guide to Spiritual Celebration
By Dr. Ron Wolfson 7 x 9, 240 pp, illus., Quality PB, 978-1-58023-122-0 **$18.95**

The Jewish Family Fun Book, 2nd Edition: Holiday Projects, Everyday Activities, and Travel Ideas with Jewish Themes *By Danielle Dardashti and Roni Sarig; Illus. by Avi Katz*
6 x 9, 304 pp, 70+ b/w illus. & diagrams, Quality PB, 978-1-58023-333-0 **$18.99**

The Jewish Lights Book of Fun Classroom Activities: Simple and Seasonal Projects for Teachers and Students *By Danielle Dardashti and Roni Sarig*
6 x 9, 240 pp, Quality PB, 978-1-58023-206-7 **$19.99**

Passover

My People's Passover Haggadah
Traditional Texts, Modern Commentaries
Edited by Rabbi Lawrence A. Hoffman, PhD, and David Arnow, PhD
A diverse and exciting collection of commentaries on the traditional Passover Haggadah—in two volumes!
Vol. 1: 7 x 10, 304 pp, HC, 978-1-58023-354-5 **$24.99**
Vol. 2: 7 x 10, 320 pp, HC, 978-1-58023-346-0 **$24.99**

Leading the Passover Journey: The Seder's Meaning Revealed, the Haggadah's Story Retold *By Rabbi Nathan Laufer*
Uncovers the hidden meaning of the Seder's rituals and customs.
6 x 9, 224 pp, Quality PB, 978-1-58023-399-6 **$18.99**; HC, 978-1-58023-211-1 **$24.99**

The Women's Passover Companion: Women's Reflections on the Festival of Freedom
Edited by Rabbi Sharon Cohen Anisfeld, Tara Mohr and Catherine Spector; Foreword by Paula E. Hyman
6 x 9, 352 pp, Quality PB, 978-1-58023-231-9 **$19.99**

The Women's Seder Sourcebook: Rituals & Readings for Use at the Passover Seder
Edited by Rabbi Sharon Cohen Anisfeld, Tara Mohr and Catherine Spector; Foreword by Paula E. Hyman
6 x 9, 384 pp, Quality PB, 978-1-58023-232-6 **$19.99**

Creating Lively Passover Seders: A Sourcebook of Engaging Tales, Texts & Activities
By David Arnow, PhD 7 x 9, 416 pp, Quality PB, 978-1-58023-184-8 **$24.99**

Passover, 2nd Edition: The Family Guide to Spiritual Celebration
By Dr. Ron Wolfson with Joel Lurie Grishaver 7 x 9, 416 pp, Quality PB, 978-1-58023-174-9 **$19.95**

Life Cycle

Marriage/Parenting/Family/Aging

The New Jewish Baby Album: Creating and Celebrating the Beginning of a Spiritual Life—A Jewish Lights Companion
By the Editors at Jewish Lights; Foreword by Anita Diamant; Preface by Rabbi Sandy Eisenberg Sasso
A spiritual keepsake that will be treasured for generations. More than just a memory book, *shows you how—and why it's important*—to create a Jewish home and a Jewish life. 8 x 10, 64 pp, Deluxe Padded HC, Full-color illus., 978-1-58023-138-1 **$19.95**

The Jewish Pregnancy Book: A Resource for the Soul, Body & Mind during Pregnancy, Birth & the First Three Months
By Sandy Falk, MD, and Rabbi Daniel Judson, with Steven A. Rapp
Includes medical information, prayers and rituals for each stage of pregnancy, from a liberal Jewish perspective. 7 x 10, 208 pp, b/w photos, Quality PB, 978-1-58023-178-7 **$16.95**

Celebrating Your New Jewish Daughter: Creating Jewish Ways to Welcome Baby Girls into the Covenant—New and Traditional Ceremonies *By Debra Nussbaum Cohen; Foreword by Rabbi Sandy Eisenberg Sasso* 6 x 9, 272 pp, Quality PB, 978-1-58023-090-2 **$18.95**

The New Jewish Baby Book, 2nd Edition: Names, Ceremonies & Customs—A Guide for Today's Families *By Anita Diamant* 6 x 9, 336 pp, Quality PB, 978-1-58023-251-7 **$19.99**

Parenting as a Spiritual Journey: Deepening Ordinary and Extraordinary Events into Sacred Occasions *By Rabbi Nancy Fuchs-Kreimer* 6 x 9, 224 pp, Quality PB, 978-1-58023-016-2 **$16.95**

Parenting Jewish Teens: A Guide for the Perplexed
By Joanne Doades
Explores the questions and issues that shape the world in which today's Jewish teenagers live and offers constructive advice to parents.
6 x 9, 176 pp, Quality PB, 978-1-58023-305-7 **$16.99**

Judaism for Two: A Spiritual Guide for Strengthening and Celebrating Your Loving Relationship *By Rabbi Nancy Fuchs-Kreimer, PhD, and Rabbi Nancy H. Wiener, DMin; Foreword by Rabbi Elliot N. Dorff*
Addresses the ways Jewish teachings can enhance and strengthen committed relationships. 6 x 9, 224 pp, Quality PB, 978-1-58023-254-8 **$16.99**

The Creative Jewish Wedding Book, 2nd Edition: A Hands-On Guide to New & Old Traditions, Ceremonies & Celebrations *By Gabrielle Kaplan-Mayer* 9 x 9, 288 pp, b/w photos, Quality PB, 978-1-58023-398-9 **$19.99**

Divorce Is a Mitzvah: A Practical Guide to Finding Wholeness and Holiness When Your Marriage Dies *By Rabbi Perry Netter; Afterword by Rabbi Laura Geller* 6 x 9, 224 pp, Quality PB, 978-1-58023-172-5 **$16.95**

Embracing the Covenant: Converts to Judaism Talk About Why & How *By Rabbi Allan Berkowitz and Patti Moskovitz* 6 x 9, 192 pp, Quality PB, 978-1-879045-50-7 **$16.95**

The Guide to Jewish Interfaith Family Life: An InterfaithFamily.com Handbook *Edited by Ronnie Friedland and Edmund Case* 6 x 9, 384 pp, Quality PB, 978-1-58023-153-4 **$18.95**

A Heart of Wisdom: Making the Jewish Journey from Midlife through the Elder Years *Edited by Susan Berrin; Foreword by Harold Kushner* 6 x 9, 384 pp, Quality PB, 978-1-58023-051-3 **$18.95**

Introducing My Faith and My Community
The Jewish Outreach Institute Guide for the Christian in a Jewish Interfaith Relationship *By Rabbi Kerry M. Olitzky* 6 x 9, 176 pp, Quality PB, 978-1-58023-192-3 **$16.99**

Making a Successful Jewish Interfaith Marriage: The Jewish Outreach Institute Guide to Opportunities, Challenges and Resources *By Rabbi Kerry M. Olitzky with Joan Peterson Littman* 6 x 9, 176 pp, Quality PB, 978-1-58023-170-1 **$16.95**

So That Your Values Live On: Ethical Wills and How to Prepare Them
Edited by Jack Riemer and Nathaniel Stampfer
6 x 9, 272 pp, Quality PB, 978-1-879045-34-7 **$18.99**

Inspiration

The Seven Questions You're Asked in Heaven: Reviewing and Renewing Your Life on Earth By Dr. Ron Wolfson
An intriguing and entertaining resource for living a life that matters.
6 x 9, 176 pp, Quality PB, 978-1-58023-407-8 **$16.99**

Happiness and the Human Spirit: The Spirituality of Becoming the Best You Can Be By Rabbi Abraham J. Twerski, MD
Shows you that true happiness is attainable once you stop looking outside yourself for the source. 6 x 9, 176 pp, Quality PB, 978-1-58023-404-7 **$16.99**; HC, 978-1-58023-343-9 **$19.99**

Life's Daily Blessings: Inspiring Reflections on Gratitude and Joy for Every Day, Based on Jewish Wisdom By Rabbi Kerry M. Olitzky 4½ x 6½, 368 pp, Quality PB, 978-1-58023-396-5 **$16.99**

The Bridge to Forgiveness: Stories and Prayers for Finding God and Restoring Wholeness By Rabbi Karyn D. Kedar
Examines how forgiveness can be the bridge that connects us to wholeness and peace.
6 x 9, 176 pp, HC, 978-1-58023-324-8 **$19.99**

A Formula for Proper Living: Practical Lessons from Life and Torah
By Rabbi Abraham J. Twerski, MD
Gives you practical lessons for life that you can put to day-to-day use in dealing with yourself and others. 6 x 9, 144 pp, HC, 978-1-58023-402-3 **$19.99**

God's To-Do List: 103 Ways to Be an Angel and Do God's Work on Earth
By Dr. Ron Wolfson 6 x 9, 144 pp, Quality PB, 978-1-58023-301-9 **$16.99**

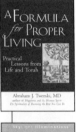

The Empty Chair: Finding Hope and Joy—Timeless Wisdom from a Hasidic Master, Rebbe Nachman of Breslov Adapted by Moshe Mykoff and the Breslov Research Institute
4 x 6, 128 pp, Deluxe PB w/ flaps, 978-1-879045-67-5 **$9.99**

The Gentle Weapon: Prayers for Everyday and Not-So-Everyday Moments— Timeless Wisdom from the Teachings of the Hasidic Master, Rebbe Nachman of Breslov Adapted by Moshe Mykoff and S. C. Mizrahi, together with the Breslov Research Institute
4 x 6, 144 pp, Deluxe PB w/ flaps, 978-1-58023-022-3 **$9.99**

God Whispers: Stories of the Soul, Lessons of the Heart By Rabbi Karyn D. Kedar
6 x 9, 176 pp, Quality PB, 978-1-58023-088-9 **$15.95**

Restful Reflections: Nighttime Inspiration to Calm the Soul, Based on Jewish Wisdom
By Rabbi Kerry M. Olitzky and Rabbi Lori Forman 4½ x 6½, 448 pp, Quality PB, 978-1-58023-091-9 **$15.95**

Sacred Intentions: Daily Inspiration to Strengthen the Spirit, Based on Jewish Wisdom
By Rabbi Kerry M. Olitzky and Rabbi Lori Forman 4½ x 6½, 448 pp, Quality PB, 978-1-58023-061-2 **$15.95**

Kabbalah/Mysticism

Seek My Face: A Jewish Mystical Theology By Rabbi Arthur Green, PhD
6 x 9, 304 pp, Quality PB, 978-1-58023-130-5 **$19.95**

Zohar: Annotated & Explained Translation & Annotation by Daniel C. Matt; Foreword by Andrew Harvey 5½ x 8½, 176 pp, Quality PB, 978-1-893361-51-5 **$15.99**
(A book from SkyLight Paths, Jewish Lights' sister imprint)

Ehyeh: A Kabbalah for Tomorrow
By Rabbi Arthur Green, PhD 6 x 9, 224 pp, Quality PB, 978-1-58023-213-5 **$16.99**

The Flame of the Heart: Prayers of a Chasidic Mystic
By Reb Noson of Breslov; Translated and adapted by David Sears, with the Breslov Research Institute
5 x 7¼, 160 pp, Quality PB, 978-1-58023-246-3 **$15.99**

The Gift of Kabbalah: Discovering the Secrets of Heaven, Renewing Your Life on Earth
By Tamar Frankiel, PhD 6 x 9, 256 pp, Quality PB, 978-1-58023-141-1 **$16.95**

Kabbalah: A Brief Introduction for Christians
By Tamar Frankiel, PhD 5½ x 8½, 208 pp, Quality PB, 978-1-58023-303-3 **$16.99**

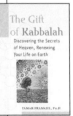

The Lost Princess & Other Kabbalistic Tales of Rebbe Nachman of Breslov
The Seven Beggars & Other Kabbalistic Tales of Rebbe Nachman of Breslov
Translated by Rabbi Aryeh Kaplan; Preface by Rabbi Chaim Kramer
Lost Princess: 6 x 9, 400 pp, Quality PB, 978-1-58023-217-3 **$18.99**
Seven Beggars: 6 x 9, 192 pp, Quality PB, 978-1-58023-250-0 **$16.99**

See also *The Way Into Jewish Mystical Tradition* in The Way Into... Series.

Meditation

Jewish Meditation Practices for Everyday Life
Awakening Your Heart, Connecting with God
By Rabbi Jeff Roth
Offers a fresh take on meditation that draws on life experience and living life with greater clarity as opposed to the traditional method of rigorous study.
6 x 9, 224 pp, Quality PB Original, 978-1-58023-397-2 **$18.99**

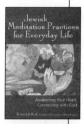

The Handbook of Jewish Meditation Practices
A Guide for Enriching the Sabbath and Other Days of Your Life
By Rabbi David A. Cooper Easy-to-learn meditation techniques.
6 x 9, 208 pp, Quality PB, 978-1-58023-102-2 **$16.95**

Discovering Jewish Meditation: Instruction & Guidance for Learning an Ancient Spiritual Practice *By Nan Fink Gefen, PhD* 6 x 9, 208 pp, Quality PB, 978-1-58023-067-4 **$16.95**

Meditation from the Heart of Judaism: Today's Teachers Share Their Practices, Techniques, and Faith *Edited by Avram Davis*
6 x 9, 256 pp, Quality PB, 978-1-58023-049-0 **$16.95**

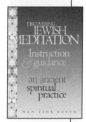

Ritual/Sacred Practices

The Jewish Dream Book: The Key to Opening the Inner Meaning of Your Dreams *By Vanessa L. Ochs, PhD, with Elizabeth Ochs; Illus. by Kristina Swarner*
Instructions for how modern people can perform ancient Jewish dream practices and dream interpretations drawn from the Jewish wisdom tradition.
8 x 8, 128 pp, Full-color illus., Deluxe PB w/ flaps, 978-1-58023-132-9 **$16.95**

God in Your Body: Kabbalah, Mindfulness and Embodied Spiritual Practice
By Jay Michaelson
The first comprehensive treatment of the body in Jewish spiritual practice and an essential guide to the sacred.
6 x 9, 272 pp, Quality PB, 978-1-58023-304-0 **$18.99**

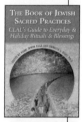

The Book of Jewish Sacred Practices: CLAL's Guide to Everyday & Holiday Rituals & Blessings *Edited by Rabbi Irwin Kula and Vanessa L. Ochs, PhD*
6 x 9, 368 pp, Quality PB, 978-1-58023-152-7 **$18.99**

Jewish Ritual: A Brief Introduction for Christians
By Rabbi Kerry M. Olitzky and Rabbi Daniel Judson
5½ x 8½, 144 pp, Quality PB, 978-1-58023-210-4 **$14.99**

The Rituals & Practices of a Jewish Life: A Handbook for Personal Spiritual Renewal *Edited by Rabbi Kerry M. Olitzky and Rabbi Daniel Judson*
6 x 9, 272 pp, illus., Quality PB, 978-1-58023-169-5 **$18.95**

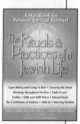

The Sacred Art of Lovingkindness: Preparing to Practice
By Rabbi Rami Shapiro 5½ x 8½, 176 pp, Quality PB, 978-1-59473-151-8 **$16.99**
(A book from SkyLight Paths, Jewish Lights' sister imprint)

Science Fiction/Mystery & Detective Fiction

Criminal Kabbalah: An Intriguing Anthology of Jewish Mystery & Detective Fiction *Edited by Lawrence W. Raphael; Foreword by Laurie R. King*
All-new stories from twelve of today's masters of mystery and detective fiction—sure to delight mystery buffs of all faith traditions.
6 x 9, 256 pp, Quality PB, 978-1-58023-109-1 **$16.95**

Mystery Midrash: An Anthology of Jewish Mystery & Detective Fiction
Edited by Lawrence W. Raphael; Preface by Joel Siegel
6 x 9, 304 pp, Quality PB, 978-1-58023-055-1 **$16.95**

Wandering Stars: An Anthology of Jewish Fantasy & Science Fiction
Edited by Jack Dann; Introduction by Isaac Asimov
6 x 9, 272 pp, Quality PB, 978-1-58023-005-6 **$18.99**

More Wandering Stars: An Anthology of Outstanding Stories of Jewish Fantasy and Science Fiction *Edited by Jack Dann; Introduction by Isaac Asimov*
6 x 9, 192 pp, Quality PB, 978-1-58023-063-6 **$16.95**

Theology/Philosophy/The Way Into... Series

The Way Into... series offers an accessible and highly usable "guided tour" of the Jewish faith, people, history and beliefs—in total, an introduction to Judaism that will enable you to understand and interact with the sacred texts of the Jewish tradition. Each volume is written by a leading contemporary scholar and teacher, and explores one key aspect of Judaism. The Way Into... series enables all readers to achieve a real sense of Jewish cultural literacy through guided study.

The Way Into Encountering God in Judaism

By Rabbi Neil Gillman, PhD

For everyone who wants to understand how Jews have encountered God throughout history and today.

6 x 9, 240 pp, Quality PB, 978-1-58023-199-2 **$18.99**; HC, 978-1-58023-025-4 **$21.95**

Also Available: **The Jewish Approach to God:** A Brief Introduction for Christians
By Rabbi Neil Gillman, PhD
5½ x 8½, 192 pp, Quality PB, 978-1-58023-190-9 **$16.95**

The Way Into Jewish Mystical Tradition

By Rabbi Lawrence Kushner

Allows readers to interact directly with the sacred mystical texts of the Jewish tradition. An accessible introduction to the concepts of Jewish mysticism, their religious and spiritual significance, and how they relate to life today.

6 x 9, 224 pp, Quality PB, 978-1-58023-200-5 **$18.99**; HC, 978-1-58023-029-2 **$21.95**

The Way Into Jewish Prayer

By Rabbi Lawrence A. Hoffman, PhD

Opens the door to 3,000 years of Jewish prayer, making available all anyone needs to feel at home in the Jewish way of communicating with God.

6 x 9, 208 pp, Quality PB, 978-1-58023-201-2 **$18.99**

Also Available: **The Way Into Jewish Prayer Teacher's Guide**
By Rabbi Jennifer Ossakow Goldsmith
8½ x 11, 42 pp, PB, 978-1-58023-345-3 **$8.99**
Download a free copy at www.jewishlights.com.

The Way Into Judaism and the Environment

By Jeremy Benstein, PhD

Explores the ways in which Judaism contributes to contemporary social-environmental issues, the extent to which Judaism is part of the problem and how it can be part of the solution.

6 x 9, 288 pp, Quality PB, 978-1-58023-368-2 **$18.99**; HC, 978-1-58023-268-5 **$24.99**

The Way Into Tikkun Olam (Repairing the World)

By Rabbi Elliot N. Dorff, PhD

An accessible introduction to the Jewish concept of the individual's responsibility to care for others and repair the world.

6 x 9, 304 pp, Quality PB, 978-1-58023-328-6 **$18.99**; 320 pp, HC, 978-1-58023-269-2 **$24.99**

The Way Into Torah

By Rabbi Norman J. Cohen, PhD

Helps guide in the exploration of the origins and development of Torah, explains why it should be studied and how to do it.

6 x 9, 176 pp, Quality PB, 978-1-58023-198-5 **$16.99**

The Way Into the Varieties of Jewishness

By Sylvia Barack Fishman, PhD

Explores the religious and historical understanding of what it has meant to be Jewish from ancient times to the present controversy over "Who is a Jew?"

6 x 9, 288 pp, Quality PB, 978-1-58023-367-5 **$18.99**; HC, 978-1-58023-030-8 **$24.99**

Theology/Philosophy

Jewish Theology in Our Time: A New Generation Explores the Foundations and Future of Jewish Belief *Edited by Rabbi Elliot J. Cosgrove, PhD*
A powerful and challenging examination of what Jews can believe—by a new generation's most dynamic and innovative thinkers.
6 x 9, 350 pp (est), HC, 978-1-58023-413-9 **$24.99**

Maimonides, Spinoza and Us: Toward an Intellectually Vibrant Judaism
By Rabbi Marc D. Angel, PhD A challenging look at two great Jewish philosophers, and what their thinking means to our understanding of God, truth, revelation and reason. 6 x 9, 224 pp, HC, 978-1-58023-411-5 **$24.99**

A Touch of the Sacred: A Theologian's Informal Guide to Jewish Belief
By Dr. Eugene B. Borowitz and Frances W. Schwartz
Explores the musings from the leading theologian of liberal Judaism.
6 x 9, 256 pp, Quality PB, 978-1-58023-416-0 **$16.99**; HC, 978-1-58023-337-8 **$21.99**

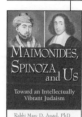

Jews and Judaism in the 21st Century: Human Responsibility, the Presence of God, and the Future of the Covenant *Edited by Rabbi Edward Feinstein; Foreword by Paula E. Hyman* Five celebrated leaders in Judaism examine contemporary Jewish life. 6 x 9, 192 pp, Quality PB, 978-1-58023-374-3 **$19.99**; HC, 978-1-58023-315-6 **$24.99**

The Death of Death: Resurrection and Immortality in Jewish Thought
By Rabbi Neil Gillman, PhD 6 x 9, 336 pp, Quality PB, 978-1-58023-081-0 **$18.95**

Ethics of the Sages: Pirke Avot—Annotated & Explained
Translation & Annotation by Rabbi Rami Shapiro
5½ x 8¼, 192 pp, Quality PB, 978-1-59473-207-2 **$16.99** *(A book from SkyLight Paths, Jewish Lights' sister imprint)*

Hasidic Tales: Annotated & Explained *Translation & Annotation by Rabbi Rami Shapiro*
5½ x 8¼, 240 pp, Quality PB, 978-1-893361-86-7 **$16.95** *(A book from SkyLight Paths, Jewish Lights' sister imprint)*

A Heart of Many Rooms: Celebrating the Many Voices within Judaism
By Dr. David Hartman 6 x 9, 352 pp, Quality PB, 978-1-58023-156-5 **$19.95**

The Hebrew Prophets: Selections Annotated & Explained
Translation & Annotation by Rabbi Rami Shapiro; Foreword by Rabbi Zalman M. Schachter-Shalomi
5½ x 8¼, 224 pp, Quality PB, 978-1-59473-037-5 **$16.99** *(A book from SkyLight Paths, Jewish Lights' sister imprint)*

A Jewish Understanding of the New Testament
By Rabbi Samuel Sandmel; Preface by Rabbi David Sandmel
5½ x 8¼, 368 pp, Quality PB, 978-1-59473-048-1 **$19.99** *(A book from SkyLight Paths, Jewish Lights' sister imprint)*

Keeping Faith with the Psalms: Deepen Your Relationship with God Using the Book of Psalms *By Rabbi Daniel F. Polish, PhD* 6 x 9, 320 pp, Quality PB, 978-1-58023-300-2 **$18.99**

A Living Covenant: The Innovative Spirit in Traditional Judaism
By Dr. David Hartman 6 x 9, 368 pp, Quality PB, 978-1-58023-011-7 **$20.00**

Love and Terror in the God Encounter: The Theological Legacy of Rabbi Joseph B. Soloveitchik *By Dr. David Hartman* 6 x 9, 240 pp, Quality PB, 978-1-58023-176-3 **$19.95**

The Personhood of God: Biblical Theology, Human Faith and the Divine Image
By Dr. Yochanan Muffs; Foreword by Dr. David Hartman
6 x 9, 240 pp, Quality PB, 978-1-58023-338-5 **$18.99**; HC, 978-1-58023-265-4 **$24.99**

Traces of God: Seeing God in Torah, History and Everyday Life *By Rabbi Neil Gillman, PhD*
6 x 9, 240 pp, Quality PB, 978-1-58023-369-9 **$16.99**; HC, 978-1-58023-249-4 **$21.99**

We Jews and Jesus: Exploring Theological Differences for Mutual Understanding
By Rabbi Samuel Sandmel; Preface by Rabbi David Sandmel
6 x 9, 192 pp, Quality PB, 978-1-59473-208-9 **$16.99** *(A book from SkyLight Paths, Jewish Lights' sister imprint)*

Your Word Is Fire: The Hasidic Masters on Contemplative Prayer
Edited and translated by Rabbi Arthur Green, PhD, and Barry W. Holtz
6 x 9, 160 pp, Quality PB, 978-1-879045-25-5 **$15.95**

I Am Jewish

Personal Reflections Inspired by the Last Words of Daniel Pearl
Almost 150 Jews—both famous and not—from all walks of life, from all around the world, write about many aspects of their Judaism.
Edited by Judea and Ruth Pearl 6 x 9, 304 pp, Deluxe PB w/ flaps, 978-1-58023-259-3 **$18.99**
Download a free copy of the *I Am Jewish Teacher's Guide* at www.jewishlights.com.

Spirituality

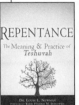

Repentance: The Meaning and Practice of *Teshuvah*
By Dr. Louis E. Newman; Foreword by Rabbi Harold M. Schulweis; Preface by Rabbi Karyn D. Kedar
Examines both the practical and philosophical dimensions of *teshuvah*, Judaism's core religious-moral teaching on repentance, and its value for us—Jews and non-Jews alike—today. 6 x 9, 256 pp, HC, 978-1-58023-426-9 **$24.99**

Tanya, the Masterpiece of Hasidic Wisdom
Selections Annotated & Explained
Translation & Annotation by Rabbi Rami Shapiro; Foreword by Rabbi Zalman M. Schachter-Shalomi
Brings the genius of the *Tanya* to anyone seeking to deepen their understanding of the soul and how it relates to and manifests the Divine Source.
5½ x 8½, 240 pp, Quality PB, 978-1-59473-275-1 **$16.99**
(A book from SkyLight Paths, Jewish Lights' sister imprint)

A Book of Life: Embracing Judaism as a Spiritual Practice
By Rabbi Michael Strassfeld 6 x 9, 544 pp, Quality PB, 978-1-58023-247-0 **$19.99**

Meaning and Mitzvah: Daily Practices for Reclaiming Judaism through Prayer, God, Torah, Hebrew, Mitzvot and Peoplehood *By Rabbi Goldie Milgram*
7 x 9, 336 pp, Quality PB, 978-1-58023-256-2 **$19.99**

The Soul of the Story: Meetings with Remarkable People
By Rabbi David Zeller 6 x 9, 288 pp, HC, 978-1-58023-272-2 **$21.99**

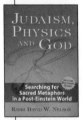

Aleph-Bet Yoga: Embodying the Hebrew Letters for Physical and Spiritual Well-Being
By Steven A. Rapp; Foreword by Tamar Frankiel, PhD, and Judy Greenfeld; Preface by Hart Lazer
7 x 10, 128 pp, b/w photos, Quality PB, Layflat binding, 978-1-58023-162-6 **$16.95**

Does the Soul Survive? A Jewish Journey to Belief in Afterlife, Past Lives & Living with Purpose *By Rabbi Elie Kaplan Spitz; Foreword by Brian L. Weiss, MD*
6 x 9, 288 pp, Quality PB, 978-1-58023-165-7 **$16.99**

First Steps to a New Jewish Spirit: Reb Zalman's Guide to Recapturing the Intimacy & Ecstasy in Your Relationship with God *By Rabbi Zalman M. Schachter-Shalomi with Donald Gropman* 6 x 9, 144 pp, Quality PB, 978-1-58023-182-4 **$16.95**

Foundations of Sephardic Spirituality: The Inner Life of Jews of the Ottoman Empire
By Rabbi Marc D. Angel, PhD 6 x 9, 224 pp, Quality PB, 978-1-58023-341-5 **$18.99**

God in Our Relationships: Spirituality between People from the Teachings of Martin Buber *By Rabbi Dennis S. Ross* 5½ x 8½, 160 pp, Quality PB, 978-1-58023-147-3 **$16.95**

Judaism, Physics and God: Searching for Sacred Metaphors in a Post-Einstein World
By Rabbi David W. Nelson 6 x 9, 352 pp, Quality PB, inc. reader's discussion guide,
978-1-58023-306-4 **$18.99**; HC, 352 pp, 978-1-58023-252-4 **$24.99**

The Jewish Lights Spirituality Handbook: A Guide to Understanding, Exploring & Living a Spiritual Life *Edited by Stuart M. Matlins*
What exactly is "Jewish" about spirituality? How do I make it a part of my life? Fifty of today's foremost spiritual leaders share their ideas and experience with us.
6 x 9, 456 pp, Quality PB, 978-1-58023-093-3 **$19.99**

Bringing the Psalms to Life: How to Understand and Use the Book of Psalms
By Rabbi Daniel F. Polish, PhD 6 x 9, 208 pp, Quality PB, 978-1-58023-157-2 **$16.95**

God & the Big Bang: Discovering Harmony between Science & Spirituality
By Dr. Daniel C. Matt 6 x 9, 216 pp, Quality PB, 978-1-879045-89-7 **$16.99**

Minding the Temple of the Soul: Balancing Body, Mind, and Spirit through Traditional Jewish Prayer, Movement, and Meditation *By Tamar Frankiel, PhD, and Judy Greenfeld*
7 x 10, 184 pp, illus., Quality PB, 978-1-879045-64-4 **$16.95**

One God Clapping: The Spiritual Path of a Zen Rabbi *By Alan Lew with Sherril Jaffe*
5½ x 8½, 336 pp, Quality PB, 978-1-58023-115-2 **$16.95**

There Is No Messiah ... and You're It: The Stunning Transformation of Judaism's Most Provocative Idea *By Rabbi Robert N. Levine, DD*
6 x 9, 192 pp, Quality PB, 978-1-58023-255-5 **$16.99**

These Are the Words: A Vocabulary of Jewish Spiritual Life
By Rabbi Arthur Green, PhD 6 x 9, 304 pp, Quality PB, 978-1-58023-107-7 **$18.95**

Spirituality/Prayer

Making Prayer Real: Leading Jewish Spiritual Voices on Why Prayer Is Difficult and What to Do about It *By Rabbi Mike Comins*
A no-holds-barred look at why so many find synagogue at best difficult, and at worst, meaningless and boring—and how to make it more satisfying.
6 x 9, 320 pp, Quality PB, 978-1-58023-417-7 **$18.99**

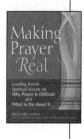

Witnesses to the One: The Spiritual History of the *Sh'ma*
By Rabbi Joseph B. Meszler; Foreword by Rabbi Elyse Goldstein
6 x 9, 176 pp, Quality PB, 978-1-58023-400-9 **$16.99**; HC, 978-1-58023-309-5 **$19.99**

My People's Prayer Book Series: Traditional Prayers, Modern Commentaries *Edited by Rabbi Lawrence A. Hoffman, PhD*
Provides diverse and exciting commentary to the traditional liturgy. Will help you find new wisdom in Jewish prayer, and bring liturgy into your life. Each book includes Hebrew text, modern translation and commentaries from all perspectives of the Jewish world.

Vol. 1—The *Sh'ma* and Its Blessings
  7 x 10, 168 pp, HC, 978-1-879045-79-8 **$24.99**
Vol. 2—The *Amidah* 7 x 10, 240 pp, HC, 978-1-879045-80-4 **$24.95**
Vol. 3—*P'sukei D'zimrah* (Morning Psalms)
  7 x 10, 240 pp, HC, 978-1-879045-81-1 **$24.95**
Vol. 4—*Seder K'riat Hatorah* (The Torah Service)
  7 x 10, 264 pp, HC, 978-1-879045-82-8 **$23.95**
Vol. 5—*Birkhot Hashachar* (Morning Blessings)
  7 x 10, 240 pp, HC, 978-1-879045-83-5 **$24.95**
Vol. 6—*Tachanun* and Concluding Prayers
  7 x 10, 240 pp, HC, 978-1-879045-84-2 **$24.95**
Vol. 7—Shabbat at Home 7 x 10, 240 pp, HC, 978-1-879045-85-9 **$24.95**
Vol. 8—*Kabbalat Shabbat* (Welcoming Shabbat in the Synagogue)
  7 x 10, 240 pp, HC, 978-1-58023-121-3 **$24.99**
Vol. 9—Welcoming the Night: *Minchah* and *Ma'ariv* (Afternoon and
  Evening Prayer) 7 x 10, 272 pp, HC, 978-1-58023-262-3 **$24.99**
Vol. 10—Shabbat Morning: *Shacharit* and *Musaf* (Morning and
  Additional Services) 7 x 10, 240 pp, HC, 978-1-58023-240-1 **$24.99**

Spirituality/Lawrence Kushner

The Book of Letters: A Mystical Hebrew Alphabet
  Popular HC Edition, 6 x 9, 80 pp, 2-color text, 978-1-879045-00-2 **$24.95**
  Collector's Limited Edition, 9 x 12, 80 pp, gold-foil-embossed pages, w/ limited-edition silkscreened
  print, 978-1-879045-04-0 **$349.00**
The Book of Miracles: A Young Person's Guide to Jewish Spiritual Awareness
  6 x 9, 96 pp, 2-color illus., HC, 978-1-879045-78-1 **$16.95** *For ages 9–13*
The Book of Words: Talking Spiritual Life, Living Spiritual Talk
  6 x 9, 160 pp, Quality PB, 978-1-58023-020-9 **$16.95**
Eyes Remade for Wonder: A Lawrence Kushner Reader *Introduction by Thomas Moore*
  6 x 9, 240 pp, Quality PB, 978-1-58023-042-1 **$18.95**

Filling Words with Light: Hasidic and Mystical Reflections on Jewish Prayer
By Rabbi Lawrence Kushner and Rabbi Nehemia Polen
  5½ x 8½, 176 pp, Quality PB, 978-1-58023-238-8 **$16.99**; HC, 978-1-58023-216-6 **$21.99**
God Was in This Place & I, i Did Not Know: Finding Self, Spirituality and
  Ultimate Meaning 6 x 9, 192 pp, Quality PB, 978-1-879045-33-0 **$16.95**
Honey from the Rock: An Introduction to Jewish Mysticism
  6 x 9, 176 pp, Quality PB, 978-1-58023-073-5 **$16.95**
Invisible Lines of Connection: Sacred Stories of the Ordinary
  5½ x 8½, 160 pp, Quality PB, 978-1-879045-98-9 **$15.95**

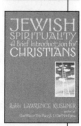

Jewish Spirituality: A Brief Introduction for Christians
  5½ x 8½, 112 pp, Quality PB, 978-1-58023-150-3 **$12.95**
The River of Light: Jewish Mystical Awareness
  6 x 9, 192 pp, Quality PB, 978-1-58023-096-4 **$16.95**
The Way Into Jewish Mystical Tradition
  6 x 9, 224 pp, Quality PB, 978-1-58023-200-5 **$18.99**; HC, 978-1-58023-029-2 **$21.95**

About Jewish Lights

People of all faiths and backgrounds yearn for books that attract, engage, educate, and spiritually inspire.

Our principal goal is to stimulate thought and help all people learn about who the Jewish People are, where they come from, and what the future can be made to hold. While people of our diverse Jewish heritage are the primary audience, our books speak to people in the Christian world as well and will broaden their understanding of Judaism and the roots of their own faith.

We bring to you authors who are at the forefront of spiritual thought and experience. While each has something different to say, they all say it in a voice that you can hear.

Our books are designed to welcome you and then to engage, stimulate, and inspire. We judge our success not only by whether or not our books are beautiful and commercially successful, but by whether or not they make a difference in your life.

For your information and convenience, at the back of this book we have provided a list of other Jewish Lights books you might find interesting and useful. They cover all the categories of your life:

Bar/Bat Mitzvah	Life Cycle
Bible Study / Midrash	Meditation
Children's Books	Men's Interest
Congregation Resources	Parenting
Current Events / History	Prayer / Ritual / Sacred Practice
Ecology / Environment	Social Justice
Fiction: Mystery, Science Fiction	Spirituality
Grief / Healing	Theology / Philosophy
Holidays / Holy Days	Travel
Inspiration	12-Step
Kabbalah / Mysticism / Enneagram	Women's Interest

Stuart M. Matlins, Publisher

Or phone, fax, mail or e-mail to: **JEWISH LIGHTS Publishing**
Sunset Farm Offices, Route 4 • P.O. Box 237 • Woodstock, Vermont 05091
Tel: (802) 457-4000 • Fax: (802) 457-4004 • www.jewishlights.com
Credit card orders: (800) 962-4544 (8:30AM–5:30PM ET Monday–Friday)
Generous discounts on quantity orders. SATISFACTION GUARANTEED. Prices subject to change.